Following Christ

R. C. SPROUL

Tyndale House Publishers, Inc.
Wheaton, Illinois

Library of Congress Cataloging-in-Publication Data

Sproul, R. C. (Robert Charles), date
    Following Christ / R. C. Sproul.
        p.   cm.
    ISBN 0-8423-5937-0
    1.Jesus Christ—Person and offices   2.Prayer.   3. God—Will.
4. Christian ethics.   5. Social ethics.   I. Title.
BT202.S6675   1991
248.4—dc20   91-22635

All Scripture references are taken from the *Holy Bible,* Revised Standard Version, unless otherwise noted. Old Testament section, copyright 1952; New Testament section, first edition, copyright 1946; New Testament section, second edition, © 1971 by the Division of Christian Education of the National Council of the Churches of Christ in the United States of America.

This book incorporates the following previously published works by R. C. Sproul:
Who Is Jesus? © 1983
Ethics and the Christian © 1983
God's Will & the Christian © 1984
Effective Prayer © 1984

Tyndale House Publishers, Inc.
Wheaton, Illinois

Printed in the United States of America

97   96   95   94   93   92   91
9   8   7   6   5   4   3   2   1

TABLE OF CONTENTS

Introduction   vii

PART ONE

WHO IS JESUS?

1. Will the Real Jesus Please Stand Up?   3
2. The Titles of Jesus   17
3. The Life of Jesus   53

PART TWO

DOES PRAYER CHANGE THINGS?

4. The Place of Prayer   107
5. The Purpose of Prayer   113
6. The Pattern of Prayer   125
7. The Practice of Prayer   149
8. The Prohibitions of Prayer   173
9. The Power of Prayer   181

PART THREE

HOW CAN I KNOW GOD'S WILL?

10. The Meaning of God's Will   197
11. The Meaning of Man's Will   227
12. God's Will and Your Job   251
13. God's Will in Marriage   273

PART FOUR

HOW SHOULD I LIVE IN THIS WORLD?

14. Ethics and Morals   295
15. Revealed Ethics   311
16. Legalism and Antinomianism   319

17. The Ethics of Materialism 341
18. The Ethics of Capital Punishment 359
19. The Ethics of War 369
20. The Ethics of Abortion 373
21. Ethics and Conscience 387

Conclusion 391

"I don't need to know any theology. All I need to know is Jesus."

Many Christians express this sentiment with firm, sincere conviction. They want a simple faith, uncluttered by the complexities of theologians.

The desire to keep the faith simple is a noble one. When things get too complicated, they become fuzzy. True devotion can falter. We must never leave Christianity in the hands of an elite group of scholars, thinking that they alone can penetrate the mystery of the Incarnation. Christianity is for everyone, strong or weak, literate or illiterate. So why complicate things with theology? Why go beyond the basics when "Christ is the answer"?

Yet the very people who say, "Jesus is all I need," are already "doing theology." Their vigorous call to keep the faith simple is actually a profound doctrinal statement. They may not realize it, but they are saying, "Jesus is relevant. Jesus means something in my life. Jesus is all-sufficient." They are saying that a relationship with Jesus is the most important thing about Christianity. All other theories and principles pale in comparison. In short, they are presenting the basics of a Christ-centered theology.

Theology simply means "the study of God." Reflecting upon the nature, person, and works of our Lord is a worthy endeavor indeed. The goal of theology is not to confuse but to clarify. Doctrine is intended to sharpen our understanding of faith, not to dull it. The assumption of classical theology is that, the more we understand Jesus, the more we will love him. Knowledge should fuel zeal. It is like the genetic code that programs the growth of all living things. The knowledge of God shapes our Christian development. The more we know, the more we should grow. Unless we know who Christ is, we cannot become more Christ-like.

Unfortunately, theologians have often disappointed us. They often shroud their words in ambiguity, trying to conceal their own unbelief. They are like the scientists who dissect a creature to learn about it, rather than letting it live and observing its actions. They tear the truth apart rather than watching how it vibrates with life and energy. They do this in the name of scientific objectivity, but they destroy their subject in the process. T. S. Eliot said, "Good prose cannot be written by people without convictions." We might say the same thing about theology.

Heisenberg's Principle of Uncertainty suggests that one cannot measure the substance and speed of an electron without changing it in some way. Theology works in a similar way. When we slow it down and box it up, we lose something essential. The only way to get at the whole truth is to see it in action. And if we really see it in action, it is bound to change our lives.

Sincere Christians recognize this. They sense the lack of warmth and religious affection in much of the academic writing they see. They find much theology cold, empty of doxology, and they smell the stench of death. So they reject it all. They are like Odysseus, who tied himself to the mast and stopped up his ears to resist the temptation of the sirens' voices. They firmly withstand the voices of scholarly skepticism.

Yet the problem is not in theology itself, but in the way it is being done. Theology can be done well when the heart responds to what the mind understands. Theology can improve the way we live our lives. It can help us serve God better.

Our ship is sailing through perilous waters. We can feel it. The world's ways are swirling around us. Ethical norms are bobbing about like driftwood. Waves of selfishness, ambition, and pleasure-seeking batter our small craft. Too many of us are tied to the mast, with our ears stopped up and our eyes closed. It is wise to resist the voices of skepticism, but the time has come to grab our maps and steer our way through this maelstrom. More than ever, we need a solid theology, a Christ-based theology, that guides us through the eddies of life. Good theology is what gives form and substance to our walk with Christ.

That is what this book is all about. Theology is not an accessory for our Christian lives. It is essential to following Christ with depth of conviction. Let us storm those ivory towers and take back theology and plug it into our everyday lives.

It has to start with *Jesus*. He is the Savior, the Mediator, the one who connects us with God the Father. He is the cornerstone of our faith. When we reach a clear understanding of who he is, we will have a better sense of who we are. There are many false ideas about Jesus around today. The world would like us to think that these are trivial differences, that everything is negotiable. But Jesus holds everything together for us. A proper understanding of his identity and his role must precede every other decision we make as Christians. That is why the first section of this book focuses on the person of Jesus.

Once we establish the idea that Jesus gives us access to the Father, we need to examine what this means. Because of Jesus, we can *pray* and expect that our prayers will be heard and, in some way, answered. But that presents us with a thorny question: If God is all-powerful, all-sovereign, can our prayers really change anything? The second section of this book tackles that question, with specific application to our everyday prayer life.

Many Christians struggle with the idea of *God's will*. It's great, they say, that I can talk to God in prayer, but how does he talk to me? I want to obey him in every decision of my life, but how do I know what he wants? The third section of this book covers these questions, with specific reference to matters of career and marriage. How do we determine God's will in these crucial areas of life?

But those are only a few of the many decisions we must make. Our society gives us many choices. It's not always easy to see what the most virtuous path is. As Christians, we need a clear sense of *ethics* based on God's Word. How should we handle our money? Is war ever justified? What about volatile issues such as abortion and capital punishment? How do we decide these matters? How can we affect our society in a Christ-like way? Section 4 wrestles with these issues in a reasoned manner. We must get beyond the slogans and into the substance of these matters.

These are all crucial issues involved in faithfully following Christ. Perhaps you are facing some of these dilemmas in your life right now. Or perhaps you're concerned about how society is dealing with these issues. God does not leave us floundering. As we study his attributes and his Word, we can come up with a *theo-logy*, an understanding of godly principles that can guide us through everyday life.

PART ONE

WHO IS JESUS?

CHAPTER 1

WILL THE REAL JESUS PLEASE STAND UP?

There are so many portraits of Jesus in the galleries of this world that it seems hopeless to clarify the confusion they have wrought in people's minds about who Christ is. So many conflicting images of him are put forward that some people have despaired of achieving an accurate picture of his true identity.

We need Christ. We need a real Christ. A Christ born of empty speculation or created to squeeze into the philosopher's pattern simply won't do. A recycled Christ, a Christ of compromise can redeem no one. A Christ watered down, stripped of power, debased of glory, reduced to a symbol or made impotent by scholarly surgery is not Christ but Antichrist.

The "anti" of Antichrist can refer either to the

prefix *against* or the prefix *instead of.* In language there is a difference; in life it is a distinction without a difference because to supplant the real Jesus with a substitute portrait is to work against Christ. To change or distort the real Christ is to oppose him with a false Christ.

No person in history has provoked as much study, criticism, prejudice, or devotion as Jesus of Nazareth. The titanic influence of this man makes him a chief target of the arrows of criticism and a prime object of revision according to the interpreter's prejudice. The historical Jesus has suffered the fate of the waxed-nose figure. His portrait has been altered to suit the fancy of those seeking to line him up on their side, to make of him an ally in a host of militant causes, many of which are mutually exclusive. In the theologian's laboratory Jesus can become a chameleon. His skin changes color to fit the backdrop painted by the theologian. Rigorous academic attempts have been made to get behind the New Testament portrait of Jesus, to discover the "real" historical Jesus. These attempts to penetrate the wall of history, to peek behind the veil of the primitive apostolic witness have taught us much about the prejudice of the scholars but have added little or nothing to our understanding of the real Jesus. What the scholars discovered behind the veil was a mirror of their own prejudice and a Jesus created in their own images. The nineteenth-century liberals found a "liberal" Jesus; the existentialists found an existential hero; and the Marxists discovered a political revolutionary. Idealists found an idealistic Jesus and pragmatists discovered a pragmatic Christ. To search behind or beyond the New Testament is to go on a snipe hunt armed with the flashlight of pride and prejudice.

Or consider the scissors-and-paste Jesus. He is fashioned by those who seek within the Bible a core or kernal of tradition about Christ that is authentic. The unnecessary extras, the implied accretions of myth and legend are excised by the scissors to expose the real Jesus. It seems so scientific, but it is all done with mirrors. The magician's art leaves us with the portrait of Rudolf Bultmann or John A. T. Robinson, and again the real Jesus is obscured. By preserving a modicum of New Testament data we think we have avoided subjectivity. But the result is the same—a Jesus shaped and formed by the bias of the scholar wielding the scissors and getting his hands sticky from the paste.

The story is told of the vagrant who knocked at the farmer's door and politely inquired about employment as a handyman. The farmer cautiously put the man to work on a trial basis to measure his skill. His first task was to split logs for firewood, which the stranger finished in record time. The next task was to plow the fields, which was done in just a few hours. The farmer was pleasantly

astonished; it seemed he had stumbled on a modern-day Hercules. The third task was less laborious. Taking the hired man to the barn, the farmer
pointed to a large pile of potatoes and instructed
him to sort them into two piles: those that were of
prime quality were to be put in one receptacle and
those of inferior grade in another. The farmer was
curious when his miracle-working laborer failed to
report in as rapidly as he had with the other tasks.
After several hours the farmer went to the barn to
investigate. No perceptible change was evident in
the pile of potatoes. One receptacle contained three
potatoes and the other had only two. "What's
wrong?" demanded the farmer. "Why are you
moving so slowly?" A look of defeat was written
on the hired man's face as he threw up his hands
and replied, "It's the decisions in life that are difficult."

The scissors-and-paste method suffers from the
problem of determining in advance what is authentic in the biblical portrait of Jesus and what is myth.
What Bultmann discards into the basket of husks,
another scholar puts into the basket of kernels.
What Bultmann calls prime, another discards as
inferior.

The problem is simple. It lies not with the
"shoddy" reporting of the New Testament authors
or the "sloppy" documents of history we call the
Gospels. It was Emil Brunner, the Swiss theologian,

who blew the whistle on nineteenth-century liberalism. Brunner's verdict was as simple as it was inflammatory. The problem, he said, is *unbelief*. In this sense it is not an academic problem or unbelief based on insufficient evidence. To withhold belief because the evidence doesn't support the claims is an honorable and wise response. To believe against poor evidence is credulity, the mark of the fool, and brings no honor to God.

But the evidence is compelling, to withhold belief is to commit an immoral act. Unbelief is judged by Jesus not as an intellectual error but as a hostile act of prejudice against God himself. It is this sort of unbelief that is destructive to the church and to the people of God.

How could such blatant unbelief not only attack the Christian church but in several cases capture whole seminaries and even entire denominations? Why wouldn't people who rejected the New Testament portrait of Jesus simply abandon Christianity altogether and leave the church to less educated mortals who need a fanciful Jesus as a religious crutch?

The nineteenth century brought an intellectual and moral crisis to the church. With the rise of liberal theology that flatly rejected the supernatural core of the New Testament, the crisis pressed hard on very practical matters. If the leaders of a church or the faculty of a seminary wake up one morning and discover they no longer believe what the Bible teaches or the church confesses, what are their options?

The most obvious option and the first expected of honorable men is that they would declare their unbelief and politely leave the church. If they control the power structures of the church, however, they have practical questions to consider. By vocation and training their jobs are tied to the church. The church represents a multi-billion-dollar financial investment, an established cultural institution with millions of active constituent members, and a proven effective vehicle for social reform. These factors make declaring unbelief to the world and closing the doors to the churches less attractive. The course of least resistance is to redefine Christianity.

Redefining Christianity is no easy task. Christianity has been given definition by two weighty factors: (1) the existence of a body of literature, indeed primary sources about the founder and teacher of the Christian faith, Jesus of Nazareth; (2) the existence of two millennia of church tradition which includes points of disagreement about particular issues of debate among denominations, but which reveals remarkable unity of confession about the essentials of Christianity. To redefine Christianity requires one to neutralize the authority of the Bible and relativize the authority of the creeds. The struggle of the church for the past 150 years has been precisely at these two points. It is not by accident that the eye of the storm of controversy within the seminaries and the church in our day has focused on issues concerning the Bible and the creeds. Why? Not simply because of words and paper but because of Christ. One must banish the Christ of the Bible and the Christ of the creeds in order to redefine Christianity.

The church is called "the body of Christ." Some refer to it as "the continuing Incarnation." Surely the church exists to embody and carry out the mission of Christ. The church is inconceivable without Christ. But the church is not Christ. It is founded by Christ, formed by Christ, commissioned by Christ, and endowed by Christ. It is ruled by Christ, sanctified by Christ, and protected by Christ. But it is not Christ. The church can preach salvation and nurture the saved, but it cannot save. The church can preach, exhort, rebuke, and admonish against sin. It can proclaim the forgiveness of sin and give theological definition to sin: but the church cannot atone for sin.

It was St. Cyprian who declared, "He cannot have God for his Father who does not have the church for his Mother." We need the church as much as a starving baby needs his mother's milk. We cannot grow or be nourished without the church. Possessing Christ and despising the church is an intolerable contradiction which none can bear.

We cannot have Christ without embracing the church. But it is possible to have the church without truly embracing Christ. St. Augustine described the church as a *corpus permixtum*, a "mixed body" of tares and wheat, of unbelievers and believers existing side by side. Unbelief can gain entrance into the church—but never into Christ.

The Christ we believe, the Christ we trust, must be true if we are to be redeemed. A false Christ or substitute Christ cannot redeem. If it is thought unlikely that the biblical Christ can redeem, it is even less likely that the speculative Christ of human invention can redeem. Apart from the Bible we know nothing of consequence concerning the real Jesus. Ultimately our faith stands or falls with the biblical Jesus. Lay aside theories of biblical inspiration if you must, doing so at your own peril, but even apart from inspiration the New Testament represents the *primary sources*—the earliest documents of those who knew him, the record of those who studied under him and were eyewitnesses to his ministry. They are the most objective historical sources we have.

Some demur at this point, calling attention to the obvious fact that the New Testament portrait of Jesus comes to us from the pens of biased men with an agenda. The Gospels are not history, they say, but *redemptive* history with the accent on efforts to persuade men to follow Jesus. Well, certainly the writers had an agenda, but it was not a hidden agenda. The apostle John says forthrightly: "These [things] are written that you may believe that Jesus is the Christ, the Son of God, and that believing you may have life in his name" (John 20:31).

The fact that the biblical writers were themselves believers and were zealous to persuade others counts for their veracity. Had they been unbelievers while exhorting others to believe, they would have been guilty of duplicity. Of course, men can be mistaken about what they proclaim, but the fact that they believed their own message, even unto death, should enhance rather than weaken their credibility.

Theirs was indeed a record of redemptive history. *Redemptive* because they were not writing from the standpoint of neutral, disinterested historians. *History* because they insisted that their testimony was true.

At this point a practical question emerges, heard from the streetwise and the hard-nosed skeptic who seeks to discredit the biblical Christ by exposing the apostolic Christ as a fantasy. If the closest associates of Jesus were biased (in that they were believers), what is the sense of laborious scholarship to discover the "real" Jesus? If all we know about Jesus is learned through the witness of the apostles—if they are the "screen" through which we must gaze to see him—what's the point of our efforts?

The answer is that the historical Jesus did not live in a vacuum; he is known at least in part by the way he transformed those around him.

I want to know the Jesus who radicalized St. Matthew, who transformed St. Peter, who turned Saul of Tarsus upside down on the Damascus Road. If these firsthand witnesses can't get me to the "real" Jesus, who can? If not through friends and loved ones, how can anyone be known?

If the apostles can't lead me to Jesus, my only options are to scale the fortress of heaven by sheer mystical subjectivism, embracing the oldest of all heresies, gnosticism, or to pitch my tent with the camp of skeptics who dismiss Jesus from the realm of significant truth altogether. Give me the biblical Christ or give me nothing. Do it quickly, please, as the options give me nothing, save the injury of fruitless laborious research.

It was Jesus who said, "What shall it profit a man, if he shall gain the whole world, and lose his own soul?" And, "What shall a man give in exchange for his soul?" (Mark 8:36-37, KJV). Jesus put an enormous price tag on the value of the human soul. For that I am grateful. I like to think my soul has worth, and I would hate to squander it on an empty Christ, a Christ of subjective speculation. But this is what we are doing when we embrace anything less than a real Christ. We are playing with human souls—the very souls Christ poured out his life to redeem.

There are different methods we could use to arrive at our picture of Jesus. We could examine the classical creeds of the church, gaining valuable insight into the collective wisdom of the ages. We could restrict our study to contemporary theology in an attempt to study Jesus in light of our own culture. Or we could try our luck at our own creativity and produce yet another speculative view.

In this essay I have chosen to look at Jesus as he is presented to us in the New Testament. Even if one rejects the revelatory character of the Bible or its divine inspiration, he must face one unassailable fact: virtually all we know about Jesus is that which is recorded in the Scriptures. The New Testament writers are the primary sources of our knowledge of Jesus. If these sources are ignored or rejected, we are left with speculation and speculation alone.

We echo the cry of Erasmus, *"Ad fontes!"* (To the sources!), as we focus attention on the New Testament. No matter what advantages we may have from two thousand years of theological reflection, those years remove us from the virginal response of the contemporaries of Jesus who knew him, who walked with him, who observed him in action, and who interpreted him from the perspective of the Old Testament Scriptures. The biblical writers themselves are the primary sources, and it is their portrait of Jesus that must take priority in any serious study of this person. Outside of the New Testament writers there amounts to no more than three paragraphs of literature written in the first century about the person and work of Jesus.

When we go back to the biblical sources, we recognize that any attempt to understand Jesus must take into account the dangers imposed by our own minds. Though the New Testament is not a product of the twentieth century, those of us who read it today are. Each of us has had some exposure to the idea of Jesus since we were children, if from no other source than from the simple displays that we see in Christmas crèches during the holiday season. Though we may not have an exhaustive knowledge of the biblical Jesus, we are not ignorant of him either. Every literate American has some information about Jesus and has some opinion about him. Those opinions may or may not be in harmony with the biblical portrait, yet we bring those assumptions to the text and sometimes create an attitude of prejudice that makes it difficult for us to hear what Jesus' contemporaries were saying.

We must also be aware that Jesus is no mere figure of historical interest whom we can study dispassionately. We are aware of the claims that Jesus is the Son of God, the Savior of the world. We realize that we must make a decision about him for or against. We are also aware that many believe such a decision determines one's eternal destiny. We sense that so much is at stake in our understanding of Jesus that we must approach the question not with indifference, but with the understanding of who Jesus is. It is a question of ultimate significance to each one of us. Whether or not Jesus brings to my life an absolute claim is something I cannot intelligently ignore.

The New Testament writers give us an eyewitness account of Jesus of Nazareth. Luke begins his Gospel with the following words:

> *Inasmuch as many have undertaken to compile a narrative of the things which have been accomplished among us, just as they were delivered to us by those who from the beginning were eyewitnesses and ministers of the word, it seemed good to me also, having followed all things closely for some time past, to write an orderly account for you, most excellent Theophilus, that you may know the truth concerning the things of which you have been informed. (Luke 1:1-4)*

Peter adds to this the following statement:

> *For we did not follow cleverly devised myths when we made known to you the power and the coming of our Lord Jesus Christ, but we were eyewitnesses of his majesty. (2 Peter 1:16)*

The biblical records claim to be firsthand accounts given to us by men who were self-consciously and openly committed to following Jesus. Let us look briefly at the testimony of those who knew him and loved him and who gave their lives for him.

CHAPTER 2

THE TITLES OF JESUS

A few years ago a distinguished professor of New Testament was invited to address an academic convocation at a large seminary. The occasion of convocation in a university or seminary is one that is attended with pomp and circumstance. The faculty are adorned in full academic regalia as they march in procession to the front of the auditorium. The guest speaker on such occasions is expected to bring an address of weighty, scholarly material. When the New Testament professor entered the hall, there was a hush of expectancy as students and faculty waited with eager anticipation for his remarks. Being an expert in the field of Christology, it was expected that the lecturer would present an address revealing his most recent research in the field. Instead, he stood at the

podium and began to recite a litany of the titles of
Jesus drawn from the Scriptures. The litany went
on for several minutes, as the full impact of the
titles in themselves, given without commentary,
was felt by the audience. The professor stood and
simply said with pauses in between:

Christ	*The Rose of Sharon*
Lord	*The Bright and Morning Star*
Rabbi	*The Alpha and Omega*
Son of Man	*The Logos*
Son of God	*The Advocate*
Son of David	*The Prince of Peace*
Lion of Judah	*The only begotten of the Father*
	The Lamb without blemish

On and on the litany went, as the man recited all
of the titles that the biblical writers had conferred
upon Jesus.

These titles reveal something of his identity and
they also give us a hint as to the meaning of his
activity. It is customary in theology to distinguish
between the person of Christ and the work of
Christ. The distinction is an important one, but it
must never involve a separation. Who Jesus is, is
known in part by what he did. On the other hand,
the significance of what he did is strongly condi-
tioned by who he is. Though we may distinguish
between person and work, we must never isolate

the one from the other. When we look at the titles conferred upon Jesus in the New Testament we see an interplay between person and work.

Space does not permit an examination of all the titles ascribed to Jesus biblically, but let us examine briefly those that are generally considered his chief titles.

Jesus as the Christ

The title *Christ* is so often used in conjunction with the name of Jesus that it has virtually become his name. One does not normally refer to Jesus as Jesus bar Joseph, or even Jesus of Nazareth. Rather, his full name is considered to be Jesus Christ. Because the term *Christ* is used as a name, the full significance of it may be lost through repetition. Actually, *Jesus* is a *name* but *Christ* is a *title*. The title *Christ* is used more often than any other title for Jesus in the New Testament. The name comes from the Greek word *christos*, which literally means "anointed." It is the Greek word that corresponds to the Hebrew word for "messiah." When Jesus is called Christ, he is being called the Messiah. If we were to translate the name and the title directly into English we would say "Jesus Messiah." With this title we are making a confession of faith that Jesus is the long awaited anointed one of Israel, the Savior who would redeem his people.

In the Old Testament, the concept of Messiah grew over a period of years as God unfolded the character and role of the Messiah progressively. Initially the term *messiah* merely meant "one who was anointed of God for a specific task." Anyone who was anointed to perform a work for God, such as a prophet, a priest, or a king, could be called messiah in the broad sense. Through the prophetic utterances of the Old Testament, a concept was developed of *the* Messiah, one who would be uniquely anointed of God to fulfill a divine task. When the New Testament writers ascribed the fulfillment of those prophecies to Jesus, they made a statement of tremendous importance. They were saying that Jesus was the one "who was to come." He fulfilled the role of all of the promises of God that converge in the person of the Messiah.

In the Old Testament the concept of the Messiah is not a simple one. It has many nuances to it, making it complex. There are different strands of messianic expectancy woven through the tapestry of the Old Testament. At first glance, some of these appear contradictory. One of the main strands of messianic expectancy is the idea of a king like David, who will restore the monarchy of Israel. There is a triumphant note in the expectation of a Messiah who will reign over Israel and put all enemies under his feet. This was the most popular variety of messianic expectancy at the time Jesus appeared on the scene. Israel had suffered under the conquest of the Romans and was bristling under the oppression of this alien yoke. A vast number of people were yearning for the fulfillment of the coming Messiah who would overthrow the Roman government and restore independence to Israel.

Another aspect of the concept of the Messiah was the notion of the suffering servant of Israel, the one who would bear the sins of the people. This concept is found most clearly in the servant songs of the prophet Isaiah, with Isaiah 53 being the chief text that the New Testament writers used to understand the ignominy of Jesus' death. The figure of a despised and rejected servant stands in stark contrast to the concept of a royal king.

A third strand of messianic expectancy is found in the so-called apocalyptic literature of the Old Testament, the highly symbolic writings of men like Daniel and Ezekiel. Herein the Messiah is seen as a heavenly being who descends from heaven in order to judge the world. It is difficult to conceive how one man could be both a heavenly being and an earthly king, a cosmic judge and a humiliated servant at the same time. Yet these are the three major varieties of messianic expectancy that were very much alive at the time of Jesus' entrance into the world. Let us look briefly again at the first strand of expectancy, that of the Son of David.

The Son of David—the Messiah

We recall that the Old Testament reign of King David had been the Golden Age of Israel. David excelled as a military hero and as a monarch. His military exploits extended the frontiers of the nation from Dan to Beersheba. During David's rule, Israel emerged as a major world power and enjoyed great military strength and prosperity. The Golden Age began to tarnish under Solomon's building program and turned to rust when the nation split under Jeroboam and Rehoboam. The memories of the great days lived on, however, in the history of the people. Nostalgia reached a peak under the oppression of the Roman government as the people of the land looked to God for a new David who would restore the former glory to Israel.

The frenzy of expectation surrounding the hope of a political Messiah was not born simply from nostalgia, but had its roots in Old Testament prophecies that gave substance to such a dream. The Psalms declared that one like David would be anointed as king by God himself. Psalm 132:11 said: "The LORD swore to David a sure oath from which he will not turn back: 'One of the sons of your body I will set on your throne.'" Psalm 89 declared, "I will establish his line for ever and his throne as the days of the heavens. . . . I will not violate my covenant, or alter the word that went forth from my lips. Once for all I have sworn by my holiness; I will not lie to David. His line shall endure for ever, his throne as long as the sun before me" (verses 29, 34-36).

Not only in the liturgy of the Psalms, but also in the Prophets we read of the future hopes of one like David. Amos, for example, proclaimed, "In that day I will raise up the booth of David that is fallen" (Amos 9:11).

These national hopes went through periods of fervor and dormancy in Israel, often depending upon the degree of political freedom the nation enjoyed. In times of crisis, in oppression, the flames of hope and expectancy were rekindled in the hearts of the populace as they yearned for the restoration of David's fallen booth.

With the advent of Jesus, the notion of the fulfillment of the seed of David's royal Messiah was sparked afresh. It was not deemed a coincidence by the New Testament authors that Jesus came from the tribe of Judah, the tribe that had been promised the royal scepter by God. It was from the tribe of Judah, the descendants of David, that the one would come who would bring the new kingdom to Israel. The New Testament writers clearly saw the fulfillment of the Old Testament hope of a royal Messiah in the person of Jesus. This is seen in the central place of importance that the ascension of Jesus is given in the New Testament. Jesus is the Son of David who announces and inaugurates the kingdom of God.

There were times in the ministry of Jesus that he had to flee from the multitudes who sought to make him king because their views of kingship were so limited and narrow. Theirs was a kingdom that would be inaugurated with no price of death and suffering. The crowds had little time for a king who was also a suffering servant. Jesus had to withdraw from the crowds repeatedly and cautioned his disciples about declaring openly that he was the Messiah. At no point did he deny that he was the Christ. When his disciples boldly proclaimed their confidence in his messiahship, Jesus accepted the designation with his blessing.

The poignant moment of messianic unveiling took place at Caesarea Philippi, when Jesus asked his disciples: "Who do the people say I am?" (Luke 9:18). The scuttlebutt of the mobs was passed on to Jesus with words like, "Some say John the Baptist; others say Elijah, and others Jeremiah or one of the prophets." Finally Jesus put the question to his inner core of disciples. "But who do you say that I am?" It was Peter who replied with fervency, "You are the Christ, the Son of the living God" (Matthew 16:13-17). Jesus' response to Peter's confession is pivotal to the New Testament understanding of the identity of Christ. Jesus replied, "Blessed are you, Simon Bar-Jona! For flesh and blood has not revealed this to you, but my Father who is in heaven." Jesus pronounced his benediction on the one to whom God revealed his true identity. He acknowledged that Peter's recognition of his identity was correct. It was not merely gleaned from an examination of external manifestations, but the scales were removed from Peter's eyes by the revelation from God the Father.

On another occasion Jesus was greeted as the "hope of Israel," the sin bearer of the nation, as John the Baptist announced to the crowds the preeminence of Jesus. John testified that Christ was greater than he and directed people to follow him. When John was arrested and cast into prison, his faith began to falter and he sent to Jesus messengers asking the pointed question, "Are you the one who is to come, or shall we look for another?" Jesus responded to the messengers by saying, "Go and tell John what you hear and see: the blind receive their sight and the lame walk, lepers are cleansed and the deaf hear, and the dead are raised up, and the poor have good news preached to them" (Luke 7:20-22). These words were not idly chosen. Jesus was calling attention to the prophecy of Isaiah 61, the text that he had read the day he entered the synagogue in Capernaum. "The Spirit of the Lord is upon me, because he has anointed me to preach good news to the poor. He has sent me to proclaim release to the captives and recovering of sight to the blind, to set at liberty those who are oppressed, to proclaim the acceptable year of the Lord" (Luke 4:18-19). After he finished reading the scroll, Jesus said, "Today this scripture has been fulfilled in your hearing" (Luke 4:21). Essentially, Jesus' reply to the message of John was this: "Tell John to read again the prophecies of Isaiah, and he will know the answer to his question."

The Suffering Servant of Israel

The figure of the servant of the Lord or "suffering servant" spoken of by the prophet Isaiah is normative to the New Testament understanding of Jesus. Debates rage as to the identity of the author of Isaiah and the identity of the servant in the author's mind. Some argue that the servant referred to Israel corporately; others apply the role to Cyrus, and some even to Isaiah himself. This debate will surely continue, but the fact that the New Testament authors found in Jesus the ultimate fulfillment of this figure in Isaiah is beyond dispute.

It is also clear that Jesus thought of his own ministry in terms of Isaiah's prophecy, as we have seen from his statement in the synagogue and from his reply to John the Baptist's inquiry.

It is not by accident that Isaiah is the most frequently quoted prophet in the New Testament. Prophecies from Isaiah quoted in the New Testament are not limited to Jesus' suffering, but refer to Jesus' entire ministry. It was the death of Christ, however, that riveted the attention of the New Tes-

tament authors to the servant prophecies of Isaiah.
Let's look at Isaiah 53:

Who has believed what we have heard?
  And to whom has the arm of the LORD been revealed?
For he grew up before him like a young plant,
  and like a root out of dry ground;
he had no form or comeliness that we should look at him,
  and no beauty that we should desire him.
He was despised and rejected by men;
  a man of sorrows, and acquainted with grief;
and as one from whom men hide their faces
  he was despised, and we esteemed him not.

Surely he has borne our griefs
  and carried our sorrows;
yet we esteemed him stricken,
  smitten by God, and afflicted.
But he was wounded for our transgressions,
  he was bruised for our iniquities;
upon him was the chastisement that made us whole,
  and with his stripes we are healed.
All we like sheep have gone astray;
  we have turned every one to his own way;
and the LORD has laid on him
  the iniquity of us all.

He was oppressed, and he was afflicted,
  yet he opened not his mouth;

like a lamb that is led to the slaughter,
  and like a sheep that before its shearers is dumb,
  so he opened not his mouth.
By oppression and judgment he was taken away;
  and as for his generation, who considered
that he was cut off out of the land of the living,
  stricken for the transgression of my people?
And they made his grave with the wicked
  and with a rich man in his death,
although he had done no violence,
  and there was no deceit in his mouth.

Yet it was the will of the LORD *to bruise him;*
  he has put him to grief;
when he makes himself an offering for sin,
  he shall see his offspring, he shall prolong his
    days;
the will of the LORD *shall prosper in his hand;*
  he shall see the fruit of the travail of his soul and
    be satisfied;
by his knowledge shall the righteous one, my servant,
  make many to be accounted righteous;
  and he shall bear their iniquities.
Therefore I will divide him a portion with the great,
  and he shall divide the spoil with the strong;
because he poured out his soul to death,
  and was numbered with the transgressors;
yet he bore the sin of many,
  and made intercession for the transgressors.

Repeated study of Isaiah 53 augments rather than diminishes our astonishment at its content. It reads like an eyewitness account of the passion of Jesus. Here the principles of corporate solidarity and imputation of sin are clearly demonstrated. The scandal of Jesus is found in the centrality of his suffering as the way of redemption. The Messiah comes not only as king, but as a servant who receives the chastisement for the iniquity of the people. In this, the one dies for the many. Any interpretation of the life and work of Jesus that fails to take this aspect seriously does radical violence to the text of the New Testament.

That the concepts of the royal king of Israel and the suffering servant of Israel were merged in one man is seen dramatically in the heavenly vision that unfolds before the apostle John on the Isle of Patmos. In this scene, recorded in the fifth chapter of Revelation, John is given a glimpse behind the veil of heaven. He hears the cry of the angel, "Who is worthy to open the scroll and break its seals?" John reports with subdued emotion that no one was found worthy of the task. His disappointment, however, gave way to grief as he records, "I wept much that no one was found worthy to open the scroll or to look into it." At that point an elder consoled him, saying, "Weep not; lo, the Lion of the tribe of Judah, the Root of David, has conquered, so that he can open the scroll and its seven seals" (5:5).

An abrupt and marked change in the mood of the narrative follows, as a sense of excited expectancy replaces the atmosphere of despair. John awaits the appearance of the triumphal Lion. The irony is completed when John sees not a lion but a slain *lamb* standing in the midst of the elders. He records that the Lamb took the scroll from the right hand of him who was seated on the throne, and thousands of angels sang, "Worthy is the Lamb who was slain, to receive . . . honor and glory and blessing!" (5:12). Here the Lion and the Lamb are one and the same person. The servant reigns as king.

Jesus as Lord

The second most frequent designation for Jesus in the New Testament is the title *Lord*. So important is this title to the biblical understanding of Jesus that it became an integral part of the earliest Christian creed. The first creed was the simple statement, "Jesus is Lord." The title *Lord* is the most exalted title conferred upon Jesus.

Sometimes it is difficult for people in the United States to grasp the full significance of the title *Lord*. An Englishman came to this country in the decade of the sixties, and upon arrival spent his first week in Philadelphia becoming acquainted with historic landmarks, such as Independence Hall and the Liberty Bell. In order to familiarize himself with

American culture, he visited several antique stores that specialized in colonial and revolutionary memorabilia. In one such shop he saw several posters and signboards that contained the slogans of the revolution, such as No Taxation Without Representation, and Don't Tread on Me. One signboard attracted his attention more than the rest. In bold letters the sign proclaimed: WE SERVE NO SOVEREIGN HERE. As he mused on this sign, he wondered how people steeped in such an antimonarchical culture could come to grips with the notion of the kingdom of God and the sovereignty that belongs to the Lord. The concept of lordship invested in one individual is repugnant to the American tradition, yet this is the boldness of the claim of the New Testament for Jesus, that absolute sovereign authority and imperial power are vested in Christ.

The New Testament word for Lord is the Greek word *kurios*. The word was used in several ways in the ancient world. In its most common usage it functioned as a polite word for *sir*. As our English word *sir* can be used in an ordinary sense and in a special sense, so it was with *kurios*. In England, men who are knighted are given the title *sir*, indicating the elevation of the common use of the word to the formal use of it.

A second use of the title *Lord* in the Greek culture was as a title given to men of the aristocratic class who were slave owners. This title was used figuratively for Jesus throughout the New Testament. He was called "Master" by his disciples. Paul frequently introduced his epistles by saying, "Paul, a *slave* of Jesus Christ." The word he used was *doulos.* There could not be a slave *(doulos)* without a lord *(kurios).* Paul declared, "You are not your own; you were bought with a price" (1 Corinthians 6:19-20). Here the believer is seen as a possession of Jesus. Jesus owns his people. He is not a despot or tyrant, as we might expect in an earthly slave/master situation. In fact, the irony of New Testament lordship is the irony that only in slavery to Christ can a man discover authentic freedom. The irony is pushed further by the New Testament teaching that it is through a slave/master relationship to Jesus that a person is liberated from bondage in this world. This strange and ironic twist in teaching is found particularly in the writings of the apostle Paul.

The third and most important meaning of the title *Lord* was the *imperial usage.* Here the title was given to one who had absolute sovereignty over a group of people. It is a usage that was usually understood politically.

Perhaps the most striking aspect about the title *Lord* was its relationship to the Old Testament. The Greek translation of the Old Testament used the word *kurios* to translate the Hebrew word *adonai,* a title used for God himself. The sacred name of God, "Yahweh," was unspoken, often replaced in the liturgy of Israel with a substitute word, or by means of circumlocution. When a substitute title was used to replace the ineffable name of God, the usual selection was the term *adonai*, a title which called attention to God's absolute rule over the earth.

In many translations of the Bible both *Yahweh* and *adonai* are translated by the English word *Lord*, though a distinction between them is found in the method of printing used. When *Yahweh* is translated, the word is usually printed with a capital letter followed by small capital letters: LORD. When *adonai* is the Hebrew word, it is printed "Lord." Psalm 8, for example, begins: "O LORD, our Lord, how majestic is thy name in all the earth!" The Hebrew would be: "O Yahweh, our adonai, how majestic . . ." Here *Yahweh* functions as the name of God and the term *adonai* is used as a title.

The Old Testament passage that is quoted more often than any other text in the New Testament is Psalm 110. Here we find something strange indeed. Psalm 110 reads, "The LORD says to my lord: 'Sit at my right hand!' " Yahweh speaks to Adonai, who is seen as David's Lord and is seated at God's right hand. In the New Testament, Jesus is the one who is elevated to the right hand of God and receives the title *Lord*. This is the title that is "above every name" and is conferred upon Jesus at his ascension. Thus, Jesus being seated at the right hand of God is elevated to the seat of cosmic authority where all authority in heaven and earth is given into his hands, and he receives the title *Adonai* that had formerly been exclusively restricted to God the Father. The exalted nature of the title can be seen not only from this context, but also from usage in its superlative form. When Jesus is called "Lord of lords" there is no doubt what is meant. Here absolute authority over all lesser authority is clearly indicated.

The title *Lord* functions so frequently in the life of the New Testament Christian community that the English word *church* derives from it. The Greek word for church is *ekklesia,* which is brought over into English in the word *ecclesiastical.* The English word *church* is similar in sound and form to other languages' word for church. *Kirk* in Scotland, *kerk* in Holland, and *kirche* in Germany all derive from the same root. That source is the Greek word *kuriache,* which means "those who belong to the kurios." Thus the word *church* in its literal origin means "the people who belong to the Lord."

One puzzling note in the New Testament is the statement, "No one can say 'Jesus is Lord' except by the Holy Spirit" (1 Corinthians 12:3). Some have pointed to this as a contradiction because Jesus says on other occasions that people do in fact profess that he is Lord without meaning it. Jesus concludes the Sermon on the Mount with the somber warning, "On that day many will say to me, 'Lord, Lord . . .' But he will say to them, "I never knew you; depart from me" (Matthew 7:22-23). Since it is evident that people can honor Christ with their lips while their hearts are far from him, and offer the words *Jesus is Lord*, what does the Bible mean when it says, "No one can say 'Jesus is Lord' except by the Holy Spirit"?

There are two ways in which we can answer this question. The first would be by asserting what is tacitly understood in the text, but left unspoken. That is, no one can say that Jesus is Lord and *mean it*, except by the Holy Spirit. That would be sound theology, and we have literary license to fill in the unstated qualifier. There may, however, be something more concrete in view here. At the time the text was written, Christians were considered enemies of the established order of Rome and guilty of treason for their refusal to subscribe to the cult of emperor worship. Repeatedly the test for loyalty to the empire was to be found in the public recitation of the words *Kaiser kurios* ("Caesar is Lord"). It was this oath that Christians refused to recite, even when it cost them their lives. When they were called upon to utter it, they would substitute the words *Iesous ho Kurios* ("Jesus is Lord"). Christians were willing to pay their taxes, to give honor to Caesar where honor was due, to render to Caesar those things that were Caesar's. But the exalted title *Lord* belonged to Jesus alone, and Christians paid with their lives to maintain that assertion.

What was in view in the biblical text, "No one can say 'Jesus is Lord' except by the Holy Spirit," may have referred to the fact that in those days people hesitated to make such a bold statement publicly unless they were prepared to take the consequences.

The Son of Man

At the Council of Chalcedon in the fifth century, the Christian church sought to find a formula that would call attention both to the full humanity of Jesus and to his full deity. The words that were settled on in A.D. 451 were the words *vere homo, vere deus*. The formula meant that Jesus was truly man and truly God, calling attention to the fact of the two natures of Jesus. In the New Testament we find that Jesus is called both the Son of Man and the Son of God. These two titles appearing in this way offer a strong temptation to assume that "Son of God" refers exclusively to Jesus' deity and "Son of Man" refers exclusively to his humanity. This way of approaching these titles would lead us into very serious error.

With the title *Son of Man* we stumble upon something strange and fascinating. This title is the third most frequently used title for Jesus in the New Testament. It occurs eighty-four times, eighty-one of them in the four Gospels. In almost every single case that we find the title used, it is used by Jesus to describe himself. Thus, though it is only third in order of frequency of those titles found describing Jesus in the New Testament, it is number one with respect to Jesus' self-designation. It was obviously his favorite title for himself. This is evidence of the integrity of the biblical writers in preserving a title for Jesus that they themselves chose so infrequently. The temptation would have been to put their own favorite title in Jesus' mouth. It is commonplace in our day to argue that the biblical portrait of Jesus is merely the creation of the early church, rather than an accurate reflection of the real historic Jesus. If this were the case, it would be extremely unlikely that the early church would put into Jesus' mouth a title they almost never used themselves to describe him.

Why did Jesus use the title *Son of Man?* Some look at the title and assume that it was because of humility that he shunned more exalted titles and selected this one as a humble means of identifying with lowly humanity. Certainly there is an element of that identification in it, but the title as it functions in the Old Testament is anything but a humble one. There are references to the figure of the Son of Man found in Daniel, Ezekiel, and some extrabiblical writings of Rabbinic Judaism. Though scholars disagree, the historic consensus is that Jesus adopts the meaning of the term *Son of Man* as it is found in Daniel's visionary work.

In the book of Daniel, the Son of Man appears in a vision of heaven. He is presented before the throne of the "ancient of days" and is given "dominion and glory and kingdom, that all peoples, nations, and languages should serve him; his dominion is an everlasting dominion, which shall not pass away, and his kingdom one that shall not be destroyed" (Daniel 7:14). Here the Son of Man is a heavenly being, a transcendent figure who will descend to the earth to exercise the role of supreme judge.

The testimony in the New Testament to the preexistence of Jesus is inseparably linked to the Son of Man motif. He is the one who has "come from above." He is sent from the Father. The theme of the *descension* of Christ is the basis for his ascension. "No one has ascended into heaven but he who has descended from heaven, the Son of man" (John 3:13).

It is not enough to declare that the New Testament writers confessed Jesus was a heavenly being. Jesus was not just any heavenly being like an angel. He was described in language restricted to deity alone. It is interesting to compare the graphic description of Daniel's vision of the Ancient of Days with John's description of the Son of Man in the book of Revelation:

ANCIENT OF DAYS

As I looked,
thrones were
placed and one
that was ancient
of days took his
seat; his raiment
was white as
snow, and the
hair of his head
like pure wool;
his throne was
fiery flames, its
wheels were
burning fire. A
stream of fire
issued and came
forth from before
him; a thousand
thousands served
him, and ten
thousand times
ten thousand
stood before him;
the court sat in
judgment, and
the books were
opened. (Daniel
7:9-10)

SON OF MAN

Then I turned to see the
voice that was speaking to
me, and on turning I saw
seven golden lampstands,
and in the midst of the lampstands one like a son of man,
clothed with a long robe
and with a golden girdle
round his breast; his head
and his hair were white as
white wool, white as snow;
his eyes were like a flame
of fire, his feet were like
burnished bronze, refined
as in a furnace, and his voice
was like the sound of many
waters; in his right hand he
held seven stars, from his
mouth issued a sharp two-
edged sword, and his face
was like the sun shining in
full strength. . . . Then I
looked, and I heard around
the throne and the living
creatures and the elders the
voice of many angels, num-
bering myriads of myriads
and thousands of thousands,

saying with a loud voice,
"Worthy is the Lamb
who was slain, to receive
power and wealth and
wisdom and might and
honor and glory and blessing!" (Revelation 1:12-16;
5:11-12)

That the Son of Man was a figure of splendor and power cannot be missed. The deity is seen not only in the Old Testament portrait, but in Jesus' understanding as well. Jesus links the Son of Man with creation by saying, "The Son of man is lord even of the sabbath" (Mark 2:28). To claim lordship over the Sabbath is to claim it over creation. The Sabbath was not merely a piece of Sinaitic legislation, but a creation ordinance given by the Lord of Creation. Jesus also said, "That you may know that the Son of man has authority on earth to forgive sins" (Luke 5:24). Here, Jesus claims an authority that, to the Jew, was a prerogative of God alone. The Jews did not miss the inference of these claims. They sought to kill him precisely because his claims to deity came through loud and clear. The Son of Man came from heaven to judge the world. He would divide the sheep from the goats; he would come in clouds of glory at the end of the age.

The Son of Man who comes from heaven, however, is not one who is exclusively deity, but is one who enters into our humanity through incarnation. It is probable that Paul's concept of Jesus as the second Adam is an elaboration of the Son of Man motif.

The Son of God

It is rare in the pages of the New Testament that God himself is heard speaking audibly from heaven. When he does, it is normally to announce something startling. God is zealous to announce from his own lips that Jesus Christ is his Son. At the baptism, the heavens open and God's voice is heard saying, "This is my beloved Son, with whom I am well pleased" (Matthew 3:17). Elsewhere the Father declares from heaven: "This is my beloved Son; listen to him" (Mark 9:7). Thus the title conferred from on high to Jesus is the title *Son of God*.

This title has engendered a great deal of controversy in the history of the church, particularly in the fourth century, which resulted in the great ecumenical Council of Nicea. In the crisis of the fourth century, the Arian movement, taking its cue from its leader, Arius, denied the Trinity, arguing that Jesus was a created being.

References from the New Testament calling Jesus the "first-born of all creation" (Colossians 1:15), "the only begotten of the Father" (John 1:14, KJV), led Arius to argue that Jesus had a beginning in time and was thus a creature. If Jesus was begotten, it could only mean that he was not eternal, and if he was not eternal, then he was a creature. To ascribe deity to Jesus was to be guilty of blasphemy because it would involve the idolatrous worship of a created being. The same controversy exists today between Christian believers and the Mormons and Jehovah's Witnesses, who acknowledge a lofty view of Jesus over angels and other creatures but deny his full deity.

The Nicene Creed provides an interesting answer to the charges of Arianism. The answer is found in the strange statement that Jesus is "begotten, not made." To the Greek, such a statement was a contradiction in terms. In normal terms begotten does imply a beginning, but when applied to Jesus, there is a uniqueness to the way in which he is begotten that separates him from all other creatures. Jesus is called the *mono genais*, the "only begotten" of the Father. There is a sense in which Jesus and Jesus alone is begotten of the Father. This is what the church was getting at when it spoke of Jesus being eternally begotten—that he was begotten, not made. This uniqueness is found not only in Jesus' eternal character, but also in the fact that Jesus' sonship carries with it a description of intimacy with the Father; to be a Son of God biblically is to be one who is in a unique relationship of obedience to the will of God.

The primary significance to sonship in the New Testament is in its figurative reference to obedience. The motif of the firstborn has more to do with preeminence than with biology. The term *begotten* is a Greek word filled with Jewish content. Nicea was not flirting with irrationality, but was being faithful to Scripture by using the strange-sounding formula "begotten, not made."

The Logos

The title *Logos* is rarely used in the New Testament for Jesus. We find it prominently in the prologue to the Gospel of John where we read, "In the beginning was the Word [*Logos*], and the Word was with God, and the Word was God." In spite of the infrequency, this title became the focal point of the theological development of the Christian church's understanding of Jesus in the first three or four centuries of church history. It was the dominant concept by which the theologians of the church considered their own doctrine of Jesus. The great minds of Alexandria, of Antioch, of East and West, poured themselves into an exhaustive study of the meaning of this title. There are significant reasons for that. The title lends itself, perhaps more than any other title, to deep philosophical and theological speculation. That is precisely because the word *logos* was already a loaded term, one pregnant with meaning against the background of Greek philosophy.

As in the case of other titles we've already considered, there is a common meaning and a more technical meaning to the word *logos*. The common meaning for the word is simply "word, thought, or concept." English translations of the New Testament normally translate *logos* by the word *word*. But from the prologue of John we see that *logos* had an exalted meaning as well. The word *logic* in our English language derives from *logos*, and we also derive a suffix that is attached to many words in our vocabulary from this term. The suffix "ology" that is attached to different academic disciplines and sciences comes from it. Theology is "theos-logos," a word or concept of God. Biology is "bios-logos," a word or concept of life.

One Christian philosopher, Gordon H. Clark, suggests that the concept of the Logos could be fittingly translated as follows: "In the beginning was logic, and logic was with God and God was logic . . . and the logic became flesh." Such a translation may raise the hackles of Christians because it seems to represent a crass form of rationalism, reducing the eternal Christ to a mere rational principle. But that is not what Dr. Clark has in mind here. He is simply saying that in God himself there is a coherence, unity, consistency, and symmetry by which all things in this world hang together under his rule. God expresses this principle of coherency that comes from within his own being by his word, which is itself coherent, consistent, and symmetrical. John's prologue goes on to say that it is the Logos that creates all things and by which all things hang together. Here Christ is identified with the eternal Logos within God himself, which brings order and harmony to the created world.

It is this principle of coherency that forms the link between John's Christianized view of the Logos and the concept that was found in ancient Greek philosophy. The ancient Greeks were preoccupied with finding the ultimate meaning of the universe and the stuff from which everything was made. They perceived the vast diversity of creative things and sought for some point of unity that would make sense of it all. As in the case of Greek art, the thinkers of the day abhorred chaos and confusion. They wanted to understand life in a unified way. Thus, in many theories of philosophy that came before the writing of the New Testament, the Greek word *logos* functioned as an important concept. We think for example of Heraclitus, an early Greek philosopher, who is still revered by many as the patron saint of modern existentialism. Heraclitus had a theory that everything was in a state of change and that all things were composed ultimately of some form of fire. But Heraclitus required some explanation for the origin and root of things, and he located that in an abstract theory of a Logos.

We find the same concept in Stoic philosophy and even earlier in pre-Socratic philosophy. In early Greek thought there was no concept of a transcendent personal God who by his wisdom and sovereignty created the world in order and harmony. At best there was a speculative postulate of an abstract principle which ordered reality and kept it from becoming a blurb of confusion. This abstract principle they would call either a "nous" (which means mind) or the "Logos," an impersonal, philosophical principle. The concept of Logos was never considered as a personal being who would become involved with the things of this world, but the idea functioned merely as an abstraction necessary to account for the order evident in the universe.

The Stoics whom Paul debated at Mars Hill had a notion that all things were composed of an ultimate seminal fire, which they called the *Logos Spermatikos*. This referred to the seminal word, the word that contains within it procreative power, the word that begets life and order and harmony. We have all heard the expression "Every person has a spark of divinity in him." Such a notion of individual private sparks of divinity does not originate from Christianity, but from the Stoics. The Stoics believed that every individual object had a piece of the divine seminal fire in it, but again, the Logos in the Stoic concept remained impersonal and abstract.

By the time the Gospels were written, the notion of Logos was a loaded philosophical category. The apostle John dropped a theological bombshell on the philosophical playground of his day by looking at Jesus and talking about him not as an impersonal concept, but as the incarnation of the eternal Logos. He does not use the term in the same way that the Greeks did, but he baptizes it and fills it with a Jewish-Christian meaning. For John, the Logos is intensely personal and radically different from that which was found in Greek speculative philosophy. The Logos is a person, not a principle.

The second scandal to the Greek mind was that the Logos should become incarnate. For the ancient Greek nothing was more of a stumbling block than the idea of incarnation. Because the Greeks had a dualistic view of spirit and matter, it was unthinkable that God, if there was one, should ever take upon himself human flesh. This world of material things was viewed as being intrinsically imperfect, and for the Logos to clothe himself in the garb of a material world would be abhorrent to anyone steeped in classical Greek philosophy. The apostle John, under the inspiration of the Holy Spirit, looked at the personal, historic Christ and saw in him the manifestation of the eternal person by whose transcendent power all things hang together. This concept, perhaps more than any other, gave clear attention to the deity of Christ in his total cosmic significance. He is the Logos that created the heaven and the earth. He is the transcendent power behind the universe. He is the ultimate reality of all things.

The Logos is said to be not only with God, but to be God. There is no more direct statement or more clear affirmation of the deity of Christ to be found anywhere in Scripture than is found in the first verse of John's Gospel, "The Word was God." We know, of course, that modern-day Jehovah's Witnesses and Mormons have tried to obviate this passage by clever distortions of the text itself. Some of their translations change the text and simply say, "The Word was like God." The Greeks had a word for "like" that is found nowhere in this text of John. The simple structure, "The Word was God" can only mean an identity between Jesus and deity. Another way the modern-day Mormons and Jehovah's Witnesses seek to get around this passage is by arguing that the definite article is not present in the text. They assert since the Bible does not say the Word was *the* God, it simply says the Word *was* God, that this does not carry with it the weight of an affirmation of deity. Thus, we would be left with the statement that the Word was *a* god. If that was what John was trying to communicate, then the problems that this solution raises are greater than those it solves. It leaves us with John affirming a crass kind of polytheism. In the context of biblical literature, it is clear that there is but one God. The Bible is monotheistic from the beginning to the end. The absence or presence of the definite article has no theological significance whatsoever in this text.

There is some difficulty with the text in that the Word is said to be both *with* God and *in* God. Here we find that the Word is on the one hand distinguished from God and, on the other, identified with God. It is because of texts like this that the church found it necessary to formulate its doctrine of God in terms of the Trinity. We must see a sense in which Christ is the same as God the Father and yet be able to distinguish him from the Father. We have the idea that God and Jesus are one in being but two in person. The idea of distinguishing and yet identifying is not something that is an intrusion on the New Testament text, but a distinction that texts like John chapter one demand. The Father and the Son are one being, yet distinguished in terms of personality as well as by the work and ministry they perform.

In the first chapter of John the idea of the Logos being "with" God is significant. The Greek language has three different words, all of which can be translated by the English word *with*. The first is the word *sun* that is rendered into English as the prefix *syn*. We find it in words such as *synchronize*, *syncretism, synagogue,* etc. A synagogue, for example, is a place where people come together with other people. To be with in the sense of "sun" is to be present in a group, to be gathered with other people. This refers to a collection of people.

The second word that can be translated by the English word *with* is the word *meta,* which means "to be alongside of." When we think of people being alongside of each other we think of them standing side by side. If I were to walk side by side with a person down the street, I would be with him in the sense of "meta."

The Greeks have a third word that can be translated "with," and it is the word *pros.* This one is found less frequently than the others, but it is in the root word for another Greek word, *prosepone,* which means "face." This kind of "withness" is the most intimate of all types. John is saying here that the Logos existed with God, *pros* God, that is, face to face in a relationship of eternal intimacy. It is this very relationship that the Old Testament Hebrew yearns to have with his God. The Logos enjoys this kind of intimate face-to-face relationship from all eternity with the Father. The Father and Son are one in their relationship as well as in their being.

In John's prologue (1:1-14), the concept of the Logos comes to a climax as we read, "And the Word became flesh and dwelt among us . . . we have beheld his glory, glory as of the only Son from the

Father." Here this "dwelling" literally means to "pitch his tent among us." Even as God dwelt with the people of Israel in the Old Testament by means of a tabernacle, so the New Testament tabernacle is the incarnate Word, the Logos who embodies the truth of God himself. He is the mind of God made flesh, coming to dwell with us in flesh and blood. When he makes his appearance, it is a manifestation of glory. As John tells us, "In him was life, and the life was the light of men."

Jesus as Savior

There are other titles of note ascribed to Jesus. He is the Rabbi, the new Adam, the Mediator. But no title captures his work more completely than the title *Savior*. The believers of the early church bore witness to this when they used the sign of the fish as their cryptic signal of recognition. The acrostic formed by the letters of the Greek word for "fish," *ixthus*, spell out: Jesus Christ, Son of God, *Savior*.

God himself named Jesus as an infant. *Jesus* means "the Lord saves" or "the one through whom the Lord saves." Thus Jesus' own name carries within it the idea of savior. His titles—Logos, Messiah, Son of Man—all indicate Jesus' qualifications to be the Savior of men. He alone has the credentials to offer atonement, to triumph over death, to reconcile people to God.

Here is where the relevance of Jesus crashes into our lives, bringing crisis in its wake. Here is where we step over the line of detached scholarly investigation into the realm of personal vulnerability. We argue endlessly over matters of religion and philosophy, about ethics and politics but each person must ultimately face the personal issue squarely: "What do I do about my sin?"

That I sin and that you sin is debated by none save the most dishonest of men. We sin. We violate each other. We assault the holiness of God. What hope do we have in such dreadful turmoil? We can deny our sin or even the existence of God. We can exclaim that we are not accountable for our lives. We can invent a God who forgives everybody without requiring repentance. All such avenues are established in delusion. There is but one who qualifies as savior. He alone has the ability to solve our most abysmal dilemma. He alone has the power of life and death.

The titles of Jesus tell us who he is. Contained in them, however, is a thesaurus of insights into what he did. His person and his work meet in the drama of life. We move now to a consideration of the chronology of his career, highlighting those episodes in which person and work merge in the divine/ human plan of redemption.

CHAPTER 3

THE LIFE OF JESUS

We meet with controversy in the person of Jesus before he is even born. The extraordinary narrative of the circumstances surrounding his conception and birth provokes howls of protest from the critics of supernaturalism. The work of demythologizing begins early, with the scissors wielded on the first page of the New Testament. Following Matthew's table of genealogy, the first paragraph of the first Gospel reads as follows: "Now the birth of Jesus Christ took place in this way. When his mother Mary had been betrothed to Joseph, before they came together she was found to be with child of the Holy Spirit" (Matthew 1:18).

Though the New Testament is replete with miracles surrounding the person of Jesus, none seems more offensive to modern man than the Virgin Birth. If any law of science is established as immutable and unbreakable, it is that human reproduction is not possible without the conjoining of the male seed and the female egg. We may have developed sophisticated methods of artificial insemination and "test tube" intrauterine implantations, but in some manner the reproduction process requires the contribution of both genders of the race to succeed.

The birth of Jesus violates the inviolable; it mutates the immutable; it breaks the unbreakable. It is alleged to be an act that is pure and simple *contra naturam*. Before we even read of the activities of Jesus' life we are thrust headfirst against this claim. Many skeptics close the door on further investigation after reading the first page of the record. The story sounds too much like magic, too much like the sort of myth and legend that tends to grow up around the portrait of famous persons.

The arguments against the Virgin Birth are many. They range from the charge of borrowing mythical baggage from the Greek-speaking world with parallels evident in pagan mythology (Ovid's *Metamorphosis* is cited as "Exhibit A") to the scientific disclaimer that the Virgin Birth represents an empirically unverifiable unique event that denies all probability quotients. Some have offered a desperate exegetical argument trying to show that the New Testament doesn't teach the idea of virgin birth. This we call the exegesis of despair.

The real problem is that of miracle. It doesn't stop with the birth of Jesus but follows him through his life, his ministry, his death, resurrection, and ascension. The life of Jesus carries the aura of miracle wherever it is described in the primary sources. A "de-miraclized" Jesus is not the biblical Jesus, but the invention of those who cannot abide the biblical proclamation. A "de-miraclized" Jesus is the Jesus of unbelief, the most mythical Jesus of all, conjured up to fit the preconceived molds of unbelief.

Behind the problem of miracle are certain assumptions about the reality of God the Creator. Matthew's infancy narrative raises questions not only about parthenogenesis but about genesis itself. Creation is the unique event to beat all unique events. It's not so amazing that a God who has the power to bring the universe into being from nothing (*ex nihilo*)—without preexistent matter to work with, without means, but by the sheer omnipotent power of his voice—can also produce the birth of a baby by supernaturally fertilizing a material egg in a woman's womb. What defies logic is that a host of theologians grant the former but deny the latter. They allow the supernatural birth of the whole but deny its possibility to the part. We have to ask the painful question: Do they really believe in God in the first place, or is espoused belief in the Creator merely a societal convention, a veil to a more fundamental unbelief?

Perhaps the most ironclad law of nature is the
law of causality. Effects require causes. If the universe is an effect, in whole or in part, then it simply
requires a cause that is sufficient to the effect. The
cause may be *greater* than its effect, but it certainly
cannot be lesser. Modern science has not repealed
the law of causality, though some injudicious thinkers have sought to do so when prejudice requires it.
The other option to causality is to have something
come from nothing—no cause is asserted; no material cause, no efficient cause, no sufficient cause, no
formal cause, no final cause. Such a theory is not
science but magic. No, it cannot even be magic;
magic requires a magician. The law that something
cannot come from nothing remains unassailable (*ex
nihilo nihil fit*).

Does not Christianity assert a universe coming
from nothing? Do we not assert an *ex nihilo* creation? Indeed we do. But that "nothing" has reference to the absence of a *material cause*. There is a
sufficient cause for the universe. There is an *efficient*
cause for the universe. There is a God who has
within himself the power to create. God has the
power of being within himself. Such an assertion is
not gratuitous, nor is it the mere dogmatic assertion
of religion. It is a dictate of science and reason. If
something *is*, then something intrinsically has the
power of being. Somewhere, somehow, something
must have the *power of being*. If not, we are left with

only two options: (l) being comes from nothing or (2) we are faced with the contradiction "nothing is." Those options would be more miraculous than miracle if such were possible.

Some seek to escape the dilemma by pointing to the universe itself or to some undiscovered part of it as the eternal source of being. They try to explain the present world by saying that a supernatural or transcendent being is not required to account for the presence of being. To argue in this manner is to slip into a serious confusion of language. The universe daily exhibits effects. Nature changes. The very meaning of *super*nature or *transcendence* refers to questions of being. A being is said to be transcendent not because it is spacially or geographically located on the far side of Mars but because it has a special power of being—a higher order of being—defined precisely as that which has the power of being within itself. Wherever or whatever it is, is beside the point. I know it does not reside in me. I am not it. My very existence depends on it—without it I pass into nothing. I know I am an effect and so was my mother and her mother before her. If we retrace the problem infinitely we compound the problem infinitely. Modern man strains out the gnat and swallows the camel when he thinks he can have an existing world without a self-existing God.

The question of the Virgin Birth is not so much a philosophical question as it is an historical one. If one whom we call God has the power of being—sovereign efficient and sufficient causal power—then we cannot rationally object to the Virgin Birth on the grounds that it couldn't happen.

The real issue is not *could* it happen but *did* it happen. It becomes then a question of history and drives us once again to the historical sources. Those sources must be accepted or rejected on the basis of their credibility, a credibility that may not be predetermined by philosophical prejudice. The purpose of this essay is not primarily to assess the veracity of these historical sources—that requires a separate work—but to rehearse their content that we may examine the only historical portrait of Jesus we have.

Matthew begins with a sober and bold declaration, "Now the birth of Jesus Christ took place *in this way.*" Matthew purports to tell us not only what happened but how it happened. He declares it happened *in this way* (Matthew 1:18).

Matthew focuses sharply on the extraordinary character of Jesus' birth, capturing the agony of Joseph's consternation. Joseph was a simple man, not privy to the sophisticated technology of our day. He knew nothing of *in vitro* fertilization and was unfamiliar with debates of parthenogenesis. He did not understand the simple rules of biology that are common knowledge to today's tenth grade high school student. He lived in a prescientific age in a prescientific community. We must remember that virgin births were as rare in the first century as they are in the twentieth. Joseph did not have to be a skilled biologist to know that babies don't come from the stork.

Joseph was vulnerable *in extremis.* He had committed his life to Mary, trusting her purity in a society where adultery was scandalous. His betrothed came to him with a crushing revelation. "Joseph, I am pregnant." Mary then proceeded to explain her condition by telling Joseph that she had been visited by an angel who declared that she would be with child by the Holy Ghost. Joseph responded by tenderly considering "to divorce her quietly." There is no evidence of acrimony or furious rage by Joseph. He chose not to have her stoned, but began thinking of ways to protect Mary from the consequences of her delusions.

It is clear from the biblical text that Joseph was the first hard-core skeptic of the Virgin Birth until an angel visited him and made him a convert to the "delusion." Nothing else would do. What man would believe such a story with less than miraculous evidence to attest it?

The road from conception to birth, from Zacharias, Elizabeth, Mary, and Joseph to the shepherds outside of Bethlehem was a road surrounded by angels. They appeared at every turn, saturating the event with the supernatural.

With the scenario of angels in full play, the critic works overtime with his scissors. He needs an electric knife to do the job as angels appear at the birth, the temptation, the resurrection, and the ascension of Jesus. They are promised as part of the retinue of his return. The word *angel* appears more frequently in the New Testament than the word *sin*. It appears more often than the word *love*. Put the scissors to angels and you are engaged, not in biblical criticism, but in wreaking biblical vandalism.

Pilgrims flock daily to the sacred sites of the life of Jesus. They follow the route of the Via Dolorosa; they argue about the authentic site of Golgotha and the garden tomb. Modern mountains compete for recognition as the locus of the Sermon on the Mount. But the field outside of Bethlehem is not under dispute as the place where the glory of God was made visible to peasant shepherds, where the feet of angels stood in the dust of earth. The panorama of blazing effulgence sent these men to Bethlehem, obeying the mandate, "Go and see."

The Baptism of Jesus

The beginning of Jesus' public ministry was marked by his coming to the Jordan River and presenting himself to John the Baptist for baptism. Baptism is commonplace for us today, one of the most established of all liturgical activities in the practice of the Christian faith. Twentieth-century Christians are not surprised by the fact that Jesus was baptized, nor are we particularly excited about the ministry of John the Baptist. To a first-century Jew, however, the activity of John the Baptist was regarded as radical.

In light of the New Testament understanding of the person of Jesus, the fact that Jesus submitted himself to baptism is a sign of cleansing from sin. Yet the New Testament teaches that Jesus was without sin. Why would the sinless Son of God come forward and present himself for baptism when it symbolized a cleansing from sin?

> In those days came John the Baptist, preaching in the wilderness of Judea, "Repent, for the kingdom of heaven is at hand." For this is he who was spoken of by the prophet Isaiah when he said, "The voice of one crying in the wilderness: Prepare the way of the Lord, make his paths straight." (Matthew 3:1-3)

The biblical narrative does not begin with the public ministry of Jesus but rather with the public ministry of John the Baptist. The voice of prophecy had been silenced in Israel for four hundred years. Between the time of Malachi and the ministry of John the Baptist there had not been heard a single word of prophetic utterance. The coming of John the Baptist marked a significant departure, not only in the national history of Israel, but in what we call redemptive history. Something new was on the scene as John came fulfilling the portrait and the character of the forerunner of the Messiah.

The last prophecy found in the last paragraph of the Old Testament reads:

> *Remember the law of my servant Moses, the statutes and ordinances that I commanded him at Horeb for all Israel. Behold I will send you Elijah the prophet before the great and terrible day of the LORD comes. And he will turn the hearts of fathers to their children and the hearts of children to their fathers, lest I come and smite the land with a curse. (Malachi 4:4-6)*

For centuries the people of Israel waited, planned, and looked for the return of Elijah. When Elijah left this world, his departure was extraordinary. He escaped the normal pangs of death, being taken up bodily into heaven in a chariot of fire. Because of his unusual departure there was a mystique attached to this man who stood at the beginning of the line of the prophetic order in the Old Testament. The last Old Testament prophet, Malachi, said that before the Messiah would appear, the first of the Old Testament prophets, Elijah, would return.

The figure of John the Baptist was a strange one. He came out of the desert, the traditional meeting place between God and his people, where prophets went to commune with God and receive their marching orders from Yahweh. He was dressed in bizarre clothes, wearing a loin cloth of camel hair. He ate wild locusts and honey, appearing like a wild man, a misfit in society. He echoed the style of Elijah. The public response to John the Baptist was electric. As the masses poured out to see him, the Sanhedrin sent delegates to the Jordan River to investigate. The first question they asked was, "Are you Elijah?" John replied mysteriously, "I am not. . . . I am the voice of one crying in the wilderness, 'Make straight the way of the Lord.'" John said he was not Elijah. When Jesus was asked the same question about John the Baptist, he declared to his disciples, "He is the Elijah who was to come" (Matthew 11:14, NIV). His declaration was couched in enigmatic words of preface, "If you are willing to accept it." Jesus was announcing that the Old Testament prophecy of Malachi was fulfilled in the ministry of John the Baptist. There was no exact identity between John and Elijah. John was not the reincarnation of Elijah, but he reestablished the ministry, the power, and the office of Elijah. He came in the spirit of Elijah, fulfilling the mission of Elijah.

When we pose the question, "Who is the greatest prophet in the Old Testament?" the list of candidates usually includes such prophetic titans as

Isaiah, Jeremiah, Ezekiel, or Daniel. One stands above them all, laying claim to this singular honor—John the Baptist. But the question inquired about the *Old* Testament prophets. John *was* an Old Testament prophet. His ministry is recorded in the books of the New Testament, but his activity took place in what was still part of Old Testament history. Jesus declared, "All the prophets and the law prophesied until John" (Matthew 11:13). The word *until* in the text carries the force of "up to and including." John both closes the Old Testament line of prophets and provides a bridge, a transition to the New.

Jesus declared that "among those born of women there has risen no one greater than John the Baptist; yet he who is least in the kingdom of heaven is greater than he" (Matthew 11:11). How can this be? Suppose I qualify for the rank of least in the kingdom. Does that make Sproul greater than John the Baptist? Greater in what sense? More devout? More righteous? More knowledgeable? God forbid. What Jesus is saying is that anyone who lives on this side of the cross, this side of the Resurrection, this side of the New Covenant, this side of the inauguration of the kingdom of God, enjoys a far better situation, a far greater blessedness than John the Baptist. John was an eyewitness of Jesus of Nazareth and the herald of the coming kingdom of God, but he died before the kingdom was inaugurated.

John belongs to the Old Testament line of prophets, yet he differs from all of them at a crucial point. The Old Testament prophets predicted that someday the Messiah would come, a "someday" obscured by vague references to the future. John was tapped by God to be the herald, the escort who ushered in the Messiah. The "someday" became John's day. His message was not "Repent for the kingdom is coming," but rather, "Repent for the kingdom of God is at hand" (Matthew 3:2). It is at hand! John used two important metaphors to call attention to the urgency of the hour. He said, "the axe is laid to the root of the trees" and "his winnowing fork is in his hand" (Luke 3:9, 17).

John's images conjure up the vision of a woodsman who goes into the forest and begins to chip away with his axe at a huge tree. He penetrates the outer edge of the wood and sees that an enormous task remains. As his work progresses the axe moves to the inner core of the tree, and the giant oak totters on one slender thread of wood. One more blow from the axe brings the tree crashing to the ground. This is the moment of breakthrough. John was declaring that the kingdom is about to come crashing through.

The image of the farmer with his fan in his hand was drawn from the agricultural environment of

John's day. It is an image we could easily misunder-
stand in our culture. When we think of someone
poised, with fan in hand, we think of visiting the
opera or seeking relief on a humid, sweltering
night. The image of a fan in the hand suggests a
kind of boredom or aloofness from one's circumstances. That is not the kind of fan John was talking
about. He was talking about the winnowing fan,
the tool farmers used to separate the wheat from
the chaff. The farmer scooped up the mixture of
wheat and chaff and pitched it in the air where the
zephyrs of wind were strong enough to carry the
chaff away. The farmer had gone beyond the time
of preparation. He had already been to the toolshed
to fetch his winnowing fork. The moment had
come to pick up the fork for the task of separation.
John speaks to the moment of history, the crisis
moment when men will be judged whether they
are for the kingdom of God or against it. The King
has arrived, and his arrival brings crisis to mankind. John sings the *agnus dei* as his eyes behold the
Christ. His lips break out in song saying, "Behold,
the Lamb of God, who takes away the sin of the
world!" (John 1:29).

The baptism John initiated had many points of
continuity and parallel with the later rite of baptism Jesus instituted which became a church sacrament, but they were not precisely the same. John's
baptism was designed and directed exclusively for

Israel, to call the Jewish nation to readiness for the coming of their king. The roots of baptism are found in the Old Testament situation where converts to Judaism from the Gentile world were subjected to a cleansing rite called proselyte baptism. For a Gentile to become a Jew he had to do three things. He had to make a profession of faith in which he embraced the teachings of the law and the prophets; he had to be circumcised; and he had to be purified by the bath of proselyte baptism. The Gentile was considered impure and unclean. To enter into the household of Israel he had to take a bath. The radical dimension of John's ministry was that he suddenly demanded that Jews submit to baptism. The rulers of Israel did not miss the scandalous offense of John's message. John was saying, "The kingdom of God is coming and you are not ready. In the sight of God you are as unclean and as impure as a Gentile." The humble people of the community acknowledged their need for the cleansing, but the clergy were furious. John's ministry stirred up so much popular reaction that the great Jewish historian Josephus gave more space to his record of John the Baptist than he did to Jesus.

When Jesus appeared at the Jordan, John burst out into a litany of praise lauding Jesus as the Lamb of God. He declared that Jesus must increase while he himself would decrease, and that he, John, was unworthy to reach down and untie Jesus' shoes.

These exalted statements fell to the ground when
Jesus stepped forward and said to John, "I need to
be baptized by you." John was incredulous and
shrank in horror at the suggestion that he should
baptize the Christ. John sought to turn the tables
and have Jesus baptize him, but Christ refused.

John's understanding of theology was limited.
He knew the Messiah must be the Lamb of God,
and he knew that the paschal lamb must be without
blemish. What distressed him was that Jesus approached the river as a soiled Jewish person who
needed to take a bath. The precise words that Jesus
spoke to John are important for our understanding
of this event: "Let it be so now; for thus it is fitting
for us to fulfill all righteousness" (Matthew 3:15).

In these words Jesus stifles a lengthy discussion
about theology. In effect he says, "Just do what I tell
you, John. There is time later to seek understanding
of it."

Jesus was baptized to fulfill all righteousness.
This was consistent with his entire mission to keep
every jot and tittle of the law. Jesus took upon
himself every obligation that God imposed upon
the Jewish nation. To be the sin-bearer of the nation
it was incumbent upon him to fulfill every requirement that God demanded of Israel. Jesus was scru-
pulous, meticulous, indeed punctilious in his zeal
for his Father's house. He was presented in the
temple as an infant, he was circumcised, he went

through bar mitzvah, and he embraced the new obligation of baptism that God had imposed upon the nation.

The baptism of Jesus carried not only the sign of his identification with a sinful people, but it also marked his consecration, his anointing for the mission the Father had given him. His baptism sealed his doom, causing his face to be set like a flint toward Jerusalem. On a later occasion Jesus spoke to his disciples saying, "Are you able . . . to be baptized with the baptism with which I am baptized?" (Mark 10:38). He was baptized to die. He was appointed to be the sacrificial lamb, and at his ordination the heavens opened and God spoke audibly, saying, "This is my beloved Son, with whom I am well pleased" (Matthew 3:17).

The Temptation of Christ

The New Testament records that immediately after Jesus underwent the rite of baptism he was driven by the Holy Spirit into the wilderness to be tempted. He had just heard the voice from heaven saying, "This is my beloved Son, with whom I am well pleased," and the Spirit had descended upon him in the form of a dove. This same Spirit "drove" Jesus (he did not invite, request, or entice him) into the wilderness.

How can the New Testament speak of God leading Jesus into temptation? We are explicitly told in James 1:13 that no one should say when he is tempted that he is tempted of God, for our temptations come as they arise out of our own lust or sinful disposition. Was Jesus an exception to this rule? The word *tempt* is used in at least two different ways in Scripture. On the one hand there is the sense of temptation that suggests an enticing or wooing into sin. God never indulges in that. On the other hand there is the temptation that carries the meaning of "being put to the test," or passing through a trial of moral probation. It is this meaning that describes the trial of Jesus in the wilderness.

Adam and Christ. The temptation of Christ offers a striking parallel to the probation of Adam in the Garden of Eden. We note both similarities and differences between the first Adam of Genesis and the one whom the New Testament calls the new Adam, Jesus. Both are tested not only for their own sakes but in behalf of others. Adam's trial is for the entire human race. As the federal head of mankind, Adam represents the human race. His fall is our fall. Jesus stands for a new humanity as he faces the ardors of the new probation.

The respective locations of the tests provide a study in contrasts. Jesus' temptation took place in a desolate section of the remote hills of the Judean wilderness, a dreadful piece of real estate. The only creatures indigenous to the area were spiders, snakes, scorpions, and a few wild birds. It was rocky, barren, and hot; fit for neither man nor beast. Adam's test took place in a garden of paradise adorned with lush and glorious surroundings. Where Adam beheld a landscape of floral luxury, Jesus stared at a rock pile.

Jesus endured temptation in isolation, in what Kierkegaard called the worst situation of human anxiety, existential solitude. Jesus was utterly alone. Adam was tested while enjoying the help and encouragement of a companion whom God had created for him. In the midst of human fellowship, indeed intimacy, Adam was tested. In the agony of deprivation of human communion, Jesus was tested.

Adam was tested in the midst of a feast. His locale was a gourmet's dream. He faced Satan on a full stomach and with a satiated appetite. Yet he succumbed to the temptation to indulge himself with one more morsel of food. Jesus was tested after a forty-day fast, when every fiber of his body was screaming for food. His hunger had reached a crescendo, and it was at the moment of consuming physical desire that Satan came with the temptation to break the fast.

It is the similarity, however, between the tests that is most important for us to grasp. The central issue, the point of attack, was the same. In neither case was the ultimate issue a matter of food; the issue was the question of believing God. It was not an issue of believing in God, but believing God. There was no doubt in Adam's mind that God existed; he had spent time in face-to-face communication with him. Jesus was equally certain of God's existence. The trial centered on believing God when it counted.

The serpent, described in Genesis as the most subtle of the beasts of the field, intruded into the idyllic domain of Adam and Eve. His initial assault was not forthright but came by way of innuendo. He raised a simple question which thinly veiled a blasphemous thought: "Did God say?" A gossamer film of doubt was suddenly applied to the integrity of God's word. "Did God say, 'You shall not eat of any tree of the garden?'" (Genesis 3:2).

A ridiculous question, so blatantly false that Eve could not miss the error of it. Like a primordial Lieutenant Columbo, the serpent set Eve up by appearing naive, by manipulating her to underestimate his cleverness. Eve was quick to correct the error. Of course God had made no such all-inclusive negative prohibition. Quite the contrary. God had declared that they could eat freely of all the trees of the garden, save one. The restriction was slight and trivial compared with the broad expanse of liberty granted in the garden.

The subtle hint was already made. The hidden agenda was doing its work, suggesting the idea that the French philosopher Jean-Paul Sartre formalized in our day: If man is not totally free, if he does not enjoy autonomy, he is not truly free at all. Unless freedom is absolute, it is but an illusion, a facade hiding the reality of servitude. This was the innuendo of the serpent, a hint received not only by Eve but by all her children. If we give our assent for our children's requests fifteen times in a row, then break the streak with one *no*, the response is immediate: "You never let me do anything!"

Give Eve credit. She met the first wave of the serpent's assault with valor. She defended the honor of God by setting the record straight. The serpent adroitly switched tactics, moving at once to the direct attack with a diabolical sledgehammer, "You will not die, . . . you will be like God" (Genesis 3:4). Satan was not offering a piece of fruit but held out the promise of deification. His words were a clear and direct contradiction to what God had said.

There is tragic irony in the motto some theologians of our day have embraced. Allergic to rationality and suspicious of logic, they glory in the mixing of Christianity and existential philosophy. The motto decrees that "Contradiction is the hallmark of truth." It is said that truth is so high, so holy that it not only transcends the power of reason, but it goes against it as well. Religious truth is not only *supra*rational, it is deemed *contra*rational as well.

Apply the motto to Adam's trial. Adam, enjoying a facility of intelligence as yet unaffected by the consequences of the Fall, hears the serpent's words. Immediately he recognizes that the serpent's words collide with God's. God said if you eat of the tree you die. The serpent said if you eat you will not die. Adam applies the canons of logic to the proposition. "If you do A, B will necessarily follow," said God. "If you do A, non B will follow," said the serpent. "Aha," muses Adam, "that violates the law of noncontradiction." Adam pursues the thought with rigorous analysis. The serpent speaks a contradiction. Contradiction is the hallmark of truth. God is truth. Q.E.D. by resistless logic, Adam's only conclusion would be that the serpent was an ambassador of God. Now it is not only Adam's privilege to eat the once forbidden fruit, but it is his moral duty. To resist the contradiction is to resist the hallmark of truth. In this mode of thinking Adam's fall was not a fall down but a great leap forward for mankind.

To call contradiction the hallmark of truth is to reach the nadir of theology. It can sink no lower. If contradiction heralds truth, we have no means to distinguish between truth and falsehood, between obedience and disobedience, between righteousness and unrighteousness, between Christ and Antichrist.

Biblically, contradiction is the hallmark of the lie. Truth may be mysterious, indeed even paradoxical, but never, never, never contradictory. The serpent spoke the first contradiction, and Jesus rightly declared him to be a liar from the beginning, the father of lies. Adam bought the lie. He grasped for the very throne of God, slandering the veracity of his Creator in the act.

Jesus faced the same issue in his trial. The same subtleness is employed with Satan's opening lines: "*If* you are the Son of God, command these stones to become loaves of bread" (Matthew 4:3). Notice Satan did not introduce the words of temptation by saying, "*Since* you are the Son of God . . ." What were the last words to ring in the ears of Christ before he entered the wilderness? God had audibly announced from heaven, "This is my beloved Son. . . ." Such words may grow difficult to trust after enduring forty days of deprivation. Jesus was hardly enjoying the prerogatives of the Prince of Heaven. Satan's subtle attack was the same point of invasion that worked so successfully in Eden, "Did God say?"

Jesus foils the subtlety by an unequivocal response: "It is written. . . ." These words were a Semitic formula for saying, "The Bible says . . ." He rebukes Satan with a citation from Scripture. "Man shall not live by bread alone, but by every word that proceeds from the mouth of God" (Matthew

4:4). It was as if Jesus was saying, "Of course I am hungry. I already know I can turn stones into bread. But some things are more important than bread. I live by the Word of God. That is my life."

The devil refused to quit. He took Jesus to the pinnacle of the temple and tested him again. "*If* you are the Son of God, throw yourself down; for it is written, 'He will give his angels charge of you'" (Matthew 4:6). Now Satan recites the Scriptures, twisting them for his own purposes. The test is clear, "If God's Word is true, put it to the test— jump, and see if the angels catch you."

Jesus answered Scripture with Scripture, reminding Satan that the Bible prohibits tempting God. Perhaps the dialogue went like this: "I perceive, Mr. Satan, that you are an astute student of the Bible. You have even committed salient parts of it to memory. But your hermeneutics are shoddy; you set Scripture against Scripture. I know the Father has promised that he would give the angels charge over me. I don't have to jump off pinnacles to confirm it. Right now the Father is testing me; I am not testing him."

Still Satan refused to surrender. He took Jesus to a high mountain and showed him all the kingdoms of the world and said, "All these I will give you, if you will fall down and worship me" (Matthew 4:9). They were in a far country beyond the eyes of observers.

No one would notice a small act of betrayal. Only a slight genuflection was necessary. Why not?

The Father had already promised Jesus all the kingdoms of the world, but the price tag was the cross. There could be no exaltation without humiliation. Satan offered an easier way. No bitter cup, no passion, no mockery. One bend of the knee and the world was Christ's.

Jesus replied, "It is written, 'You shall worship the Lord your God and him only shall you serve'" (Matthew 4:10). There could be no compromise. Can you hear the dialogue couched in twentieth-century terms? Satan charges, "Jesus, you are rigid and narrow-minded. Are you so pedantic about Scripture that you will choose death rather than compromise a single line of it? Don't you understand that the Law you cite is out of date? It comes from the Pentateuch, and we now know that Moses didn't even write it. It reflects the primitive beliefs of unsophisticated man, encased in primitive mythology and superstitious taboos."

"I am sorry," said Jesus. "It is Scripture and the Scripture cannot be broken."

Jesus believed God, and Satan departed from him. Where Adam collapsed, Jesus conquered. Where Adam compromised, Jesus refused to negotiate. Where Adam's trust in God faltered, Jesus' never wavered. The second Adam triumphed for himself and for us.

One parallel remains to be noted. At the end of Jesus' trial, angels appeared to minister to him, precisely as the Father had promised. Adam saw an angel too. His angel was carrying a flaming sword as he stood guard at the gates of Paradise. That sword banished Adam to live east of Eden.

The Passion of Christ

If there is any event that has transpired on this planet too high and too holy for us to comprehend, it is the passion of Christ—his death, his atonement, and his foresakenness by the Father. We would be totally intimidated to speak of it at all were it not for the fact that God in his Word has set before us his revelation of its meaning. In this section we focus our attention on the biblical interpretation of Christ's death on the cross.

Any time we discuss a historical event, we review the facts, and sometimes we argue about what really took place, what was said, what was observed. But once we agree on the facts (or agree to disagree), we are still left with the most important question we can ask: What is the meaning of the event?

The people who witnessed Christ stumbling to Golgotha, who saw him delivered to the Romans, and who watched his crucifixion, understood the significance of this event in a variety of ways. There were those present who thought that they were viewing the just execution of a criminal. Caiaphas, the high priest, said that Christ's death was expedient and that he had to die for the good of the nation. He saw the crucifixion as an act of political appeasement. A centurion who watched how Jesus died said, "Truly this man was the Son of God!" (Matthew 27:54). Pontius Pilate, the two thieves who were crucified next to Jesus—everyone, it seems, had a different understanding of what the cross signified.

The cross has been a favorite theme of theological speculation for two thousand years. If we would peruse the various theological schools of thought today, we would find a multitude of different theories competing with one another as to what really happened on the cross. Some say it was the supreme act of illustrating sacrificial love. Others say it was the supreme act of existential courage, while still others say it was a cosmic act of redemption. The dispute goes on.

However, in the Scriptures we have not only the record of the events, primarily in the Gospels, but we also have God's interpretation of those events, primarily in the Epistles. In Galatians 3:13, Paul discusses the meaning of the cross, summarizing the entire teaching of the chapter in a single verse: "Christ redeemed us from the curse of the law, having become a curse for us—for it is written, 'Cursed be every one who hangs on a tree.'"

This curse motif would have been understood clearly by a knowledgeable Jew in the ancient world, but in our day it has a foreign sound to it. To us, the very concept of "curse" smacks of something superstitious. When I hear the word *curse* I think of Oil Can Harry in the *Perils of Pauline*, who says, "Curses, foiled again" when the hero saves the heroine from his clutches. Or, we think of the behavior of primitive tribes who practice voodoo, in which tiny replica dolls are punctured by pins as a curse is put on an enemy. Or, we think of the curse of the mummy's tomb in Hollywood horror movies with Vincent Price and Bella Lugosi. A curse in our day and age is considered something that belongs in the realm of superstition.

In biblical categories, a curse has quite a different meaning. In the Old Testament, the curse refers to the negative judgment of God. It is the antonym, the opposite, of the word *blessing*. Its roots go back to the giving of the law in the book of Deuteronomy when the covenant is established with Israel. There is no covenant without sanctions attached to it, provisions for reward for those who keep the terms of the covenant and provisions of punishment for those who violate the covenant. God says to his people, "See, I am setting before you today a blessing and a curse—the blessing if you obey the commands of the

LORD your God that I am giving you today; the curse if you disobey the commands of the LORD your God and turn from the way that I command you today by following other gods which you have not known" (Deuteronomy 11:26-28, NIV). The curse is the judgment of God on disobedience, on the breaking of the holy law of God.

The meaning of the curse may be grasped more fully by viewing it in contrast to its opposite. The word *blessed* is often defined in Hebrew terms quite concretely. In the Old Testament, after fellowship with God was violated in Eden, people could still have a proximate relationship with God, but there was one absolute prohibition. No one was allowed to look into the face of God. That privilege, the beatific vision, is reserved for the final fulfillment of our redemption. This is the hope that we have, that someday we will be able to gaze unveiled, directly into the face of God. We are still under the mandate, "man shall not see [God] and live" (Exodus 33:20). It was always the Jewish hope, however, that someday this punishment for the fall of man would be removed. The Hebrew benediction illustrates this.

> The LORD *bless you and keep you.*
> The LORD *make his face to shine upon you, and be*
>   *gracious to you:*
> The LORD *lift up his countenance upon you, and*
>   *give you peace. (Numbers 6:24-26)*

This is an example of Hebrew parallelism. Each of the three stanzas are saying the same thing: May the Lord bless; May the Lord make his face shine; May the Lord lift up his countenance upon you. The Israelite understood blessedness concretely: to be blessed was to be able to behold the face of God. One could enjoy the blessing only in relative degrees, as the closer one got to the ultimate face-to-face relationship, the more blessed he was. Conversely, the farther removed from that face-to-face relationship, the greater the curse. So by contrast, in the Old Testament the curse of God involved being removed from his presence altogether. The full curse precluded a glimpse, even at a distance, of the light of his countenance. It forbade even the refracted glory of one ray of the beaming light radiating from the face of Yahweh. To be cursed was to enter into the place of absolute darkness outside the presence of God.

This symbolism was carried out through the history of Israel and extended to the liturgy of the Jewish people. It applied to the position of the tabernacle, the tent of meeting, which was designed to symbolize the promise that God would be in the midst of his people. God ordained that the people would pitch their tents by tribes in such a way that they were gathered around the central point of the community where the tabernacle, the dwelling place of Yahweh, stood. Only the high priest was permitted to enter into the midst of the tabernacle, the Holy of holies, and only on one day a year, on the Day of Atonement. Even then, only lengthy ablutions and cleansing rights made it possible for him to enter into the sacred place. God was in the midst of his people, but they could not enter the inner sanctum of the tabernacle, which symbolized his dwelling place.

On the Day of Atonement, two animals were involved in the liturgical ceremonies, a lamb and a scapegoat. The priest sacrificed the lamb on the altar for the sins of the people. The priest also took the scapegoat and placed his hands upon it, symbolizing the transfer of the sins of the nation to the back of the goat. Immediately the scapegoat was driven outside the camp into the wilderness, into that barren place of remote desolation—to the outer darkness away from any proximity to the presence of God. The scapegoat received the curse. He was cut off from the land of the living, cut off from the presence of God.

In order to grasp the significance of this action as it relates to Christ's death, we must turn to the New Testament, to John 1:1. John begins his Gospel, "In the beginning was the Word, and the Word was with God, and the Word was God." The mystery of the Trinity has puzzled our minds for centuries. We know that there is a sense in which the Father and the Son are one, yet they are to be distinguished, and they exist in a very unique relationship. The relationship, as John explains it, is described by the word *with*. And the Word was *with* God. Literally, John is saying that Father and Son have a face-to-face relationship, precisely the type of relationship Jews were denied with the Father. The Old Testament Jew could go into the tabernacle and be "with" (*sun*) God, but no one could ever be *pros* God.

When we examine the Crucifixion, it is important for us to remember that Jesus' relationship with the Father represents the ultimate in blessedness and that its absence is the essence of the curse. When we read the narrative of the passion of Jesus, certain things stand out. The Old Testament teaches us that his own people delivered him to the Gentiles, to strangers and foreigners to the covenant. After his trial before the Jewish authorities, he was sent to the Romans for judgment. He was not executed by the Jewish method of stoning, for the circumstances of world history at that time precluded that option. When capital punishment was exercised under the Roman occupation, it had to be done by the Roman courts, so execution had to be by the Roman method of crucifixion. It is significant that Jesus was killed at the hands of the Gentiles *outside the camp*. His death took place outside the city of Jerusalem; he was taken to Golgotha. All of these activities, when woven together, indicate the reenactment of the drama, of the scapegoat who received the curse.

Paul tells us that in the Deuteronomic law the curse of God is upon anyone who hangs from a tree, a curse not necessarily given to those who suffer death by stoning. Jesus hangs on a tree, fulfilling in these tiny details all of the Old Testament provisions for the execution of divine judgment. The New Testament sees the death of Jesus as more than an isolated act or illustration of courage or love, though his death may illustrate those things. Rather it is seen as a cosmic event, an atoning death; it is a curse that is poured out upon Christ for us.

The Swiss theologian Karl Barth said that the most important word in the whole New Testament is the little four-letter Greek word, Y'uper *(huper)*. The word *huper* means simply "in behalf of." The death of Jesus is in behalf of us. He takes the curse of the law for me and for you. Jesus, himself, said it in many different ways: "I lay down my life for the sheep. . . . No one takes it from me, but I lay it down of my own accord" (John 10:15, 18). "For even the Son of Man did not come to be served, but to serve, and to give his life as a ransom for many" (Mark 10:45, NIV). These New Testament images underscore the concept of substitution.

I once delivered a public lecture on the relationship between the old and new covenants when, in the middle of my lecture, a man jumped up in the back of the room. He became outraged when I suggested that Jesus Christ's death was an atoning death, a substitutionary death on behalf of other people. He shouted from the back of the room, "That's primitive and obscene." I replied, "Those are the two best descriptive words I have heard to characterize the Cross." What could be more primitive? A bloody enactment like this, with all the drama and ritual, is reminiscent of primitive taboos. It is so simple that even the most uneducated, the most simpleminded person, can understand it.

God provides a way of redemption for us that is not limited to an intellectual elite, but is so crass, so crude, that the primitive person can comprehend it, and, at the same time, so sublime that it brings consternation to the most brilliant theologians. But I particularly like the second word, *obscene.* It is a most appropriate word because the cross of Christ was the most obscene event in human history. Jesus Christ became an obscenity. The moment that he was on the cross, the sin of the world was imputed to him like it was to the back of the scapegoat. The obscenity of the murderer, the obscenity of the prostitute, the obscenity of the kidnapper, the obscenity of the slanderer, the obscenity of all those sins, as they violate people in this world, were at one moment, focused on one man. Once Christ embraced that, he himself became the incarnation of sin, the absolute paragon of obscenity.

It is an obscene symbol that we display to the world, the symbol of the cross. There is a sense in which Christ on the cross was the most filthy and grotesque person in the history of the world. In and of himself he was a lamb without blemish—sinless, perfect, and majestic. But by imputation, all of the ugliness of human violence was concentrated on his person.

Once sin was concentrated on Jesus, God cursed him. When the curse of the law was poured out upon Jesus, he experienced pain that had never been suffered in the annals of history. I have heard graphic sermons about the excruciating pain of the nails in the hands, of hanging on a cross, and of the torturous dimensions of crucifixion. I am sure that they are all accurate and that it was a dreadful way to be executed, but literally thousands of people in world history have undergone the excruciating pain of crucifixion. Only one man has ever felt the pain of the fullness of the unmitigated curse of God upon him. When he felt it, he cried out, "My God, my God, why have you forsaken me?" (Mark 15:34, NIV). Some say he did that simply to quote Psalm 22. Others say he was disoriented by his pain and didn't really understand what was happening. God certainly *did* forsake him. That is the whole point of the atonement. Without forsakenness, there is no curse. God, at that moment in space and time, turned his back on his Son.

The intimacy of the *pros* relationship that Jesus experienced with the Father was ruptured (at least in his human nature). At that moment God turned out the lights. The Bible tells us that the world was encompassed with darkness, God himself bearing witness to the trauma of the hour. Jesus was forsaken, he was cursed, and he felt it. The word *passion* means "feeling." In the midst of forsakenness, I doubt if he was even aware of nails in his hands or thorns in his brow. He was cut off from the Father. It was obscene, yet it was beautiful, because by it we can someday experience the fullness of the benediction of Israel. We will look unveiled into the light of the countenance of God.

The Resurrection of Jesus

The life of Jesus follows a general pattern of movement from humiliation to exaltation. The movement is not strictly linear, however, as it is interposed along the way with vignettes of contrast. The birth contains both ignominy and majesty. His public ministry attracts scorn and praise, rejection and welcome, cries of "Hosannah" and "Crucify him." Nearing the shadow of death, he exhibits the translucent breakthrough of transfiguration.

The transition from the pathos of the Cross to the grandeur of the Resurrection is not abrupt. There is a rising crescendo that swells to the moment of breaking forth from the grave clothes and the shroud of the tomb. Exaltation begins with the descent from the cross immortalized in classical Christian art by the *Pieta*. With the disposition of the corpse of Jesus the normal rules were broken. Under normal judicial circumstances the body of a crucified criminal was discarded by the state, being thrown without ceremony into Gehenna, the city garbage dump outside of Jerusalem. There the body was incinerated, being subject to a pagan form of cremation, robbed of the dignity of traditional Jewish burial. The fires of Gehenna burned incessantly as a necessary measure of public health to rid the city of its refuse. Gehenna served Jesus as an apt metaphor for hell, a place where the flames are never extinguished and the worm does not die.

Pilate made an exception in the case of Jesus. Perhaps he was bruised of conscience and was moved by pity to accede to the request for Jesus to be buried. Or, perhaps he was moved by a mighty Providence that would ensure the fulfillment of the prophecy of Isaiah that he would make his grave with the rich or the fulfillment of his promise that he would not let his Holy one see corruption. The body of Christ was anointed with spices and wrapped in fine linen to be laid in the tomb belonging to the patrician, Joseph of Arimathea.

For three days the world was plunged into darkness. The women of Jesus' entourage wept bitterly, taking but small consolation in the permission to perform the tender act of anointing his body. The disciples had fled and were huddled together in hiding, their dreams shattered by the cry, "It is finished." For three days God was silent. Then he screamed. With cataclysmic power God rolled the stone away and unleashed a paroxysm of creative energy of life, infusing it once more into the still body of Christ. Jesus' heart began to beat, pumping glorified blood through glorified arteries, sending glorified power to muscles atrophied by death. The grave clothes could not bind him as he rose to his feet and quit the crypt. In an instant the mortal became immortal and death was swallowed up by victory. In a moment of history Job's question was answered once and for all: "If a man die, shall he live again?"

Here is the watershed of human history where the misery of the race is transformed into grandeur. Here the kerygma, the proclamation of the early church, was born with the cry "He is risen." We can view this event as a symbol, a lovely tale of hope. We can reduce it to a moralism that declares, as one preacher put it, "The meaning of the Resurrection is that we can face the dawn of each new day with dialectical courage."

Dialectical courage is the variety invented by Frederick Nietzsche, the father of modern nihilism.

Courage that is dialectical is a courage-in-tension. The tension is this: Life is meaningless, death is ultimate. We must be courageous knowing that even our courage is empty of meaning. This is denial of resurrection bathed in the despair of a truncated existential hope.

The New Testament proclaims the Resurrection as sober historical fact. The early Christians were not interested in dialectical symbols but in concrete realities. Authentic Christianity stands or falls with the space/time event of Jesus' resurrection. The term *Christian* suffers from the burden of a thousand qualifications and a myriad of diverse definitions. One dictionary defines a Christian as a person who is civilized. One can certainly be civilized without affirming the Resurrection, but one cannot then be a Christian in the biblical sense. The person who claims to be a Christian while denying the Resurrection speaks with a forked tongue. From such turn away.

The resurrection narrative offended David Hume's test of probability quotients; it is consigned by Rudolf Bultmann to the husk of mythology that is unnecessary to the kernel of biblical truth. For Paul Van Buren, the death-of-God theologian, the Resurrection is not even taught in the Bible as a real historical event. He dubs it a "discernment situation" in which the disciples suddenly came to "understand" Jesus, "seeing" him in a new light.

Van Buren's treatment violates every canon of sober literary analysis of the biblical text. That the New Testament writers were purporting to declare that a dead man came back to life is beyond serious literary dispute. One may reject the idea, but not that the idea is proclaimed.

Even Bultmann concedes the historical reality of the "Easter-faith" of the early church. He reverses the biblical order, however, by arguing that it was the Easter-faith of the early church that caused the proclamation of the Resurrection. The Bible argues that it was the Resurrection that caused the Easter-faith of the early church. This subtle difference in causal nexus is the difference between faith and apostasy. The biblical writers claimed to be eyewitnesses of the risen Christ and certified the integrity of their faith with their own blood. The ancient church was willing to die for it; the modern church negotiates it, as evidenced by one major denomination's reluctance to reaffirm the bodily resurrection on the grounds that it is divisive. Faith in the resurrection of Christ is indeed divisive as it divided the Christians from the gladiators and prompted the hostile Nero to illumine his garden with human torches.

The resurrection of Jesus is radical in the original sense of the word. It touches the *radix*, the "root" of the Christian faith. Without it Christianity becomes just another religion designed to titillate our moral senses with platitudes of human wisdom. The apostle Paul spelled out the clear and irrefutable consequences of a "resurrectionless" Christianity. If Christ is not raised, he reasoned, we are left with the following list of conclusions:

1. *Our preaching is futile.*
2. *Our faith is in vain.*
3. *We have misrepresented God.*
4. *We are still in our sins.*
5. *Our loved ones who have died have perished.*
6. *If all we have is hope, we are of all men most to be pitied.*

These six consequences sharply reveal the inner connection of the Resurrection to the substance of Christianity. The resurrection of Jesus is the *sine qua non* of the Christian faith. Take away the Resurrection and you take away Christianity.

The biblical writers do not base their claim of resurrection on the basis of its internal consistency to the whole of faith, however. It is not simply a logical deduction drawn from other doctrines of faith. It is not a matter that we must affirm the Resurrection because the options to it are grim. Resurrection is not affirmed because life would be hopeless or intolerable without it. The claim is based not on speculation but on empirical data. They saw the risen Christ. They spoke with him and ate with him. Neither his death nor resurrection were done in a corner like Joseph Smith's alleged reception of special revelation. The death of Jesus was a public spectacle and a matter of public record. His resurrection was witnessed by more than five hundred people at one time. The Bible presents history on this matter.

The strongest objection raised against the biblical account of Jesus' resurrection is the same objection raised against other biblical miracles, namely that such an event is impossible. It is ironic that the New Testament approaches the question of Christ's resurrection from exactly the opposite direction. In Peter's speech on Pentecost he declared: "But God raised him up, having loosed the pangs of death, because it was not possible for him to be held by it" (Acts 2:24).

To set forth the principle stated here I must indulge myself with the use of a double negative. It was impossible for Christ *not* to have been raised. For death to have held Christ would have required the supreme and unthinkable violation of the laws of death. It is viewed by modern man as an inexorable law of nature that what dies, stays dead. But that law is a law of fallen nature. In the Judeo-Christian view of nature, death enters the world as a judgment upon sin. The Creator decreed that sin was a capital offense. The soul that sins shall die. "In the day that you eat of it you shall die" (Genesis 2:14), was the original warning. God granted an extension of life beyond the day of sin, but not indefinitely. The original sanction was not completely rescinded. Mother Nature became the paramount executioner. Adam was created with both the possibility of death (*posse mori*) and the possibility of avoiding it (*posse non mori*). By his transgression he forfeited the possibility of avoidance of death and incurred, as judgment, the impossibility of not dying (*non posse non mori*).

Jesus was not Adam. He was the New Adam. He was free from sin, both original and actual. Death had no legitimate claim on him in himself. He was punished for the sin imputed to him, but once the price was paid and the imputation was lifted from his back, death lost its power. In death an atonement was made; in resurrection the perfect sinlessness of Jesus was vindicated. He was, as the Scriptures assert, raised for our justification as well as his own vindication.

Hume's probability quotients discard the Resurrection because it was a unique event. He was right on one count. It was a unique event. Though Scripture relates other resurrection accounts such as the raising of Lazarus, they were all in a different category. Lazarus died again. The uniqueness of Jesus' resurrection was tied to another aspect of his uniqueness. It was tied to his sinlessness, a dimension of the person of Jesus that would be even more unique if uniqueness were capable of degrees.

For God to allow Jesus to be forever bound by death would have been for God to violate his own righteous character. It would have been an injustice, an act that is supremely impossible for God to commit. The surprise is not that Jesus rose, but that he stayed in the tomb as long as he did. Perhaps it was God's condescension to human weakness of unbelief that inclined him to keep Christ captive, to ensure that there would be no doubt he was dead and the Resurrection would not be mistaken for a resuscitation.

The Resurrection sets Jesus apart from every other central figure of world religions. Buddha is dead. Mohammed is dead. Confucius is dead. None of these were sinless. None offered atonement. None were vindicated by resurrection.

If we stagger with unbelief before the fact of resurrection we would do well to consider the plight of the two walking to Emmaus that weekend. Luke records the event for us (Luke 24:13ff.). As they were walking away from Jerusalem, Jesus joined them incognito. They presumed to inform Jesus about the events of the Crucifixion and were obviously impatient with his apparent ignorance of the matters. When they related the report of the women concerning the Resurrection, Christ rebuked them:

"O foolish men, and slow of heart to believe all that the prophets have spoken! Was it not necessary that the Christ should suffer these things and enter into his glory?" And beginning with Moses and all the prophets, he interpreted to them in all the scriptures the things concerning himself.

One of the most painful rebukes we can suffer is the one contained in the four miserable words, "I told you so."

When the two had their eyes opened and they recognized Jesus that night, they said to each other, "Did not our hearts burn within us while he talked to us on the road, while he opened to us the scriptures?"

A Christian is not a skeptic. A Christian is a person with a burning heart, a heart set aflame with the certainty of the Resurrection.

The Ascension of Christ

My graduate work in theology in Amsterdam provoked a crisis in my Christian life. The crisis was triggered by a technical study of the doctrine of the Ascension. Like most Protestants I had neglected this theme, considering it a concluding unscientific postscript to the life of Christ, not worthy of special commemoration like Christmas and Easter. The actual event is described only twice in the New

Testament. I am now convinced that no single event in the life of Jesus is more important than the Ascension, no, not even the Cross or the Resurrection. It is dangerous business to assign relative values to the episodes of Christ's life and ministry, but if we underestimate the significance of the Ascension, we sail in perilous waters.

What could be more important than the Cross? Without it we have no atonement, no redemption. Paul resolved to preach Christ and him crucified. Yet without the Resurrection we would be left with a dead Savior. Cross and resurrection go together, each borrowing some of its value from the other. But the story does not end with the empty tomb. To write *finis* there is to miss a climactic moment of redemptive history, a moment toward which both Old and New Testaments move with inexorable determination. It is the apex of Christ's exaltation, the acme of redemptive history to this point. It is the pregnant moment of Christ's coronation as King. Without it the Resurrection ends in disappointment and Pentecost would not be possible.

My crisis experience in Holland was provoked by a study of one obscure statement from the lips of Christ. On an occasion when Jesus told his disciples of his impending death, he said, "Where I am going you cannot follow me now" (John 13:36) and "A little while, and you will see me no more" (John 14:18). Jesus continued his discourse by explaining,

"It is to your advantage that I go away" (John 16:7). Here Jesus was making a value judgment about his departure. The thrust of his comment was to suggest that his absence was better for his disciples than his presence. This must have strained the understanding of his friends to the uttermost limits. *Prima facia* it is unthinkable that under any circumstances people could benefit more from the absence of Jesus than from his presence, save for those unfortunates who face his judgment and would welcome a respite from him. The Christian longs for the abiding presence of Christ. The contemporary Christian grows wistful imagining what it must have been like to have seen and known the incarnate Christ when he walked the earth. Millions travel annually to Palestine just to see the footprints that are left. Surely the church has either failed to grasp the import of Jesus' words or has simply been unable to believe them. We live as if there had been no ascension.

The disciples were slow in grasping the expediency of Jesus' departure. They resisted his determination to go to Jerusalem and took umbrage at his announcements of his coming death. Between the Resurrection and the Ascension new light dawned on them as they began to undergo a remarkable change of attitude. The culmination in the change was evidenced by their immediate reaction to Jesus' visible elevation into heaven. The normal human reaction to scenes of departure was shattered by their behavior. The record says, the disciples "returned to Jerusalem *with great joy*" (Luke 24:52).

Parting may be sweet sorrow, but the normal measure of sweetness is unable to turn sorrow into rejoicing. When men ship out for war or sailors go to sea, there are more tears than smiles on the faces of loved ones left behind. I remember tugging at my father's dufflebag when he started for the troop train at the end of a furlough during World War II. There was no joy in it. I remember the end of Christmas vacation, and the ritual that took place at the Greyhound bus terminals during my college days when I would put my fiancée on a bus to return to school after enjoying a brief interlude together. I did not return to my school rejoicing.

To be sure, the disciples had to be prodded by an angel to leave the spot where Christ departed on the Mount of Olives. They stood there transfixed, savoring the vision of the glory cloud enveloping Jesus. They were rooted to the spot, spellbound by the vista of majesty surrounding them. Their reverie was broken by the words of the angel: "Men of Galilee, why do you stand looking into heaven? This Jesus, who was taken up from you into heaven, will come in the same way as you saw him go into heaven" (Acts 1:11).

They returned to Jerusalem. They must have

been giddy: laughing, skipping, and singing the whole way. They recalled the words of Jesus in the upper room of the promise of another Comforter who would come. They were glad in heart because they finally understood where Jesus was going and why he was going there.

Earlier Christ had said, "No one has ascended into heaven but he who descended from heaven" (John 3:13). He was speaking of himself. These words placed the Ascension squarely in the category of the unique event. In his ascension Jesus displayed again that he was *sui generis*. No one before or since has "ascended" to heaven. The prerequisite for ascension was a prior descension. As the only-begotten incarnate Christ, Jesus was singularly qualified for this event. Others had gone to heaven. Enoch was "translated" and Elijah was "taken up." One could "ascend" a ladder (as Jesus spoke to Nathaniel that he would see angels ascending and descending on the Son of Man and as Jacob beheld in his midnight dream at Bethel), or one could "ascend" to Jerusalem, moving to a higher elevation from sea level. The term could be used figuratively to refer to the elevation of a king to his royal office. But no one ever had "ascended to heaven" in the sense in which Jesus was speaking.

The ascension of Jesus was the supreme political event of world history. He ascended not so much to a place as to an office. He departed from the arena of humiliation and suffering to enter into his glory. He, in one moment, leapfrogged from the status of despised Galilean teacher to the cosmic King of the universe, jumping over the heads of Pilate, Herod, and Caesar Augustus. The Ascension catapulted Jesus to the right hand of God, where he was enthroned as King of kings and Lord of lords. Here the political "expediency" of his departure stands out in bold relief.

The implications of this event for the church are staggering. It means that though we suffer persecution and the scorn of hostile power structures—though we groan under the demeaning status of an unwelcome minority—our candidate sits in the seat of sovereign authority. The kingdom of God is not an unrealized dream or religious fantasy. The investiture of our king is a *fait accompli*. His reign is neither mythical nor illusory. It corresponds to a real state of affairs. At this very moment the Lord God omnipotent reigns with his Son at his right hand, in the seat of imperial authority. To be sure, the kingdom is yet to be consummated—that is future. It has however been inaugurated. That is past. He reigns in power, possessing all authority in heaven and earth. That is present. His kingdom is invisible but no less real. It is left to his church to make his invisible kingship visible.

Christ's succession to the right hand of God is inseparably linked to the coming of Pentecost. In a certain sense Jesus lacked the authority to dispatch the Spirit prior to his ascension. One of the first acts of authority he exercised after his enthronement was to endow his church with power from on high. His disciples were given a great commission, a mandate to penetrate the whole world bearing witness to the kingdom. These were and are to be the authentic witnesses of Yahweh. But no border was to be crossed or mission undertaken until first the Spirit came down. The disciples returned to Jerusalem rejoicing for the purpose of their wait; they were waiting for Pentecost. When the new King of the cosmos sent the Holy Ghost, the power of the kingdom was unleashed on the world.

Christ's elevation was not only political, it was also sacerdotal. He assumed not only the scepter of the King but the garments of the High Priest as well. In his ascension Jesus entered the sanctuary as well as the palace. Not only does Jesus *sit* at the right hand of God, he kneels. He has entered the *sanctus sanctorum*, the holy of holies, to make daily intercession for his people. We are a people whose King prays for us by name.

Do you wonder then at the disciples' joy? Once they understood where Jesus was going and why he was going there, the only appropriate response was celebration. They danced back to Jerusalem. His physical presence was gone, but his spiritual and political presence was enhanced, giving rise to the creedal affirmation: "Touching his humanity, Jesus is no longer present with us: touching his deity, he is never absent from us." His words console his "absent" bride: "Lo, I am with you always, to the close of the age" (Matthew 28:20).

PART TWO

Does Prayer
Change Things?

CHAPTER 4

THE PLACE OF PRAYER

What is the goal of the Christian life? Godliness born of obedience to Christ. Obedience unlocks the riches of the Christian experience. Prayer is what prompts and nurtures obedience, putting the heart into the proper "frame of mind" to desire obedience.

Of course, knowledge is also important because without it, we cannot know what God requires. However, knowledge and truth will remain abstract unless we commune with God in prayer. It is the Holy Spirit who teaches, inspires, and illumines God's Word to us. He mediates the Word of God and assists us in responding to the Father in prayer.

Prayer has a vital place in the life of the Christian. First, it is an absolute prerequisite for salvation. Some people cannot hear; yet though deaf, they can be saved. Some may not be able to see; yet though blind, they can be saved. Knowledge of the Good News—salvation through the atoning death and resurrection of Jesus Christ—will come from one source or another, but in the final analysis, a person must humbly ask God for salvation. The prayer of salvation is the one prayer of the wicked God has said he will hear.

What do those in heaven have in common? Several things. They have all been justified, having put their faith in the atonement of Christ. They are all praising God. And they have all prayed for salvation. To be without prayer is to be without God, Christ, the Holy Spirit, and the hope and reality of heaven.

Second, one of the surest marks of the Christian is his prayer life. One might pray and not be a Christian, but one could not possibly be a Christian and not pray. Romans 8:15 tells us that the spiritual adoption that has made us sons of God causes us to cry out in verbal expressions: "Abba! Father." Prayer is to the Christian what breath is to life, yet no duty of the Christian is so neglected.

Prayer, at least private prayer, is difficult to do out of a false motive. One might preach out of a false motive, as do the false prophets; one might be involved in Christian activities out of false motives. Many of the externals of religion might be done from false motives, but it is highly unlikely that anyone would commune with God out of some improper motive. Matthew 7 tells us that in the "last day," many will stand at the Judgment and tell Christ of their great and noble deeds done in his name, but his response will be that he does not know them.

So, we are invited, even commanded, to pray. Prayer is both a privilege and a duty, and any duty can become laborious. Prayer, like any means of growth for the Christian, requires work. In a sense, prayer is unnatural to us. Though we were created for fellowship and communion with God, the effects of the Fall have left most of us lazy and indifferent toward something as important as prayer. Rebirth quickens a new desire for communion with God, but sin resists the Spirit.

We can take comfort from the fact that God knows our hearts and hears our unspoken petitions more than the words that emanate from our lips. Whenever we are unable to express the deep feelings and emotions of our souls or when we are completely unclear about what it is for which we ought to be praying, the Holy Spirit intercedes for us. Romans 8:26-27 says, "the Spirit helps us in our weakness; for we do not know how to pray as we ought, but the Spirit himself intercedes for us with sighs too deep for words. And he who searches the hearts of men knows what is the mind of the Spirit, because the Spirit intercedes for the saints according to the will of God." When we don't know how to pray or what to pray for in a given situation, the Holy Spirit assists us. There is reason to believe from the text that if we pray incorrectly, the Holy Spirit corrects the error in our prayers before he takes them before the Father, for verse 27 tells us that he "intercedes for the saints according to the will of God."

Prayer is the secret of holiness—if holiness, indeed, has anything secretive about it. If we examine the lives of the great saints of the church, we find that they were great people of prayer. John Wesley once remarked that he didn't think much of ministers who didn't spend at least four hours per day in prayer. Luther said that he prayed regularly for an hour every day except when he experienced a particularly busy day. Then he prayed for two hours.

The neglect of prayer is a major cause of stagnation in the Christian life. Consider the example of Peter in Luke 22:39-62. Jesus went to the Mount of Olives to pray as was his custom and told his disciples, "Pray that you may not enter into temptation." The disciples fell asleep instead. The next thing Peter did was try to take on the Roman army with a sword; then he denied Christ. Peter did not pray and as a result fell into temptation. What is true of Peter is also true of all of us: we fall in private before we ever fall in public.

Is there a right and wrong time for prayer? Isaiah 50:4 talks about the morning as the time when God gives the desire to pray on a daily basis and about renewed confidence in God. But there are other passages that give times of prayer during all times of the day. No part of the day is set apart as being more sanctified than another. Jesus prayed in the morning, during the day, and sometimes all night long. There is evidence that he had a time set aside for prayer; however, considering the relationship Jesus had with the Father, we know that communion between them never stopped.

First Thessalonians 5:17 commands us to pray without ceasing. It means that we are to be in a continual state of communion with our Father.

CHAPTER 5

THE PURPOSE OF PRAYER

Nothing escapes God's notice; nothing oversteps the boundaries of his power. God is authoritative in all things. If I thought even for one moment that a single molecule were running loose in the universe outside the control and domain of Almighty God, I wouldn't sleep tonight. My confidence in the future rests in my confidence in the God who controls history. But how does God exercise that control and manifest that authority? How does God bring to pass those things he has sovereignly decreed?

Augustine said that nothing happens in this universe apart from the will of God and that, in a certain sense, God ordains everything that happens. Augustine was not, however, attempting to absolve men of their responsibility for their actions.

Our concern, though, in this chapter, is to answer the question, If God is sovereign over the actions and intents of men, why pray at all? A secondary concern revolves around the question, Does prayer really change anything?

Let me answer the first question by stating that the sovereign God commands by his sovereign, holy Word that we pray. Prayer is not optional for the Christian; it is required.

We might ask, "What if it doesn't do anything?" That is not the issue. Regardless of whether it does any good to pray, if God commands us to pray, we must pray. It is reason enough that the Lord God of the universe, the Creator and Sustainer of all things, commands it. Yet he not only commands us to pray, but also invites us to make our requests known. Jesus says that we have not because we ask not. James tells us that the effectual, fervent prayer of a righteous man accomplishes much. Time and again the Bible says that prayer is an effective tool. It is useful; it works.

John Calvin, in the *Institutes of the Christian Religion*, makes some profound observations regarding prayer:

> But some will say, "Does he not know without a monitor, what our difficulties are, what is meet for our interests? So it seems, in some measure, superfluous to solicit him by our prayers, as if he were

winking or even sleeping until aroused by the sound of our voices."

Those who argue this way attend not to the end for which the Lord told us to pray. It was not so much for his sake, as for ours. He wills indeed, as is just, that due honor be paid him, acknowledging that all which men desire or feel to be useful and pray to obtain, is derived from him, but even he benefit of the homage which we thus pay him redounds to ourselves. Hence, the holy patriarchs, the more confidently they proclaimed the mercies of God to themselves and to others, felt the more incitement to pray. . . .

It is very much in our interests that we be constantly supplicating him, first that our heart might always be inflamed with the serious and ardent desire of seeking, loving, and serving him as the sacred anchor in every necessity. Secondly, that no desire, no longing whatever that we are ashamed to make him the witness, enter our minds while we learn to place all of our wishes in his sight, and thus pour out our heart before him. Lastly, that we might be prepared to receive all of his benefits with true gratitude and thanksgiving, while our prayers remind us that they proceed from his hand. (Book 3, chapter 20, section 3)

Prayer, like everything else in the Christian life, is for God's glory and for our benefit, in that order.

Everything that God does, everything that God allows and ordains, is in the supreme sense for his glory. It is also true that while God seeks his own glory supremely, man benefits when God is glorified. We pray to glorify God, but we also pray to receive the benefits of prayer from his hand. Prayer is for our benefit, even in light of the fact that God knows the end from the beginning. It is our privilege to bring the whole of our finite existence into the glory of his infinite presence.

One of the great themes of the Reformation was the idea that all of our life is to be lived under the authority of God, to the glory of God, in the presence of God. Prayer is not simply soliloquy, a mere exercise in therapeutic self-analysis, or a religious recitation. Prayer is discourse with the personal God himself. There, in the act and dynamic of praying, I bring my whole life under his gaze. Yes, he knows what is in my mind, but I still have the privilege of articulating to him what is there. He says, "Come. Speak to me. Make your requests known to me." And so we come in order to know him and to be known by him.

There is something erroneous in the question, If God knows everything, why pray? The question assumes that prayer is one-dimensional and is defined simply as the prayer of supplication, or intercession. On the contrary, prayer is multidimensional. God's sovereignty casts no shadow over the prayer of adoration. God's foreknowledge or determinate counsel does not negate the prayer of praise. The only thing it should do is give us greater reason for expressing our adoration for who God is. If God knows what I'm going to say before I say it, his knowledge, rather than limiting my prayer, enhances the beauty of my praise.

My wife and I are as close as two people can be. Often I know what she's going to say almost before she says it. And the reverse is also true. But I still like to hear her say what is on her mind. If that is true of man, how much more true is it of God? We have the matchless privilege of sharing our innermost thoughts with God. Of course, we could simply enter our prayer closet, shut the door, let God read our mind, and call that prayer. But that's not communion, and certainly not communication.

We are creatures who communicate primarily through speech. Spoken prayer is obviously a form of speech, a way for us to commune and communicate with God. There is a certain sense in which God's sovereignty should influence our attitude toward prayer, at least with respect to adoration. If anything, our understanding of God's sovereignty should provoke us to an intense prayer life of thanksgiving. Because of such knowledge we would really see that every benefit, every good and perfect gift, is really an expression of the abundance of his grace. The more we understand God's sovereignty, the more our prayers will be filled with thanksgiving.

In what way does God's sovereignty negatively affect the prayer of contrition, of confession? Perhaps we could draw the conclusion that our sin is ultimately God's responsibility, that our confession is an accusation of guilt against God himself. Every true Christian knows that he cannot blame God for his sin. I may not understand the relationship between divine sovereignty and human responsibility, but I do realize that what stems from the wickedness of my own heart may not be assigned to the will of God. So we must pray because we are guilty, pleading the pardon of the Holy one whom we have offended.

But what about intercession and supplication? It's nice to talk about the religious, spiritual, and psychological benefits (and whatever else might derive from prayer), but what about the real question, Does prayer make any difference? Does it really change anything? Someone once asked me that question, only in a slightly different manner: "Does prayer change God's mind?" My answer brought storms of protest. I said simply, "No." Now, if the person had asked me, "Does prayer change *things?*" I would have answered, "Of course!"

The Bible says that there are certain things that God has decreed from all eternity. Those things will

inevitably come to pass. If you were to pray individually or if you and I were to join forces in prayer
or if all the Christians of the world were to pray
collectively, it would not change what God, in his
hidden counsel, determined to do. If we decided to
pray for Jesus not to return, he would still return.
You might ask, though, "Doesn't the Bible say that
if two or three agree on anything, they'll get it?"
Yes, it does, but that passage is talking about church
discipline, not prayer requests. Second, we must
take all the biblical teaching on prayer into account
and not isolate one passage from the rest. We must
approach the matter in light of the whole of Scripture, resisting an atomistic reading.

Again, you might ask, "Doesn't the Bible say
from time to time that God repents?" Yes, the Old
Testament certainly says so. The book of Jonah tells
us that God "repented of" the evil he had planned
for the people of Tarshish. In using the concept of
repentance here, the Bible is describing God, who is
Spirit, in what theologians call "anthropomorphic"
language. Obviously, the Bible does not mean that
God repented in the way we would repent; otherwise we could rightly assume that God had sinned
and therefore would need a savior himself. What it
clearly means is that God removed the threat of
judgment from the people. The Hebrew word
nacham, translated "repent" in the King James Version, means "comforted" or "eased" in this case.

God was comforted and felt at ease that the people had turned from their sin, and therefore he revoked the sentence of judgment he had previously imposed.

When God hangs his sword of judgment over people's heads and they repent and he then withholds his judgment, has he really changed his mind, like a chameleon?

The mind of God does not change; God is not a thing. *Things* change, and they change according to his sovereign will, which he exercises through secondary means and secondary activities. The prayer of his people is one of the means he uses to bring things to pass in this world. So if you ask me if prayer changes things, I answer with an unhesitating "Yes!"

It is impossible to know how much of human history reflects God's immediate intervention and how much reveals God working through human agents. John Calvin's favorite example of this was the book of Job. The Sabeans and the Chaldeans had raided Job's donkeys and camels. Why? Because Satan had stirred their hearts to do so. But why? Because Satan had received permission from God to test Job's faithfulness in any way he so desired, short of taking Job's life. Why had God agreed to such a thing? For three reasons: (1) to silence the slander of Satan; (2) to vindicate himself; and (3) to vindicate Job from the slander of Satan.

All of these reasons are perfectly righteous justifications for God's actions.

God's purpose in allowing Job's animals to be stolen was to vindicate himself and Job from the slander of Satan—a righteous reason. Satan's purpose in stirring up these two groups was to cause Job to blaspheme God—an altogether wicked motive. But we notice that Satan does not do something supernatural to accomplish his ends. He chooses human agents—the Sabeans and Chaldeans, who were evil by nature—to steal Job's animals. The Sabeans and Chaldeans were known for their thievery and murderous way of life. Their will was involved, but there was no coercion; God's purpose was accomplished through their wicked actions.

The Sabeans and Chaldeans were free to choose, but for them, as for us, freedom always means freedom within limits. We must not, however, confuse human freedom and human autonomy. There will always be a conflict between divine sovereignty and human autonomy. There is never a conflict between divine sovereignty and human freedom. The Bible says that man is free, but he is not an autonomous law unto himself.

Suppose the Sabeans and Chaldeans had prayed, "Lead us not into temptation, but deliver us from the evil one." I'm absolutely certain that Job's animals would still have been stolen. But I'm equally certain that the Sabeans and Chaldeans would not have been responsible because their prayer would have altered the entire situation. There is freedom within limits, and within those limits, our prayers can change things. The Scriptures tell us that Elijah, through prayer, was given power to command the rain. He was not dissuaded from praying by his understanding of divine sovereignty.

No human being has ever had a more profound understanding of divine sovereignty than Jesus. No man ever prayed more fiercely or more effectively. Even in Gethsemane he requested an option, a different way. When the request was denied, he bowed to the Father's will. The very reason we pray is because of God's sovereignty, because we believe that God has it within his power to order things according to his purpose. That is what sovereignty is all about—ordering things according to God's purpose. So then, does prayer change God's mind? No! Does prayer change things? Yes, of course!

The promise of the Scriptures is that "the prayer of a righteous man has great power in its effects" (James 5:16). The problem is that we are not all that righteous. What prayer most often changes is the wickedness and the hardness of our own hearts. That alone would be reason enough to pray, even if none of the other reasons were valid or true.

In a sermon entitled "The Most High, a Prayer-

Hearing God,"Jonathan Edwards gives us two reasons why God requires prayer:

> With respect to God, prayer is but a sensible acknowledgement of our dependence on him to his glory. As he hath made all things for his own glory, so he will be glorified and acknowledged by his creatures; and it is fit that he should require this of those who would be subjects of his mercy . . . it is a suitable acknowledgement of our dependence on the power and mercy of God for that which we need, and but a suitable honor paid to the great Author and Fountain of all good.
>
> With respect to ourselves, God requires prayer of us. . . . Fervent prayer in many ways tends to prepare the heart. Hereby is excited a sense of our need . . . whereby the mind is more prepared to prize the mercy we seek. Our prayer to God may excite in us a suitable sense and consideration of our dependence on God for the mercy we ask, and a suitable exercise of faith in God's sufficiency, so that we may be prepared to glorify his name when the mercy is received.[*]

All that God does is for his glory first and for our benefit second. We pray because God commands us to pray, because it glorifies him, and because it benefits us.

[*]Jonathan Edwards, *The Work of Jonathan Edwards* (Carlisle, Penn.: Banner of Truth, 1974), 116.

CHAPTER 6

THE PATTERN OF PRAYER

Jesus performed many miracles. During the course of his ministry, he walked on water, turned water into wine, healed the sick, raised the dead. As John said, "There are also many other things that Jesus did; were every one of them to be written, I suppose that the world itself could not contain the books that would be written" (John 21:25).

I have always been amazed that the disciples didn't ask Jesus how to walk on water, how to still the tempest, or how to do any of his other miracles. They did, however, ask Jesus to teach them about prayer. Note that they did not ask Jesus to teach them *how* to pray; instead they begged, "Teach us *to* pray" (Luke 11:1). I'm certain that the disciples clearly saw the inseparable relationship between the power Jesus manifested and the hours he spent in solitude, conversing with his Father.

The instruction Jesus gives regarding prayer comes to us from the Sermon on the Mount, found in both Matthew 6 and Luke 11. Jesus prefaces his remarks on the pattern for prayer with these words:

> *And when you pray, you must not be like the hypocrites; for they love to stand and pray in the synagogues and at the street corners, that they may be seen by men. Truly, I say to you, they have received their reward. But when you pray, go into your room and shut the door and pray to your Father who is in secret; and your Father who sees in secret will reward you.*
>
> *And in praying do not heap up empty phrases as the Gentiles do; for they think that they will be heard for their many words. Do not be like them, for your Father knows what you need before you ask him. Pray then like this . . . (Matthew 6:5-9)*

Notice that Jesus says, "Pray this way," not "Pray this prayer" or "Pray these words." There is some question as to whether Jesus ever meant for us to repeat the prayer. I'm not attacking the use of the Lord's Prayer; there's certainly nothing wrong with its use in the personal life of the believer or the devotional life of the church. Yet Jesus was not so much giving us a prayer to recite as a pattern to show us the way in which to pray. Jesus was providing us with an outline of priorities or those things that *ought* to be priorities in our prayer life. Let's look at the sections of the Lord's Prayer one at a time.

Our Father

The first two words of the prayer are radical as used in the New Testament. The word *Father* was not the basic form of address for God found in the Old Covenant community. His name was ineffable; he was not to be addressed with any degree of intimacy. Seldom was the term *Father* used to speak of God in the Old Testament. Of all the terms used to address God in prayer by the Old Covenant community, *Father* is not among them. But here, in the New Testament, Jesus brings us into an intimate relationship with the Father, breaking down the partition symbolized by the veil in the temple. Now Jesus gives us the incomparable privilege of calling God "Father."

Jesus was the first on record to take prayer and make it a personal discourse with God. Jesus, who spoke Aramaic, used the Aramaic word *Abba*, best translated "Dad" or "Poppa." We can almost hear the cry of alarm from the disciples and see the looks of astonishment on their faces: "You don't mean it, Jesus. You can't be serious! We're not even allowed to speak the name of God aloud. We don't even call him *Father*, much less *Dad!*"

Ironically today we live in a world that assumes God is the Father of everyone, that all men are brothers. We hear this in the cliché "the fatherhood of God and the brotherhood of man." But nowhere in Scripture does it say that all men are brothers. It does say, however, that all men are my *neighbors*.

There is a restricted sense in which God is the Father of all men as the giver and sustainer of life, the progenitor par excellence of the human race. But nothing in the Bible indicates that an individual may approach God in a familiar sense. The only exception is when that person has been adopted into God's family, having expressed saving faith in the atonement of Christ and having submitted to his lordship. Then and only then is one afforded the privilege of calling God his Father. To those who have received him, God "gave the right [authority, privilege] to become children of God (John 1:12, NIV). Only then does God call men "sons." The Greek word *exousia* translated "right to become" denotes the freedom to act and the authority for that action. Calling God "Father" without the proper credentials of sonship is an act of extreme presumption and arrogance.

We don't find the idea of universal fatherhood and brotherhood in the introduction to the Lord's Prayer. This cultural tacit assumption causes us to miss what Jesus is saying. In the first place, the fatherhood of God cannot be taken for granted by anyone in the world. Jesus is the one person with the ultimate right to address God in this way, for Jesus alone is the *monogenes*, "the only begotten of the Father," having existed from all eternity in a unique filial relationship with the Father.

If there is a universal fatherhood and brotherhood in any sense whatsoever, it would have to be in the context of Jesus' discussion with the Pharisees in John 8. The Pharisees were claiming to be children of Abraham, offspring of God by ancestral association. Jesus challenges them on this point, saying "If you were Abraham's children, you would do what Abraham did, but now you seek to kill me, a man who has told you the truth which I heard from God; this is not what Abraham did. . . . You are of your father the devil, and your will is to do your father's desires" (8:39-40, 44).

There is a clear distinction between the children of God and the children of the devil. God's children hear his voice and obey him. The children of the devil do not listen to God's voice; they disobey him by doing the will of their father, Satan. There are only two families, and everyone belongs to one or the other. Both groups have one thing in common, however. The members of each family do the will of their respective fathers, whether it be God or Satan.

If we go through the New Testament, making inquiry as to who are the sons of God, the answer is clear. The New Testament is neither vague nor enigmatic on this point. Romans 8:14-17 says this:

> *Those who are led by the Spirit of God are sons of God. For you did not receive a spirit that makes you a slave again to fear, but you received the Spirit of sonship. And by him we cry, "Abba, Father." The Spirit himself testifies with our spirit that we are God's children. Now if we are children, then we are heirs—heirs of God and co-heirs with Christ.* (NIV)

In verse 14 of this passage, the pronoun *those*, *autoi* in the Greek, is in what is called the *emphatic* form to indicate an exclusiveness. The verse is best translated, "For all who are being led by the Spirit of God, these *alone* are the sons of God" or "these *only* are the sons of God." Paul teaches that it is *only* by the Holy Spirit that we can call God our Father. The significance of this in the New Testament is that we are sons, not illegitimate children, because we are in union with Christ. Our sonship is not automatic, not inherited; it is not a genetic necessity, but rather it is derived. The New Testament word for this transaction is *adoption*. Because of our adoptive relationship with God through Christ, we become joint heirs with Christ.

It is only because we are in Christ and Christ is in

us that we have the privilege of addressing God as our Father and of approaching him in a filial relationship. Martin Luther once said that if he could just understand the first two words of the Lord's Prayer, he would never be the same again.

The word *our* signifies that the right to call God "Father" is not mine alone. It is a corporate privilege belonging to the entire body of Christ. When I pray, I do not come before God as an isolated individual, but as a member of a family, a community of saints.

Who Art in Heaven

Another debate raging at the time Jesus delivered these words was over the precise location of God's presence. In the discussion between Jesus and the woman at the well, Jesus was quick to point out that God is spirit, and as such could not be pinpointed to one particular place. He was neither at Mt. Gerizim, as she thought, nor in Jerusalem, as some of the Jews believed.

To be sure, God is omnipresent. There are no finite restrictions to his divine presence, yet Christ spoke of the Father's being in heaven. Why? Christ was speaking about God's transcendence. Since God is not part of this worldly process, he is not part of nature. He cannot be confined to a locality.

The God whom we address is the God who is above and beyond the finite limits of the world.

The opening line of the Lord's Prayer presents a dynamic tension for us. Although we are to come before the Lord in an attitude of intimacy, there is still an element of separation. We can come to God and call him Father, but this filial relationship does not allow us to have the type of familiarity that breeds contempt. We are to come with boldness, yes, but never with arrogance or presumption. The "Our Father" speaks of the nearness of God, but the "who art in heaven" points to his otherness, his being set apart. The point is this: When we pray, we must remember who we are and whom we are addressing.

Hallowed Be Thy Name

No matter how close God invites us to come, there is still an infinite gulf between our sinfulness and his majesty. He is the heavenly one; we are of the earth. He is perfect; we are imperfect. He is infinite; we are finite. He is holy; we are unholy. We must never forget that God is wholly "Other" than we.

The sacred "otherness" of God is a fact the sons of Aaron forgot, but they forgot it only once. In Leviticus 10:1-3 we read:

> *Now Nadab and Abihu, the sons of Aaron, each took his censer, and put fire in it, and laid incense*

on it, and offered unholy fire before the LORD, such as he had not commanded them. And fire came forth from the presence of the LORD and devoured them, and they died before the LORD. Then Moses said to Aaron, "This is what the LORD has said, 'I will show myself holy among those who are near me, and before all the people I will be glorified.'"

God demands to be treated as holy, for he is holy. He is jealous for his honor. He does not plead for respect in this passage. Rather, it is a statement of fact: "I will be treated as holy." We must never make the fatal mistake of Nadab and Abihu and approach the sovereign God in a flippantly casual attitude.

Looking at the first petition of the Lord's Prayer, we can see that this is the first priority of which Jesus speaks. His initial request is that the name of God be hallowed. It is the Greek word *hagios*, which is literally translated "holy." The top priority for the Christian is to see that God's name be kept holy, for it is holy. If that were the only prayer request the Christian community ever made and they made it earnestly and regularly, I suspect the revival we pray for and the reformation we so earnestly desire would be accomplished in no time. Everything— our work, our ministry, and all aspects of our daily lives—would be affected.

In the Old Testament the stated purpose for Israel's

election and for their religious and dietary laws and ceremonies was to establish them as a holy nation, set apart from the commonplace cultures of antiquity. Was it for their honor? No, it was for God's honor. God's honor must become the obsession of the Christian community today. Honor must go not to our organizations, our denominations, our individual modes of worship, or even our particular churches, but to God alone.

Consider the words given in Ezekiel 36:22: "Thus says the Lord GOD: It is not for your sake, O house of Israel, that I am about to act, but for the sake of my holy name, which you have profaned among the nations to which you came." What a shift. The nation chosen to have the matchless privilege of showing forth the greatness of God had instead chosen to profane his name publicly. God had to rebuke them for their treason. In the final analysis, our names, our organizations, and our efforts are all meaningless unless we honor God's name.

Today a frightening lack of fear of God prevails in our land. Martin Luther once remarked that those around him spoke to God "as if he were a shoe clerk's apprentice." If that was true in Martin Luther's day, how much more so today? And yet, the top priority that Jesus establishes is that the name of God be hallowed, honored, and exalted.

God's name is an expression of himself. We are the image-bearers of God. Where God is not respected,

it is inevitable that his image-bearers will also suffer a loss of respect.

Thy Kingdom Come

One central motif in the Scriptures is the kingdom
of God. It was the main thrust of Jesus' teaching
and preaching. Jesus came as the fulfillment of
John the Baptist's message, which was clear, precise, and simple: "Repent, for the kingdom of God
is at hand."

Jesus focused on the kingdom in the Sermon on
the Mount, the keynote address of his preaching.
Dealing with the reality of the kingdom of God, it
was more than simply an ethical presentation of
principles for good living. Jesus was talking about
the character traits of people who live a redeemed
life-style within the kingdom of God.

The kingdom concept is difficult for us to understand in our present-day culture. Ours is a democ-
racy, where the mere idea of a monarchy is
repugnant. Remember that we are heirs of the rev-
olutionaries who proclaimed, "We will serve no
sovereign here!" Our nation is built on a resistance
to sovereignty. Americans have fought battles and
entire wars to be delivered from monarchy. How
are we to understand the minds of New Testament
people who were praying for the Son of David to
restore a monarchy and the throne of Israel?

The King has come. Christ sits exalted at the right hand of God and reigns as King. But Jesus is not merely the spiritual King of the church, where his only responsibility is to exercise authority over our piety, as if there were a separation between church and state. Jesus is King of the universe. That is the fact of the Ascension. This reality, however, is not believed or acknowledged by the world. Though that kingship is an established fact right now, it is *invisible* to the world in which we live. In heaven, there is no question about it. On the earth, there is considerable question about it. Jesus is saying that we must pray that the kingdom of God will become visible on the earth, that the invisible will be made visible.

Rebellion against God's authority is nothing new or unique to our day or to Western culture. In Psalm 2:2-3, we read: "The kings of the earth set themselves, and the rulers take counsel together, against the LORD and his anointed, saying, 'Let us burst their bonds asunder, and cast their cords from us.'"

What is God's response to this uprising? "He who sits in the heavens laughs; the LORD has them in derision" (Psalm 2:4).

God is not amused for long, for we read in verses 5 and 6, "Then he will speak to them in his wrath, and terrify them in his fury, saying, 'I have set my king on Zion, my holy hill.'"

The Lord speaks to those who have rebelled

against him—those involved in this cosmic Declaration of Independence—and declares, "I have installed my King, I have anointed my Christ, and you had better submit to that." Reading further in verse 10, we learn something else:

> Now therefore, O kings, be wise; be warned, O rulers of the earth. Serve the LORD with fear, . . . lest he be angry, and you perish in the way; for his wrath is quickly kindled. Blessed are all who take refuge in him.

Christians are to pray for the manifestation of the reign of Christ and the emergence of his kingdom. If that is our prayer, it is our responsibility to show our allegiance to the King. People won't have to guess about whom we are exalting.

Thy Will Be Done

This phrase is not asking that God's determinate counsel come to pass or that God usher in those things that he has foreordained from eternity. Rather, we are praying for obedience to the revealed preceptive will of God—what he has made plain to us by way of his commandments. This third petition is a prayer for obedience on the part of God's people, that those who are the people of God will obey the mandates of God.

On Earth As It Is in Heaven

The angels in God's court do as he says and desires. His people on earth do not. God is the covenant Maker; we are the covenant breakers, frequently on a collision course with the will of the Father.

There is a sense in which the first three petitions are all saying the same thing. The honoring of God's name, the visibility of his kingdom, and the obedience to his will are virtually the same concept repeated three different ways. They are inseparably related. God is honored by our obedience. His kingdom is made visible by our obedience, and quite obviously his will is done when we are obedient to that will. These are the priorities Jesus has laid down.

We do not come rushing into God's presence arrogantly, assaulting him with our petty requests, forgetting whom we are addressing. We are to make certain that we have properly exalted the God of creation. Only after God has been rightly honored, adored, and exalted, do the subsequent petitions of God's people assume their proper place.

Give Us This Day Our Daily Bread

God provides for his people. It is noteworthy that the request here is for daily bread, not daily steak or daily prime rib. God provides the necessities, but not always the niceties.

Look at the experience of the Israelites after their deliverance from the land of Egypt. God miraculously provided the people with bread in the form of manna. Then what happened? First, they stopped thanking him, for his provision. Second, they stopped asking him for his provision, and third, they began grumbling about his provision. Finally, they began reminiscing about how good things had been in Egypt. They dreamed about the cucumbers, the melons, the leeks, and the garlic they had had in Egypt—all the while forgetting about the oppression, the hardships, and the tortures they had endured at the hands of Pharaoh. They grumbled about having to eat manna for breakfast, manna for lunch, and manna for dinner. The Israelites ate manna soufflé, manna pie, manna meringue, boiled manna, baked manna, and broiled manna. Soon, they cried out for meat.

Their story is relayed to us in Numbers 11:18-20:

> *Say to the people, "Consecrate yourselves for tomorrow, and you shall eat meat; for you have wept in the hearing of the LORD, saying, 'Who will give us meat to eat? For it was well with us in Egypt.' Therefore the LORD will give you meat and you shall eat. You shall not eat one day, or two days, or five days, or ten days, or twenty days, but a whole*

month, until it comes out at your nostrils and becomes loathsome to you."

God says, "You want meat. I'll give you meat, and you're going to eat meat until you're sick of it."

One of the things that betrays our fallen condition is the self-made man concept, which takes credit for the bounty of our goods and forgets the Source of all our provision. We must remember God is the one who gives us all we have in the ultimate sense.

Forgive Us Our Debts As We Also Have Forgiven Our Debtors

This is an extremely dangerous prayer to pray, but it contains a principle that the New Testament takes very seriously. The supreme warning from Jesus is that God will judge us according to how we have judged other people. Since man is saved by grace, what better evidence could there be of a man's salvation than that he offers to others the grace he himself has so generously received? If that grace is not conspicuous in our lives, we may validly question the genuineness of our own alleged conversion.

We must take God seriously on this point. In Matthew 18:23-35, Jesus tells the story of two men who owed money. One owed roughly $10 million, and the other owed about $18. The one who owed the large sum had his debt forgiven by the man to whom he owed that debt. But he, in turn, would not forgive the man who owed him the paltry sum of $18. Interestingly enough, both men asked for the same thing—more time—not a total release from the debt.

It was comical for the man with the exorbitantly large debt to ask for more time, since even by today's wage standards, the amount owed was an astronomical figure. The daily wage at that time was approximately eighteen cents per day. The man with the small debt could have paid his debt in three months. His request for more time was not unreasonable, but his creditor, rather than expressing the forgiveness he had received, began to harass him. The point should be clear. Our offenses to each other and the offenses people do to us are like an $18 debt, while the innumerable offenses we have committed against the Lord God Omnipotent are like the $10 million debt.

Jonathan Edwards, in his famous sermon "The Justice of God in the Damnation of Sinners," said that any sin is more or less heinous, depending upon the honor and majesty of the one whom we had offended. Since God is of infinite honor, infinite majesty, and infinite holiness, the slightest sin is of infinite consequence. Such seemingly trivial sins are nothing less than "cosmic treason" when viewed in light of the great King against whom we have sinned. We are debtors who cannot pay, yet we have been released from the threat of debtors' prison. It is an insult to God for us to withhold forgiveness and grace from those who ask us, while claiming to be forgiven and saved by grace ourselves.

There is another important point to consider here. Even in our act of forgiveness there is no merit. We cannot commend ourselves to God and claim forgiveness merely because we have shown forgiveness to someone else. Our forgiveness in no way obligates God toward us. Luke 17:10 clearly points out that there is no merit even in the best of our good works: "When you have done all that is commanded you, say, 'We are unworthy servants; we have only done what was our duty.'"

We deserve nothing for our obedience because obedience—even to the point of perfection—is the minimal requirement of a citizen of God's kingdom. Obedience is his duty. The only thing we could claim would be a lack of punishment, but certainly no reward, because we have done only what is expected. Obedience never qualifies as service "above and beyond the call of duty." We are merely in a position to prostrate ourselves before God and beg his forgiveness. But, if we do, we must be prepared to show that forgiveness ourselves; otherwise our position in Christ dangles precariously. The bottom line of what Jesus is saying is this: "Forgiven people forgive other people." We dare not claim to be possessors of his life and nature and at the same time fail to exhibit that life and nature.

To carry the thought further, if God has forgiven someone, can we do any less? It would be incredible to think that we, who are so guilty, would refuse to forgive someone who has been forgiven by God, who is completely guiltless. We are to be mirrors of grace to others, reflecting what we have received ourselves. This implements the Golden Rule in practical terms.

Forgiveness is not a private matter but a corporate one. The body of Christ is a group of people who live daily in the context of forgiveness. What distinguishes us is the fact that we are forgiven sinners. Jesus calls attention, not only to the horizontal elements in the petition, but also to the vertical. We are to pray every day for the forgiveness of our sins.

Some may ask at this point, "If God has already forgiven us, why should we ask for forgiveness? Isn't it wrong to ask for something he's already given us?" The ultimate answer to questions like this is always the same. We do it because God commands it. First John 1:9 points out that one mark of a Christian is his continual asking for forgiveness. The verb tense in the Greek indicates an ongoing process. Forgiveness sets the Christian apart. The unbeliever represses his sinfulness, but the Christian is sensitive to his unworthiness. Confession takes up a significant portion of his prayer time.

Personally I find it a bit frightening to ask God to forgive us to the extent we forgive others. It's almost like asking God for justice. I warn my students, "Don't ask God for justice. You just might get it." If God, in fact, forgave me in exact proportion to my willingness to forgive others, I am afraid I would be in deep trouble.

The mandate to forgive others as we have been forgiven applies also to the matter of self-forgiveness. When we confess our sins to God, we have his promise that he will forgive us. Unfortunately, we don't always believe that promise. Confession requires humility on two levels. The first level is the actual admission of guilt; the second level is the humble acceptance of pardon.

A man distraught about a guilt problem once came to me, saying, "I've asked God to forgive me of this sin over and over, but I still feel guilty. What can I do?" The situation did not involve the multiple repetition of the same sin, but the multiple confession of a sin committed once.

"You must pray again and ask God to forgive you," I replied. A look of frustrated impatience came into his eyes. "But, I've done that!" he exclaimed. "I've asked God over and over again to forgive me. What good will it do to ask him again?"

In my reply I applied the proverbial firm force of

the board to the head of the mule: "I'm not suggesting that you ask God to forgive you for that sin. I'm
asking you to seek forgiveness for your arrogance."

The man was incredulous. "Arrogance? What
arrogance?" The man was assuming that his repeated entreaties for pardon were proof positive of
his humility. He was so contrite over his sin that he
felt he had to repent for it forever. His sin was too
great to be pardoned by one dose of repentance. Let
others get by on grace. He was going to suffer for
his sin no matter how gracious God was. Pride had
fixed a barrier to this man's acceptance of forgiveness. When God promises us that he will forgive us,
we insult his integrity when we refuse to accept it.
To forgive ourselves after God has forgiven us is a
duty as well as a privilege.

Do Not Lead Us into Temptation, But Deliver Us from Evil

At first glance this section of the Lord's Prayer
seems to be two separate petitions, but that is not
the case. It follows the literary form of parallelism
used in the Old Testament—two different ways of
saying the same thing. Jesus is not suggesting that
God will tempt us to evil, if we do not petition him
otherwise. James 1:13 specifically says that God

tempts no one. God may *test*, but he never *tempts* to evil. A test is for growth; temptation is toward evil.

Not all temptation is from Satan, for James also says that we are tempted by our own lust. Satan is not innocent of evil; nevertheless the evil inherent within the heart of man is capable of tempting man without Satan's help.

The plea to avoid temptation and the petition for deliverance from evil are one and the same. The King James Version is not the best translation of this text, because the evil is not in the general sense of which Jesus speaks. In Greek, the word for *evil* is neuter in gender; in this section of the Lord's Prayer, the word is masculine in gender. Jesus is saying that we should ask the Father to deliver us from the *evil one*, from onslaughts Luther called the "unbridled assaults of Satan," the enemy who would destroy the work of Christ in this world.

Jesus is telling us to ask the Father to build a hedge around us. The petition is not designed to avoid the trials of this world, but to protect us from naked exposure to the attacks of Satan. In his "High Priestly Prayer," Jesus asks the Father not to take his disciples out of the world, but rather to "keep them from the evil one [*poneros*]" (John 17:15).

We are asking for God's redemptive presence. Without that presence we are easy prey for the enemy. Think of Peter, who had just finished rhapsodizing to Jesus about the extent of his commitment, the depth of his love and devotion, and the intensity of his loyalty. Looking at him and foretelling his denial, Jesus said, "Simon, Simon, behold, Satan demanded to have you, that he might sift you like wheat, but I have prayed for you that your faith may not fail" (Luke 22:31-32). In other words, Jesus was telling Peter that on his own he would be putty in the hands of Satan. Were it not for the intercession of Christ on Peter's behalf, Peter would have been lost; his faith would have failed.

Not only do we have Jesus to intercede for us to protect us from the enemy, but we ourselves are also to ask God to keep us safe from the enemy's hand.

In six petitions, Jesus has outlined the pattern and the priorities for our prayer lives. The close of the Lord's Prayer—"for Thine is the kingdom and the power, and the glory forever. Amen"—is not in the best manuscripts. In all probability it was not in the original text, but was a common conclusion for prayers in the early church. However, it is a fitting and truthful ending. It hearkens back to the prayer's opening, raising a doxology to the one who hears our petitions.

CHAPTER 7

THE PRACTICE OF PRAYER

The Lord's Prayer was given to the church in response to the disciples' request that Jesus teach them to pray. In the masterful example of the Lord's Prayer we have seen the priorities of prayer. We can also detect a pattern of prayer, a fluid movement that begins with adoration and moves finally to petition and supplication.

The acrostic "ACTS" has been useful to follow as a pattern for prayer. Each letter in the acrostic represents a vital element of effective prayer:

A — ADORATION
C — CONFESSION
T — THANKSGIVING
S — SUPPLICATION

The complete acrostic "ACTS" suggests the dynamic dimension of prayer. Prayer is action. While it may be expressed in a spirit of serene quietness, it is action, nevertheless. When we pray, we are not passive observers or neutral, detached spectators. Energy is expended in the exercise of prayer.

The Bible tells us that it is the *fervent*, effectual prayer of the righteous man that avails much. Fervency characterized Jesus' agony in Gethsemane, where his sweat fell to the ground as droplets of blood. Fervency describes Jacob's all-night wrestling match with the angel at Peniel. Prayer is an exercise of passion, not of indifference.

Jesus told the parable of the persistent widow taking her case to an unjust judge. The judge, an unscrupulous man with no regard for man or for God, heard the widow's pleas. He was not moved by a sudden burst of compassion, but rather was worn out by her repeated entreaties. In short, the woman became a pest, driving the judge to action by her relentless nagging.

The point of the parable is not that God is indifferent to our needs and must be nagged if we are to be heard. It is not a question of a parallel between the unjust judge and God, the perfectly just Judge. It is a contrast. Jesus frequently uses the "how much more" motif in his parables. Here he states, "And will not God vindicate his elect, who cry to him day and night?" (Luke 18:7). The point of comparison/

contrast is this: If a human, unjust judge will hear the petition of a fervent woman, *how much more* will our heavenly just Judge hear our petitions?

The persistent woman is likened to the saints who *cry* day and night. Like King David, whose pillow was saturated with his tears, the saints come to God with genuine emotion, even with tears.

Fervency is an appropriate form of active prayer. Frenzy is not. A fine line exists between the two. Both possess passion; both are loaded with emotion. Fervency crosses over into frenzy at two points: the mental and the emotional. Fervency becomes frenzy when the mind stops thinking and the emotions slip out of control. The frenzied prayer lapses into the incoherence of the whirling dervish, and God is not honored.

Frenzy, the counterfeit of fervency, is a contrived attempt to simulate godly fervor. Those who deliberately manipulate people's emotions are served warning here. There is something holy, something sovereign, about genuine spiritual fervor that cannot be manufactured artificially. It is easy to confuse frenzy and fervor. The confusion is deadly.

Adoration

As in the pattern of the Lord's Prayer, the most appropriate way to begin prayer is with adoration. Sadly, we are most often moved to prayer by our desires for supplication. We go to God when we want something from him. We are in such a hurry to mention our requests and articulate our needs (which God already knows) that we either omit adoration altogether or skip over it quickly in a perfunctory manner.

To omit adoration is to cut the heart out of prayer. It is one thing to be fervent in supplication, particularly while praying in a foxhole; it is another thing to be fervent in adoration. The prayers of the great saints, the prayer warriors of church history, are marked by their fervent adoration of God.

God forbid that we should ever second-guess the teaching of Christ, but I must confess to being at least mildly surprised by Jesus' response to the disciples' request about prayer. When they said, "Teach us to pray," I would have anticipated a different response from his lips than the one he gave by way of the Lord's Prayer. I would have anticipated a response something like this: "Do you want to learn how to pray? Read the Psalms."

I'm surprised Jesus didn't refer the disciples to the Psalms. There we find not only the heart of David exposed, but also a divinely inspired treasury of adoration filled with models for us to follow.

Our hesitancy and weakness in expressing adoration may have two root causes. The first is our simple lack of suitable vocabulary. We tend to be inarticulate when it comes to adoration. It was Edgar Allan Poe who said that prose is a more fitting vehicle to communicate instruction than poetry. The aim of poetry is to lift the soul to loftly heights. No wonder the Psalms were written in poetic form. Here the loftiest heights of verbal expression are reached in the service of the soul's praise for God.

Many people in the charismatic movement have declared that one of the chief reasons for their pursuit of the gift of tongues is a keen desire to overcome or bypass the deficiency of an impoverished vocabulary, by way of a special prayer language. People often feel their own language is inadequate to express adoration. This sense of inadequacy from having to use the same tired, haggard words yields frustration. A similar view is expressed by Charles Wesley in his hymn "O for a Thousand Tongues." The hymn complains that the restriction to one tongue is a lamentable hindrance to praise, to be relieved only by the addition of nine hundred and ninety-nine other tongues.

The Psalms were written in simple but powerful vocabulary through which the hearts of several writers expressed reverence for God *without bypassing the mind.* Opening their mouths, the psalmists uttered praise. That praise was given under the inspiration of the Holy Spirit to be sure, but by men whose minds were steeped in the things of God.

Another great barrier to articulate praise is

ignorance. We suffer not so much from a limited vocabulary as from a limited understanding of the one whom we are adoring. Our worship also suffers from a lack of knowledge of God.

Consider the love-struck teenager who writes love notes to his girlfriend during study hall. The youth may be shy and reticent, but give him a pen and the object of his romance and suddenly he is another Shakespeare. Oh, the love notes may be maudlin and less than sophisticated from a literary standpoint, but there is no lack of words. The boy is in love. His heart moves his pen.

How does one pen love letters to an unknown God? How do the lips form words of praise to a nebulous, unnamed Supreme Being? God is a person, with an unending personal history. He has revealed himself to us not only in the glorious theater of nature, but also in the pages of sacred Scripture. If we fill our minds with his Word, our inarticulate stammers will change to accomplished patterns of meaningful praise. By immersing ourselves in the Psalms, we will not only gain insight into the how of praise, but also enlarge our understanding of the one whom we are praising.

Why should we adore him? Because that is our duty as human beings. We have been called to fill the earth with the glory of God. We are created in his image to reflect his glory; our major function is to magnify the Lord. Likewise we are to adore him, but not to flatter him, as if to "set him up" for our supplications. We note that the angels in heaven are described as surrounding the throne of God with praise and adoration.

Why is adoration so important to us in practical terms? Because the whole life of the Christian—which is to be a life of obedience and service—is motivated and enriched when holiness and the dignity of God are etched into our minds. Before I can be motivated to do something difficult for someone, I need to have a certain amount of respect for that person. When someone asks me to go out into the world and endure persecution and hostility from angry and contrary people, I have to respect that person deeply. Only then does that task become easier.

When we begin our prayers with adoration, we are setting the tone for our coming to God in confession, in thanksgiving, and in supplication. Hebrews 4:16 tells us that we are to enter into the Holy of Holies *boldly*, for the veil has been removed by the Cross. The sword the angel wielded at the gate to paradise has been removed. Christ has given us access to the Father. Yet, if we look at the history of the church, people have kept a respectful distance, thinking that God remained aloof from them. Prayer became so formal that the church and its people reacted with equal intensity in the opposite direction.

Today we have "conversational prayer." Our talking to God goes something like this: "Uh, hi there, God. How's it going? Not going too good for me today, but, uh, you know, you and me, God, we'll make out somehow, huh?" This is a rather casual approach to God. Historically there is a reason for it. It represents an overreaction to formalism by embracing what turns out to be the informality that breeds contempt. Designed to eliminate artificiality, it has, nevertheless, created the worst kind of artificiality. A creature has not yet been made who would have the audacity to speak to God like this in his immediate presence.

God has invited us to come freely into his presence, but we must realize that we are still coming before *God*. When confronted with the Lord God Omnipotent himself, who would speak as if to a friend at a baseball game? We may come boldly, but never arrogantly, never presumptuously, never flippantly, as if we were dealing with a peer.

When we begin our prayer with adoration and praise, we acknowledge the one to whom we are speaking. The grammar need not be perfect, nor the words lofty and eloquent; but they must reflect the respect and the honor due God. There is a sense in which adoration introduces us into the proper mode by which we confess and give our thanks and make our supplications.

Several recent books would have us believe that

all we have to do is follow certain steps and God will give us whatever we ask. The authors say, in effect, "Follow this procedure or use these specific words and know for certain that God will give in to your requests." That's not prayer; that's magic. That's not faith, but superstition. These are gimmicks intended to manipulate the sovereign God. But the one who prays forgets the one to whom he is speaking. The sovereign God cannot be manipulated, for he knows the hearts of all who pray to him. True prayer presupposes an attitude of humble submission and adoration to the Almighty God.

Confession

After expressing adoration, we must come with hearts of confession. Remember that we have no right to come before God at all, apart from the finished work of Christ. We can make no claim, in and of ourselves, to the ear of God. We have no intrinsic right to his presence. The Scriptures tell us that God is too holy to even look at sin. God delights in the prayers of the righteous, but we are not very righteous in our daily lives. Nevertheless, the God we serve invites us into his presence *in spite of our sin.*

In our study of the Lord's Prayer, we have already considered some of the important elements of confession. As the model prayer indicates, confession is to be a normal part of our conversation with God. Confession is not a frivolous matter to be engaged in only at appointed times and dates throughout the year. Confession should be a daily activity for the Christian, whose entire pilgrimage is characterized by the spirit of repentance. The principal reason why confession must be on a daily basis is because our sins are committed on a daily basis against divine law. We do things we ought not to do and leave undone those things God commands us to do. We run up a daily indebtedness before God. Consequently, our daily prayers must include genuine acts of confession.

It is no accident that the Roman Catholic church elevated the rite of penance to the level of a sacrament. Because the sacrament of penance was at the eye of the tornado of the Protestant Reformation, a backlash of negativism toward penitence set in among Protestants. Here is the classic case of overreaction and the throwing out of the baby with the bath water. The Reformers sought not the elimination of repentance and confession, but the reformation of the church's practice of these things.

The Roman Catholic sacrament of penance contains several elements: verbal confession, priestly absolution, and "works of satisfaction," that are required to fulfill the demands of the sacrament.

The works of satisfaction may be for perfunctory tasks such as saying so many Hail Marys or Our Fathers or even more rigorous acts of penance. The works of satisfaction are designed to accrue "congruous merit" for the penitent Christian, making it fitting for God to restore the grace of justification.

It was this third aspect of the sacrament of penance that created so much controversy in the sixteenth century. The works of satisfaction, in the Reformers eyes, cast a shadow on the sufficiency and the efficacy of Christ's finished work of satisfaction in our behalf on the cross. The "congruous merit" of which Rome spoke obscured the biblical doctrine of justification by faith alone.

In the controversy over penance, the Protestant Reformers did not repudiate the importance of confession, nor did they necessarily repudiate the concept of confessing one's sin to another person. They did, of course, challenge elements of required confession to a priest. Nevertheless, they acknowledged that confessing one's sins to another human being is biblical. The principle of priestly absolution was not a major issue. The Roman Catholic church has always taught that the priestly words *Te absolvo* ("I absolve you") find their strength in the premise of Jesus to the church that "whatever you bind on earth shall be bound in heaven, and whatever you loose on earth shall be loosed in heaven" (Matthew 16:19), granting the spokesmen of the church a right to speak the pardon of Christ to penitent people.

The Roman Catholic church understands that the power to forgive sins does not reside ultimately in the priest. The priest is merely a spokesman for Christ. In practice the priestly absolution differs very little from the Protestant minister's "Assurance of Pardon," which is given from pulpits across the land every Sunday.

Saint John tells us, "If we confess our sins, he is faithful and just to forgive us our sins, and to cleanse us from all unrighteousness" (1 John 1:9, KJV). Here we find the promise of God to forgive our confessed sins. To ignore or to neglect this promise is to steer a perilous course. God commands us to confess our sins and promises to forgive our sins. That we should confess our sins daily is clear. What confession means and what it involves are matters that need some elaboration.

We can distinguish between two kinds of repentance: attrition and contrition. Attrition is counterfeit repentance, which never qualifies us for forgiveness. It is like the repentance of a child who, caught in the act of disobeying his mother, cries out, "Mommy, Mommy, I'm sorry. Please don't spank me." Attrition is repentance motivated strictly by a fear of punishment. The sinner confesses his sin to God, not out of genuine remorse, but out of a desire to secure a ticket out of hell.

True repentance reflects contrition, a godly remorse for offending God. Here the sinner mourns his sin, not for the loss of reward or for the threat of judgment, but because he has done injury to the honor of God. The Roman Catholic church uses a prayer in the confession called "The Act of Contrition" to express the sinner's repentance:

> O my God, I am heartily sorry for having offended thee. I detest all my sins because of thy just punishment, but most of all because I have offended thee, O my God, who art all good and deserving of all my love. I firmly resolve, with the help of thy grace, to sin no more and to avoid the near occasion of sin.

This prayer goes beyond attrition, the mere fear of punishment, to a godly sorrow for offending God. Notice that the sinner acknowledges that God is *all good* and deserving of our love. This acknowledgment silences all attempts at self-justification.

The prayer includes a firm statement of resolve not to commit the sin again, a willingness to abandon the evil pattern and to avoid even the occasion of it. A humble recognition of dependence upon divine mercy and assistance is also included.

Of course, it is possible to use this prayer in a perfunctory manner, merely reciting it as a formal exercise with no heartfelt remorse. Still, the words of the prayer capture the elements of true contrition.

Contrition has lost much of its meaning in our culture. It is not difficult to convince people that they are sinners, for not one in a thousand is going to say that he is perfect. The common response is, "Sure, I'm a sinner. Isn't everyone? Nobody's perfect." There are few, if any, who claim they are blameless, that they have lived lives of ethical consistency, keeping the Golden Rule in every situation. The rub is in acknowledging the intensity of our sin, the extreme godlessness of our actions. Because we are all sinners and know that we share a common guilt, our confession tends to be superficial, often not characterized by earnestness or a sense of moral urgency.

Psalm 51, a contrite sinner's prayer for pardon, is delivered by King David after he has committed adultery with Bathsheba. David does not approach God with excuses. He does not ask God to consider the circumstances that produced his sin or the loneliness of his government position. David does not seek to minimize the gravity of his sin in God's presence. There are no rationalizations and no attempts at self-justification, which are so characteristic of guilty people.

David says, "I know my transgressions, and my sin is ever before me. . . . Thou art justified in thy sentence and blameless in thy judgment" (verses 3-4). In other words, David believes that God is absolutely justified if he gives him nothing but absolute punishment. David exhibits what God has said he will not despise: a broken and contrite heart.

David pleads for restoration to God's favor:

> Create in me a clean heart, O God, and put a new and right spirit within me. Cast me not away from thy presence, and take not thy holy Spirit from me. Restore to me the joy of thy salvation, and uphold me with a willing spirit. (verses 10-12)

He understood the most crucial element of confession: total dependence upon God's, mercy. David could not atone for his own sins. There was nothing he could do and nothing he could say to undo what he had done. There was no way for him to "make it up to God." David understood what Jesus later made clear—that we are debtors who cannot pay our debts.

Confession is like a declaration of bankruptcy. God requires perfection. The slightest sin blemishes a perfect record. All the "good deeds" in the world cannot erase the blemish and move us from imperfection to perfection. Once the sin has been committed, we are morally bankrupt. Our only hope is to have that sin forgiven and covered through the atonement of the one who is altogether perfect.

When we sin, our only option is repentance. Without repentance there is no forgiveness. We must come before God in contrition. David put it this way:

You do not delight in sacrifice. . . . The sacrifices of God are a broken spirit; a broken and contrite heart, O God, you will not despise. (Psalm 51:16-17, NIV)

Here David's profound thoughts reveal his understanding of what many Old Testament persons failed to grasp—that the offering of sacrifices in the temple did not gain merit for the sinner. Sacrifices pointed beyond themselves to the perfect Sacrifice. The perfect atonement was offered by the perfect Lamb without blemish. The blood of bulls and goats does not take away sin. The blood of Jesus does. To avail ourselves of the atonement of Christ, to gain that covering, requires that we come before God in brokenness and contrition. The true sacrifices of God are a broken spirit and a contrite heart.

There was an important element of surprise in David's experience of forgiveness. He had begged God to wash away his sin and to make him clean. In a certain sense, forgiveness must never be a surprise. We should never be surprised when God keeps his word. In 1 John 1:9,

God tells us that if we confess our sins, he will be faithful to forgive those sins. God keeps his promises; man does not. God is the covenant Maker; we are covenant breakers.

Looking at the issue from another perspective, however, we ought to be surprised *every time* we experience forgiveness. We ought never to take God's mercy and forgiveness for granted, even though we live in a culture that does. It is terrifying to consider the ease with which we take God's grace for granted. I occasionally ask collegians, seminarians, seminary professors, and ministers the questions, "Is God obligated to be loving? Is he bound to forgiveness and grace?" Again and again their answers are in the affirmative: "Yes, of course, it's God's nature to be loving. He's essentially a God of love. If he didn't show love, he wouldn't be God. If God is God, then he *must* be merciful!"

He *must* be merciful? If God must be merciful, then his mercy is no longer free or voluntary. It has become obligatory; if so, then it is no longer mercy, but justice. God is never required to be merciful. As soon as we think God is obligated to be merciful, a red light should flash in our brains, indicating that we are no longer thinking about mercy, but about justice. We need to do more than sing "Amazing Grace"—we need to be repeatedly amazed by grace.

Thanksgiving

Thanksgiving must be an integral part of prayer. It should be inseparably related to our petitions of supplication; otherwise thanksgiving is illegitimate. The Scriptures tell us to come to God and make all of our requests known with thanksgiving. Thanksgiving is an acknowledgment of God and his benefits. In Psalm 103:2, David extols: "Bless the LORD, O my soul, and forget not all his benefits."

Ingratitude is a serious matter. The Scriptures have much to say about it. The failure to be grateful is the mark both of the pagan and the apostate.

In Romans 1:21, Paul calls attention to two primary sins of the pagan. He says, "For although they knew God they did not honor him as God or give thanks to him." Honor and thanksgiving may be distinguished, but not separated. God is honored by thanksgiving and dishonored by the lack of it. All that we have and all that we are we owe ultimately to the benevolence of our Creator. To slight him by withholding appropriate gratitude is to exalt ourselves and debase him.

The pagan must be distinguished from the apostate. The pagan has never entered into the household of faith. He is a stranger to the covenant community. Idolatry and ingratitude characterize him. An apostate is one who joins the church, becomes a member of the visible covenant community, and then repudiates the church, leaving it for a life of secular indulgence. The apostate is "one who forgets." He has a short memory.

Jesus' encounter with the ten lepers illustrates the importance of thanksgiving. Countless sermons have been preached about the healing of the ten lepers, focusing attention on the theme of gratitude. The thrust of many of these sermons has been that Jesus healed ten lepers, but that only one of them was grateful. The only polite response to such preaching is to call it what it is—nonsense. It is inconceivable that a leper enduring the abject misery he faced daily in the ancient world would not be grateful for receiving instant healing from the dreadful disease. Had he been one of the lepers, even Adolph Hitler would have been grateful.

The issue in the story is not one of *gratitude*, but of *thanksgiving*. It is one thing to feel grateful; it is another thing to express it. Lepers were cut off from family and friends. Instant cleansing meant release from exile. We can imagine them deliriously happy, rushing home to embrace their wives and children, to announce their healing. Who would not be grateful? But only one of them postponed his return home and took time to *give* thanks. The account in Luke 17 reads: "Then one of them, when he saw that he was healed, turned back, praising God with a loud voice; and he fell on his face at Jesus' feet, *giving him thanks.* Now he was a Samaritan" (verses 15-16; italics mine).

All of our prayers are to include thanksgiving. Like the leper we must pause, turn back, and give thanks. We are so indebted to God that we can never exhaust our opportunities for expressing gratitude.

Forgetting the benefits of God is also the mark of the carnal Christian, one who lives by his feelings. He is prone to a roller-coaster spiritual life, moving quickly from ecstatic highs to depressing lows. In the high moments he feels an exhilarating sense of God's presence, but he plunges to despair the moment he senses an acute absence of such feelings. He lives from blessing to blessing, suffering the pangs of a short memory. He lives always in the present, savoring the "now" but losing sight of what God has done in the past. His obedience and service are only as strong as the intensity of his last memory of blessing.

If God never grants us another glimpse of his glory in this life, if he never grants us another request, if he never gives us another gift from the abundance of his grace, we still would be obligated to spend the rest of our lives praising him for what he has already done. We have already been blessed enough to be moved daily to thanksgiving. Nevertheless, God continues to bless us.

Supplication

Someone once said to me, "With so many people starving, it might be wrong for me to pray for a rug for my living room." Yet, the God who cares about the empty stomachs of the world is the same God who cares about empty living rooms. What is important to us may also be important to our Father. If we are not sure about the propriety of our request, we should tell that to God. James 1:5 says, "If any of you lacks wisdom, let him ask God, who gives to all men generously and without reproaching, and it will be given him." The Greek phrase translated "without reproaching," literally means "without throwing it back in your face." We don't need to be afraid of the reproach of God, provided we are sincerely seeking his will in a given situation.

Nothing is too big or too small to bring before God in prayer, as long as it is not something we know to be contrary to the expressed will of God. It would obviously be quite inappropriate to ask God to make us competent thieves. We must not tempt God as the man who revealed during a national television interview that he had made a pact with God. He declared that he had promised God that if God were to bless his two brothels, he would spend the rest of his life serving him. Assuming that our request is not blatantly opposed to the will of God as made clear in his Word, then no supplication is illegitimate, if it can be made with thanksgiving.

But, what if our prayers seem to go unanswered? Sometimes we feel as if our prayers lack the power to penetrate the ceiling. It is as if our petitions fall upon deaf ears, and God remains unmoved or unconcerned about our passionate pleading. Why do these feelings haunt us?

There are several reasons why we are sometimes frustrated in prayer. I will review some of the more important ones:

1. We pray in vague generalities. When all our prayers are either vague or universal in scope, it is difficult for us to experience the exhilaration that goes with clear and obvious answers to prayer. If we ask God to "bless everyone in the world" or to "forgive everyone in town," it would be difficult to "see" the prayer answered in any concrete way. Having a broad scope of interest in prayer is not wrong, but if all prayer is so general, then no prayer will have specific and concrete application.

2. We are at war with God. If we are out of harmony with God or in open rebellion toward him, we can hardly expect him to turn a benevolent ear toward our prayers. His ear is inclined to those who love him and seek to obey him. He turns his ear away from the wicked. Thus an attitude of reverence toward God is vital to the effectiveness of our prayers.

3. We tend to be impatient. When I pray for patience, I tend to ask for it "right now!" It is not uncommon for us to wait years, indeed decades, for our most sincere petitions to become realized. God is rarely in a hurry. On the other hand, our fidelity to God tends to depend on "prompt and courteous" acts by God. If God tarries, our impatience gives way to frustration. We need to learn patience, asking God for his peace.

4. We have short memories. It is easy for us to forget the benefits and gifts given by the hand of God. This is the mark of the apostate—he forgets the benefits of God. The saint remembers the gifts of God and doesn't require a fresh one each hour to keep his faith intact.

Though God does heap grace upon grace, we should be able to rejoice in God's benefits even if we never receive another benefit from him. Remember the Lord when you go before him. He will not give you a stone when you ask him for bread.

CHAPTER 8

THE PROHIBITIONS OF PRAYER

Very few prohibitions regarding prayer are found in the Scriptures. In Psalm 66:18, the Psalmist David penned these divinely inspired words: "If I had cherished iniquity in my heart, the Lord would not have listened." The Hebrew verse could also be translated, "If I *had* iniquity in my heart, the Lord would not have heard."

In either case, David is laying down a condition under which the prayer would be not only ineffective, but unheard. The Hebrew word translated "cherished" is *raah*, meaning merely "to see." In other words, if I look at my life and see sin and nurture it, my prayers are an exercise in futility.

Does this mean that if sin is present in our lives, God refuses to hear our prayers? No. If this were so, all prayer would be futile. However, if our hearts are hardened in a spirit of impenitence, our prayers are not only futile, but also in mockery of God.

King David in Psalm 66 is reminding himself that there is a time when prayer is a presumptuous, arrogant, detestable, and obnoxious deed perpetrated upon the Almighty. This psalm contains seventeen verses of joy and praise to God for his mighty deeds. And then, suddenly there appears the grim reminder of how the entire story could have been so drastically different. We are alerted to the importance of properly approaching God in prayer. If there is anything worse than not praying, it would be praying in an unworthy manner.

Other Scripture references reflect this attitude. Psalm 109:7 suggests that the prayers of wicked men should be counted as sin. John 9:31 specifically states the Lord does not hear sinners. Proverbs 15:29 says, "The LORD is far from the wicked, but he hears the prayer of the righteous." Proverbs 28:9 says that the prayer of the disobedient or rebellious is an "abomination" to the Lord. It is something disgusting or loathsome to him.

James, however, tells us that the prayers of *righteous* men accomplish much. But we are not righteous in our daily lives, I'm afraid. Yes, we are clothed with the righteousness of Christ, so that as far as our position before God is concerned, we are righteous; but the practical manifestation of what we are in Christ is sadly inconsistent and woefully inadequate.

Theologians sometimes define a concept by saying what something does *not* say as well as by what it does say. What the psalmist is *not* saying is that if he had been guilty of sin, the Lord would not have heard him. The psalmist is not saying that if he had sin in his heart, God would not have heard him.

David was constantly confessing sin in the Psalms. We know that he is not saying that one must be holy in order to pray; otherwise no one would ever pray. In fact, being a sinner is one of the prerequisites for entrance into the kingdom of God. Jesus said that he did not come to call the righteous, but sinners, to repentance. Looking again to the Lord's Prayer as a pattern, we note that confession is an integral part of prayer. Without the confession of sin, says 1 John 1:9, there is no forgiveness of sin.

A former mentor of mine, Dr. John Gerstner, tells of an occasion when at one of his meetings, a woman announced to him that she had not sinned for over twenty years. Dr. Gerstner said that he felt sorry for her because that could only mean that she had not prayed in over twenty years, at least not in the way the Lord had told us to pray.

I am not suggesting that the more we sin, the more qualified we are for prayer; that would obviously be a false conclusion. But confessing sin, asking for forgiveness of our "debts," or trespasses, is

an integral part of the practice of prayer, as outlined
by our Lord himself. In fact, the more godly we are,
the more devout we will strive to be and the more
painfully aware of our sin we will be. It is much the
same as walking toward a mountain. The closer we
get to that mountain, the bigger it appears.

Think about the fairy tale *The Princess and the Pea*,
for example. The princess had been gone for some
time, and many had tried to lay claim to her throne.
To prove true royalty, a scheme was concocted.
Many mattresses were stacked on top of one another, with one small pea hidden far down the
stack. None of the false princesses had any notion
that anything was there, but the true princess could
not sleep because of the extreme discomfort the pea
gave her. She was extraordinarily sensitive to the
presence of the tiny pea.

The lesson for Christians should be clear. When
we have that kind of sensitivity to sin, we have
royal sensitivity. The closer we are to God, the more
the slightest sin will cause us deep sorrow.

We can be sure that being guilty of sin does not
disqualify us from the privilege of coming into
God's presence. The psalmist is not talking about
committing sin, but *allowing* for it. The Puritans
spoke of this concept of allowing for sin. It is not so
much the victory over sin we need to look at as it is
the battle itself. We are in a battle with sin constantly, and we never emerge unscathed.

One of the marks of a true Christian is that he never quits fighting. He doesn't always win, though he will win the ultimate battle because of Christ. If a person ever does give up the fight, then he has truly embraced the evil, legitimizing it. In short, he condones, even allows, it.

In a sermon on the first beatitude, "Blessed are the poor in spirit," the English Puritan preacher Charles Haddon Spurgeon said that "the proud sinner wants Christ, and his own parties; Christ, and his own lusts; Christ, and his own waywardness. The one who is truly poor in spirit wants only Christ, and he will do anything, and give anything to have him!" This is what Psalm 66 is suggesting. The very idea of a person trying to pray, while cherishing some sin, while holding on to a sin he is not willing to relinquish to the lordship of Christ, casts a dark shadow of doubt on the validity of his sonship.

The Scripture cites other practical applications of this concept. First Peter 3:7 says:

> *Likewise you husbands, live considerately with your wives, bestowing honor on the woman as the weaker sex, since you are joint heirs of the grace of life, in order that your prayers may not be hindered.*

The Greek word translated "hindered" is *ekkepto*, which literally means "cut off." If discord in the marital relationship is not being dealt with, prayers are cut off. This echoes the initial warning of Psalm 66.

A second example is taken from Matthew 5:23-24:

> *If you are offering your gift at the altar, and there remember that your brother has something against you, leave your gift there before the altar and go; first be reconciled to your brother, and then come and offer your gift.*

Here Jesus is saying that if there are unresolved conflicts in our lives, our worship is blemished. He is setting down priorities. First, we are to give heed to those things that require attention; then we are to come and offer our worship. Though the passage does not speak specifically of prayer, the principle of settling accounts is constant.

When we petition God with unconfessed, hence unpurged, sin lurking in our hearts, we are like the irate college student who confronted his professor about a failing grade. The professor listened politely to the student's frustrations, but remarked that, in his honest professional estimation, the student had received the grade he deserved. The student countered that not only he but also several others in the class felt it was unfair.

The professor, with understandably aroused curiosity, asked what they thought should be done. To that, the student explained, "They've decided that you should be shot. But there's one small problem. Not one of them owns a gun." The professor breathed a sigh of relief and expressed his deepest regret over the "plight" of these students. "But *you* do," the young man said. This student then had the audacity to ask the kindly professor if he could borrow his gun so that the students might shoot him.

In a similarly audacious manner, if we see iniquity in our lives and harbor it in our hearts when we pray, we are asking God for the strength we need to curse him. We are petitioning God for more strength to disobey him further. Just as the professor was not about to lend his gun to those who would kill him, God is not about to honor our requests made out of sinful hearts.

CHAPTER 9

THE POWER OF PRAYER

We are moved by the litany of faith that the author of Hebrews records in chapter 11 of that book. There we have the "Roll Call of Faith," which catalogues the heroic acts of biblical men and women of faith. Their acts are partially summarized in verses 33 and 34:

> *Who through faith conquered kingdoms, enforced justice, received promises, stopped the mouths of lions, quenched raging fire, escaped the edge of the sword, won strength out of weakness, became mighty in war, put foreign armies to flight.*

The Scriptures do not provide a similar catalogue of the heroes of prayer, but such a list could easily be compiled. Using the same format as does the writer of Hebrews, let us examine a partial list of the accomplishments of prayer:

- By prayer, Esau's heart was changed toward Jacob, so that they met in a friendly, rather than hostile, manner (Genesis 32).

- By the prayer of Moses, God brought the plagues upon Egypt and then removed them again (Exodus 7–11).

- By prayer, Joshua made the sun stand still (Joshua 10).

- By prayer, when Samson was ready to perish with thirst, God brought water out of a hollow place for his sustenance (Judges 15).

- By prayer, the strength of Samson was restored. And he pulled down the temple of Dagon on the Philistines, so that those whom he killed as he died were more than all he had killed in his life prior to that (Judges 16).

- By prayer, Elijah held back the rains for three and a half years. And then by prayer, caused it to rain again (1 Kings 17–18).

- By the prayer of Hezekiah, God sent an angel and killed in one night 185,000 men in Sennacherib's army (2 Kings 19).

• By the prayer of Asa, God confounded the army of Zerah (2 Chronicles 14).

And time would fail me to tell of Abraham, who prayed for and received a son at the age of one hundred years; and Moses, who received help at the Red Sea; and the Israelites, who were delivered from Egypt after much prayer; and David, who escaped the treachery of Saul by prayer; and Solomon, who received great wisdom as the result of prayer; and Daniel, who was able to interpret dreams after prayer. People were delivered from peril, healed from diseases, saw loved ones cured, and witnessed innumerable miracles as the result of fervent prayer.

James, if anything, was understating the case when he wrote that the effective prayer of a righteous man can accomplish much.

The power of prayer is neither automatic nor magical. Conditions are attached to the promises of the Bible regarding prayer. At times Jesus uses a kind of "shorthand," delivering brief aphorisms about prayer to encourage his people in its practice. We are reminded of statements like "Ask, and it will be given you" (Matthew 7:7); "If two of you agree on earth about anything they ask, it will be done for them by my Father in heaven" (Matthew 18:19); and "Whatever you ask in prayer, you will receive, if you have faith" (Matthew 21:22).

Shorthand summaries like these have provoked

bizarre theories of prayer where people have violently isolated these passages from everything else Jesus and the Bible say about prayer. Distortions also abound when we approach these aphorisms simplistically. Consider the earlier statement about any two people agreeing. It would not be difficult to find two Christians who agree that ridding the world of cancer or wars would be a good idea. Their prayer in this matter would not automatically accomplish their desire. The Word of God indicates that wars, poverty, and disease will be present at the time of Christ's return. To expect their absolute elimination before the appointed time is to grasp prematurely the future promises of God. What life will be like in heaven would be delightful to us now, but all our prayers cannot force God to give us this future situation in this present world.

We still must suffer the ravages of sin, disease, and death. We entreat God to comfort us, to deliver us, to heal us—but we cannot demand these things in an absolute way.

The idea that God "always wills healing" has been a destructive distortion in the Christian community. The pastoral problems emanating from this are enormous. I was once approached by a young man stricken with cerebral palsy. His Christian faith was vibrant, his attitude was contagious with pleasant optimism, his productivity exceptional. He had graduated from college with a superior record. His question to me was poignant: "Dr. Sproul, do you think I am demon possessed?" The question was accompanied by tears. The man's life had been hurled into chaos.

Aghast at this question, I replied, "Why would you even ask such a question?"

The young man proceeded to relate a series of events triggered by an encounter with some Christian friends who had "claimed" the promise of Scripture and "agreed" that the young man be healed of cerebral palsy. They had laid hands on him, praying "the prayer of faith" and claiming a healing for him. When it was apparent that he had not been healed, they first chastised him for his lack of faith. Next they claimed he was guilty of some heinous secret sin that was blocking the healing. Finally they concluded that he was demon possessed and left him with a tortured soul. His "friends" never considered that the error might be their own. They had given the impression of being zealous, Spirit-filled Christians. Their actions revealed at best immaturity; at worst, arrogance and presumption.

Prayer is not magic. God is not a celestial bellhop ready at our beck and call to satisfy our every whim. In some cases our prayers must involve travail of the soul and agony of heart such as Jesus himself experienced in the Garden. Sometimes the immature Christian suffers bitter disappointment not because God failed to keep his promises, but because well-meaning Christians made promises "for" God that God himself never authorized.

The simple summaries Jesus gives are designed to encourage us to pray. We have not, he said, because we ask not. The pattern seems simple. We are to ask and we will receive. Elsewhere the New Testament expands the conditions, giving us a fuller view of what is involved in effective prayer. Below are five texts with the conditions that qualify the statements Jesus gives.

1. John 9:31—"We know that God does not listen to sinners, but if any one is a worshiper of God and does his will, God listens to him."
(REVERENCE & OBEDIENCE)

2. John 14:13—"Whatever you ask in my name, I will do it, that the Father may be glorified in the Son."
(IN ACCORDANCE WITH THE CHARACTER OF CHRIST)

3. John 15:7—"If you abide in me, and my words abide in you, ask whatever you will, and it shall be done for you."
(MUTUAL COMMUNION WITH CHRIST)

4. 1 John 3:22—"And we receive from him whatever we ask, because we keep his commandments and do what pleases him."
(OBEDIENCE)

> *5. 1 John 5:14—"And this is the confidence which*
> *we have in him, that if we ask anything according*
> *to his will he hears us."*
> (ACCORDANCE WITH THE WILL OF GOD)

As these passages reveal, there is more to receiving what we desire from God than the mere asking. Trust in God is not enough. There must be proper reverence for God, obedience to his will, and an ongoing communion with Christ. The request must be made in accordance with the revealed will of God, in accordance with the nature and character of God.

The Bible enjoins us to pray "in the name of Jesus." The invoking of Jesus' name is not a magical incantation; its significance lies deeper. In the culture in which the Bible was written, a person's name indicated the sum total of his attributes and character. To ask for something in Jesus' name is not to tag on a phrase at the end of a prayer. Rather, it means that we believe that our request is what Jesus himself would ask for. We are showing that we are so closely aligned with the mind of Christ that we can make our request in his stead.

We have seen that there are certain prerequisites we must follow as we pray. If we ask anything, we must trust in God, knowing that our request is in accordance with the will of the Father and the nature and purpose of Christ. We must have a proper reverence for God as well as the assurance that we are being obedient to what he has revealed to us. We must maintain continuous communion with Christ. After all of these prerequisites have been met, we may have confidence that our prayer will be answered. The crucial thing to notice here is that if we are meeting these prerequisites, we will not ask for anything out of the will of God.

Another reason our prayers are not always answered as we desire is given to us in James 4:3. We are told that we don't have because we ask with improper motives, asking in prayer things in the pursuit of wicked pleasures. God is not going to give us the things we would misuse. Nor is he going to answer those requests made in ignorance, which would prove disastrous.

Moses is a prime example. In Exodus 33:18, he prays, "Show me thy glory." Moses has talked with God, seen God do various miracles: the burning bush, sending the plagues, parting the Red Sea, but now Moses wants the big one: "God, those other things were great, but now let me have it all. Let me see your face!"

In verses 19 and 20, God says:

> *I will make all my goodness pass before you, and will proclaim before you my name "The LORD"; and I will be gracious to whom I will be gracious, and will show mercy on whom I will show mercy. But . . . you cannot see my face; for man shall not see me and live.*

God was doing Moses a monumental favor by refusing to honor his request. If God had granted Moses his wish, it would have cost him his life. No man can see God and live. Moses should have rejoiced that God said no.

Another reason that we fail to see the desired answers to our prayers may be because we are praying for things we already have in Christ. In John 4, Jesus is speaking with the woman at the well. He tells her that if she realized to whom she was speaking, she would have known what to request. The same is true of us. If we really knew who God is and all that he has already given us in Christ, our prayer lives would be far different from what they are.

We ask God for his presence, yet he has promised never to leave us or forsake us. We ask God to give us peace, but Ephesians says that Christ is our peace. Imagine sitting down to a marvelous Thanksgiving feast, a table overflowing with foods of all kinds, and asking the hostess for something to eat. It is possible to pray ourselves right into a state of unbelief by continuing to pray for those things we already have in Christ.

The Power of the Intercessor

Prayer is the priestly function of carrying a petition to God. In Old Testament times two major classes of mediators functioned between God and his people: prophets and priests. Stated simply, the prophet was ordained by God to speak his divine Word to the people. The prophet spoke to the people for God. Conversely, the priest was ordained by God to be a spokesman for the people. The priest spoke to God for the people.

In the New Testament, Christ exercises the offices not only of prophet and priest but also of King. In his priestly role he made the perfect sacrifice, offering the perfect atonement once and for all. Yet the Cross was not the end of Christ's priestly office. In his ascension he entered the heavenly holy of holies, and continues to act as our Great High Priest. There he prays for his people, interceding with the Father on our behalf. The power of Christ's prayers is immeasurable. It can be illustrated not only by the miracles he performed on earth, but also by his prayers of intercession during his earthly ministry.

Consider the cases of Judas and Simon Peter. Both were disciples who had committed heinous acts of treachery against Jesus in his darkest hour. Judas committed suicide, whereas Simon was restored and became the "Rock" of the early church in Jerusalem. Why?

One critical difference between these men may be seen in Jesus' announcements of their forthcoming treachery. About Judas he said, "Truly, truly, I say to you, one of you will betray me" (John 13:21).

When the disciples asked Jesus to identify the traitor, he replied, "It is he to whom I shall give this morsel when I have dipped it." Then Jesus dipped the morsel, gave it to Judas and said, "What you are going to do, do quickly" (John 13:26-27).

Later that evening in his great prayer of intercession, Jesus said, "While I was with them, I kept them in thy name, which thou hast given me; I have guarded them, and none of them is lost but the son of perdition, that the scripture might be fulfilled" (John 17:12). Here Jesus prayed *about* Judas, but not *for* Judas, and called him the "son of perdition."

In the case of Peter's denial Jesus announced to him:

> "*Simon, Simon, behold, Satan demanded to have you, that he might sift you like wheat, but I have prayed for you that your faith may not fail; and when you have turned again, strengthen your brethren.*" (Luke 22:31-32)

Notice that Jesus did not say, "If you have turned again, strengthen your brethren," but "when you have turned." Jesus was confident of Peter's restoration. We cannot help but draw the conclusion that Jesus' confidence was in large measure due to his earlier words: "but I have prayed for you."

Jesus prayed about Judas. He prayed for Simon Peter. He made intercession for Peter. He acted as

Peter's Priest. At this very moment Christ is acting as our High Priest, interceding for us.

This is the jubilant conclusion of the author in Hebrews 4:14-16.

> *Since then we have a great high priest who has passed through the heavens, Jesus, the Son of God, let us hold fast our confession. For we have not a high priest who is unable to sympathize with our weaknesses, but one who in every respect has been tempted as we are, yet without sin. Let us then with confidence draw near to the throne of grace, that we may receive mercy and find grace to help in time of need.*

May these words become life to our souls as we appropriate them for ourselves.

Tapping into Prayer's Power

Prayer requires structure, but not at the expense of spontaneity. I have tried to give direction to avoid harmful pitfalls in our pilgrimage. No band director tells his musicians to play whatever is on their hearts and then expects to hear "The Star-Spangled Banner." There must be order, and the procedure must be somewhat regulated. However, room still exists for individual self-expression within the limits of reverence and order.

Why do we pray?

- We pray because God has commanded it and because he is glorified when we pray.

- We pray because it prepares our hearts for what we will receive from him.

- We pray because much is accomplished by prayer, by which God gives us our instructions, our marching orders.

- We pray to adore God, to praise him, to express our wonder at his majesty, his sovereignty, and his mighty acts.

- We pray to confess to God our shortcomings, numerous as they are, and to experience grace, mercy, and forgiveness at his hand.

- We pray to thank him for all that he is and all that he has done.

- And we pray to make our supplication known to him, to fulfill the invitation he has left us.

When we pray, we must remember who God is and who we are before him. We must remember first and foremost that God's name is to be kept holy. We must remember that he is the Source of our provision and that all good things come from him. We are to live in such a way that we will make visible the kingdom of God in this world. We must always be confessing sin, for that is one of the surest marks of a Christian. And we are to pray that God will protect us from the evil one.

We must always remember that God is God and owes no man anything. As the psalmist says, "He does whatever he pleases" (Psalm 115:3). We have been invited to come boldly before God, but never flippantly, arrogantly, or presumptuously. Ecclesiastes 5:2 reminds us that we are not to be "hasty to utter a word before God, for God is in heaven, and you upon the earth."

Finally, if there is a secret to learning how to pray, it is no different from that of any other endeavor. To become accomplished in anything, you must practice. If you want to learn how to pray, then pray—again and again and again . . .

PART THREE

CAN I KNOW GOD'S WILL?

CHAPTER 10

THE MEANING OF GOD'S WILL

Alice in Wonderland came to a fork in the road. Icy panic stung her as she stood frozen by indecision. She lifted her eyes toward heaven, looking for guidance. Her eyes did not find God, only the Cheshire cat leering at her from his perch in the tree above. "Which way should I go?" blurted Alice.

"That depends . . . ," said the cat, fixing a sardonic smile on the confused girl.

"On what?" Alice managed to reply.

"On your destination. Where are you going?" queried the Cheshire fiend.

"I don't know . . . ," stammered Alice.

"Then," said the cat, with grin spreading wider, "it doesn't matter."

It matters to the Christian. Every Christian has a

destiny in the kingdom of God. We are a pilgrim
people, a people on the move—our destination
matters. The days of wandering in the wilderness
are over. The Promised Land has been reached and
made secure. Yet we still seek a better country, an
eternal city whose builder and maker is God.
Though we do not wander aimlessly or grope in
darkness for a clue to our future, the specifics of our
personal futures are, nevertheless, unknown to us.
We must still walk by faith rather than by sight.

We are certain that there is a future for the people
of God. The ultimate destination is clear. But what
of tomorrow? We feel anxious about the future as
other people do. With the child we ask, "Will I be
pretty? Will I be rich? What will happen to me?"

Concern for our hidden destiny can fill us with
fear. The paralyzing power of worry can obstruct
our progress. As long as there have been people,
there have been soothsayers and wizards exploiting our anxieties. If prostitution is the world's oldest profession, surely fortune-telling is the second
oldest. "Tell me of tomorrow" is the plea of the
stock market speculator, the competitive businessman, the sports forecaster, and the young couple in
love. The student asks, "Will I graduate?" The manager muses, "Will I be promoted?" The person in
the doctor's waiting room clenches his hands and
asks, "Is it cancer or indigestion?"

People have examined lizard entrails, snake

skins, the bones of owls, the Ouija board, the daily horoscope, and the predictions of Jimmy the Greek—all to gain a small margin of insurance against an unknown future. The Christian asks, "What is the will of God for my life?"

To search for the will of God can be an exercise in piety or impiety, an act of humble submission, or an act of outrageous arrogance—depending on what will of God we are looking for. To try to look behind the veil at what God has not been pleased to reveal is to tamper with holy things that are out of bounds. John Calvin put it this way, "Where God has closed his holy mouth, I will desist from inquiry."

On the other hand, it is a delight to God to hear the prayers of his people when they individually ask, "Lord, what do you want me to do?" The Christian pursues God, looking for his marching orders, seeking to know what course of action is pleasing to him. This search for the will of God is a holy quest—a pursuit that is to be undertaken with vigor by the godly person.

The Biblical Meaning of the Will of God

We yearn for simple answers to difficult questions. We want clarity. We desire to cut through the entanglements to the heart of the question. Sometimes the answers are simple enough in themselves, but the process of finding them is laborious and confusing along the way. Sometimes the answers are *simplistic*, giving us temporary relief from the pressures and the burdens of confusing questions. However, there is a profound difference between the *simple* answer and the *simplistic* answer. The simple answer is correct; it accounts for all the data found in the complex problem. It is clear and can be easily grasped in its fullness. It abides, being able to stand the test of rigorous questioning.

The simplistic answer is a counterfeit. On the surface it appears to be the genuine article, but under closer scrutiny it yields its bogus flaws. The simplistic answer may account for some of the data but not all of it. It remains fuzzy. Worst of all, it does not abide; it fails the test of deeper questioning. It does not satisfy in the long haul.

One of the most excruciating questions of all theology is the question, Why did Adam fall? The simplistic answer, commonly heard, is that Adam fell by his own free will. Such an answer is satisfying until we probe the question more deeply. Suppose we ask, "How could a righteous creature created by a perfect Creator sin? How could Adam make an evil choice while possessing no prior inclination or disposition to evil? Was he simply deceived or coerced by Satan? If so, why would Adam then be blameworthy?" If he had been merely deceived, then the fault is all Satan's. If he had been coerced, then it was not a free choice. If he sinned

because he had a prior desire or inclination to sin,
then we must ask, "What was the source of his evil
desire? Did God put it there?" If so, then we cast a
shadow on the integrity of the Creator.

Perhaps the simplest way to expose the weak
character of the simplistic answer that Adam fell by
his own free will is to ask our question another way.
"Why did Adam exercise his own free will to sin?"
Here it simply won't do to answer, "Because he
chose to." This answer is a mere repetition of the
question in a declarative form.

I would like to offer a simple answer to the difficult question of Adam's fall, but I simply can't. The
only response I can give to the question is that I
simply don't know the answer.

Some readers will surely chasten me at this point
by saying to themselves, "I know the answer!
Adam fell because it was the will of God."

But I immediately ask, "In what sense? Did God
force Adam to fall and then punish him for doing
what he had no power to avoid?" To ask such an
impious question is to answer it. Certainly it must
have been the "will of God" in some sense, but the
crucial question remains, "In what sense?"

So, here we are, pressed squarely against a biting
question that involves the whole matter of the will
of God. We want to know how the will of God
worked in Adam's life; but more personally, we

want to know how the will of God works in our own lives.

When questions are difficult and complex, it is a good rule to collect as much data about them as we possibly can. The more clues the detective has to work with, the easier the solving of the crime *usually* is (note the word *usually*). Sometimes the detective suffers from having too many clues, which only serve to compound the difficulty of the solution. The corporate executive faced with major decision-making responsibilities knows the importance of sufficient data and record keeping. His maxim may be: "If you have enough data, the decisions jump out at you." Again we must add the qualifier *usually*. Sometimes the data is so complex that it jumps out like screaming banshees, defying our ability to sort through it all.

I emphasize the point of data, complexity, and simplicity because the biblical meaning of the will of God is a very complicated matter. To approach it simplistically is to invite disaster. At times, wrestling with the complexities of the biblical concept of the will of God can give us an Excedrin headache.

Yet ours is a holy quest, a pursuit that is worth a few headaches along the way. If we proceed in a simplistic way, we run the clear and present danger of changing the holy quest into an unholy presumption.

We note at the outset that the Bible speaks of the

"will of God" in more than one way. This is the problem that complicates our quest and serves as a warning against simplistic solutions. In the New Testament there are two different Greek words, both of which can be, and have been, translated by the English word *will*. Now it would seem that all we need is to identify precisely the meanings of the two words and check out the Greek text every time we see the word *will*, and our problems will be solved.

Alas, it doesn't work that way. The plot thickens when we discover that each of the two Greek words has several nuances of meaning. Simply checking the Greek text for word usage is not enough to solve our difficulty. But it helps. Let's examine the two words briefly to see if they shed any light on our quest. The two Greek words are *boule* and *thelema*.

The Meaning of Boule

The term *boule* has its roots in an ancient verb which meant a "rational and conscious desire," as opposed to *thelema*, meaning "an impulsive or unconscious desire." The ancient subtle distinction was between rational desire and impulsive desire. As the Greek language developed, however, this distinction was softened, and eventually the words became used at times as synonyms, with authors switching from one to the other for purposes of stylistic change.

In the New Testament the use of *boule* usually refers to a plan based upon careful deliberation and is most often used with respect to the counsel of God. *Boule* frequently indicates God's providential plan, which is predetermined and inflexible. Luke is fond of using it this way, as we read in the book of Acts: "This Jesus, delivered up according to the definite plan *[boule]* and foreknowledge of God, you crucified and killed by the hands of lawless men" (Acts 2:23).

Here the resolute decree of God is in view, which no human action can set aside. God's plan is impregnable; his "will" is unalterable.

The word *thelema* is rich in its diversity of meanings. It refers to what is agreeable, what is desired, what is intended, what is chosen, or what is commanded. Here we have the notions of consent, desire, purpose, resolution, and command. The force of the various meanings is determined by the context in which *thelema* appears.

The Decretive Will of God

Theologians describe that will by which God decrees things to come to pass according to his supreme sovereignty as the "decretive will of God." This is also sometimes called "God's sovereign efficacious will"; by it God brings to pass whatsoever he wills. When God sovereignly decrees something in this sense, nothing can thwart its coming to pass.

When God commanded the light to shine, the darkness had no power to resist the command. The "lights" came on. This is God's "determinate counsel" spoken of in the Bible. God did not persuade the light to shine. He did not negotiate with elemental powers to form a universe. He did not achieve a plan of redemption by trial and error; the Cross was not a cosmic accident exploited by the Deity. These things were decreed absolutely. Their effects were efficacious (producing the desired result) because their causes were sovereignly decreed.

A serious danger faces those who restrict the meaning of the will of God to the sovereign will. We hear the Muslim cry, "It is the will of Allah." We slip at times into a deterministic view of life that says, "Que será, será" —What will be, will be. In so doing, we are embracing a sub-Christian form of fatalism, as if God willed everything that happened in such a way as to eliminate human choices.

Classical theologians insist on the reality of man's will in acting, choosing, and responding. God works his plan through *means*, via the real choices of willing and acting creatures. There are secondary as well as primary causes. To deny this is to embrace a kind of determinism that eliminates human freedom and dignity.

Yet there is a God who is sovereign, whose will is greater than mine. His will restricts my will. My will cannot restrict his will. When he decrees something sovereignly, it will come to pass—whether I like it or not, whether I choose it or not. He is sovereign. I am subordinate.

The Preceptive Will of God

When the Bible speaks of the will of God, it does not always mean the decretive will of God. The decretive will of God cannot be broken, cannot be disobeyed. It will come to pass. On the other hand, there is a will that can be broken: "the preceptive will of God." It can be disobeyed. Indeed, it is broken and disobeyed every day by each one of us.

The preceptive will of God is found in his law. The precepts, statutes, and commandments that he delivers to his people make up the preceptive will. They express and reveal to us what is right and proper for us to do. The preceptive will is God's rule of righteousness for our lives. By this rule we are governed.

It is the will of God that we sin not. It is the will of God that we have no other gods before him; that we love our neighbor as we love ourselves; that we refrain from stealing, coveting, and committing adultery. Yet the world is filled with idolatry, hatred, thievery, covetousness, and adultery. Here the will of God is violated. His law is broken.

One of the great tragedies of contemporary Christendom is the preoccupation of so many Christians with the secret decretive will of God to the exclusion and neglect of the preceptive will. We want to peek behind the veil, to catch a glimpse of our personal future. We seem more concerned with our horoscope than with our obedience, more concerned with what the stars in their courses are doing than with what we are doing.

With respect to God's sovereign will, we assume we are passive. With respect to his preceptive will, we know that we are active and therefore responsible and accountable. It is easier to engage in ungodly prying into the secret counsel of God than to apply ourselves to the practice of godliness. We can flee to the safety of the sovereign will and try to pass off our sin to God, laying the burden and responsibility of it on his unchanging will. Such characterizes the spirit of Antichrist, the spirit of lawlessness, or antinomianism, that despises God's law and ignores his precepts.

Protestants are particularly vulnerable to this distortion. We seek refuge in our precious doctrine of justification by faith alone, forgetting that the very doctrine is to be a catalyst for the pursuit of righteousness and obedience to the preceptive will of God.

Biblical Righteousness

Habakkuk's famous statement "the just shall live by faith" (Habakkuk 2:4, KJV) is found three times in the New Testament. It has become a slogan of evangelical Protestantism, whose emphasis has been upon the doctrine of justification by faith alone. This slogan, containing a hint of the essence of the Christian life, has its focal point in the biblical concept of righteousness.

One of Jesus' most disturbing comments was the statement, "Unless your righteousness exceeds that of the scribes and Pharisees, you will never enter the kingdom of heaven" (Matthew 5:20). It is easy for us to assume that Jesus meant that our righteousness must be of a higher sort than that characterized by men who were hypocrites. The image that we have of scribes and Pharisees from the New Testament period is that of unscrupulous, ruthless practitioners of religious deceit. We must bear in mind, however, that the Pharisees as a group were men historically committed to a very lofty level of righteous living. Yet Jesus tells us that our righteousness must exceed theirs. What did he mean?

When we consider the biblical notion of righteousness, we are dealing with a matter that touches virtually every plane of theology. In the first place, there is the righteousness of God by which all standards of rightness and wrongness are to be measured. God's character is the ultimate foundation and model of righteousness. In the Old Testament, righteousness becomes defined in terms of obedience to the commandments delivered by God, who himself is altogether righteous. Those commands include not only precepts of human behavior with respect to our fellow human beings but also matters of a liturgical and ceremonial nature.

In Old Testament Israel and among the New Testament Pharisees, liturgical righteousness was substituted for authentic righteousness. That is to say, men became satisfied with obeying the rituals of the religious community, rather than fulfilling the broader implications of the law. The Pharisees, for example, were rebuked by Jesus for tithing their mint and cumin while omitting the weightier matters of the law: justice and mercy. Jesus indicated that the Pharisees were correct in giving their tithes, but were incorrect in assuming that the liturgical exercises had completed the requirements of the law. Here liturgical righteousness had become a substitute for true and full obedience.

Within the evangelical world, *righteousness* is a

rare word indeed. We speak of morality, spirituality, and piety. Seldom, however, do we speak of righteousness. Yet the goal of our redemption is not piety or spirituality but righteousness. Spirituality in the New Testament sense is a means to the end of righteousness. Being spiritual means that we are exercising the spiritual graces given by God to mold us after the image of his Son. That is, the discipline of prayer, Bible study, church fellowship, witnessing, and the like are not ends in themselves, but are designed to assist us in living righteously. We are stunted in our growth if we assume that the end of the Christian life is spirituality.

Spiritual concerns are but the beginning of our walk with God. We must beware of the subtle danger of thinking that spirituality completes the requirements of Christ. To fall into such a trap—the trap of the Pharisees—is to substitute liturgical or ritualistic practices for authentic righteousness. By all means we are to pray and to study the Bible; we are to bear witness in evangelism. But we must never, at any point in our lives, rest from our pursuit of righteousness.

In justification we become righteous in the sight of God by means of the cloak of Christ's righteousness. However, as soon as we are justified, our lives must give evidence of the personal righteousness that flows out of our justification. It is interesting to me that the whole biblical concept of righteousness is contained in one Greek word, *dikaios*. That same Greek word is used to refer in the first instance to the righteousness of God; in the second instance, to what we call justification; and in the third instance, to the righteousness of life. Thus, from beginning to end—from the nature of God to the destiny of man—our human duty remains the same—a call to righteousness.

True righteousness must never be confused with self-righteousness. Since our righteousness proceeds from our justification, which is based upon the righteousness of Christ alone, we must never be deluded into thinking that our works of righteousness have any merit of their own. Yet as Protestants, zealously maintaining our doctrine of justification by faith alone, we must be ever mindful that the justification which is by faith alone is never *by a faith that is alone*. True faith is a faith that manifests itself in righteousness exceeding that of the Pharisees and the scribes, for it is concerned with the weightier matters of the law: justice and mercy.

We are called to bear witness to the righteousness of God in every area of life—from our prayer closets to our courtrooms, from our pews to our marketplaces. The top priority of Jesus is that we seek first the kingdom of God and his righteousness. All other things will be added to that.

"Everybody do your own thing." This worn-out cliché from the sixties characterizes the spirit of our age. Increasingly freedom is being equated with the inalienable right to do whatever you please. It carries with it a built-in allergy to laws that restrain, whether they be the laws of God or the laws of men.

This pervasive anti-law, or antinomian, attitude is so reminiscent of the biblical epoch that provoked God's judgment because "every man did what was right in his own eyes" (Judges 17:6). The secular world reflects this attitude in the statement "Government can't legislate morality." Morality is a private matter, outside of the domain of the state and even of the church.

What has occurred is a shift in word meaning so subtle that many have missed it. The original intent of the concept "You cannot legislate morality" was to convey the idea that passing a law prohibiting a particular kind of activity would not necessarily eliminate such activity. The point of the phrase was that laws do not *ipso facto* produce obedience to those laws. In fact, on some occasions the legal prohibition of certain practices has incited only greater violation of established law. "Prohibition" is an example.

The contemporary interpretation of legislating morality differs from the original intent. Instead of saying the government *cannot* legislate morality, it says the government *may* not legislate morality. That means the government should stay out of moral issues such as the regulation of abortion, deviant sexual practices, marriage and divorce, and so on, since morality is a matter of conscience in the private sector. For the government to legislate in these areas is often viewed as an invasion of privacy by the state, representing a denial of basic freedoms for the individual.

If we take this kind of thinking to its logical conclusion, we leave the government with little to do. If the government may not legislate morality, its activity will be restricted to determining the colors of the state flag, the state flower, and perhaps the state bird. (But even questions of flowers and birds may be deemed "moral" as they touch on ecological issues, which are ultimately moral in character.) The vast majority of matters that concern legislation are, in fact, of a decidedly moral character. The regulation of murder, theft, and civil rights are moral matters. How a person operates his automobile on the highway is a moral issue since it touches on the well-being of fellow travelers.

Questions relating to the legalization of marijuana often focus on the fact that a majority of certain age groups are violating the law. The argument goes like this: Since disobedience is so widespread, doesn't this indicate that the law is bad? Such a conclusion is a blatant non sequitur.

Whether or not marijuana should be decriminalized should not be determined by levels of civil disobedience. The point is, however, that a vast number of Americans reflect an antinomian spirit regarding marijuana. Such disobedience is hardly motivated by noble aspirations to a higher ethic suppressed by a tyrannical government. Here the law is broken as a matter of convenience and physical appetite.

Within the church the same spirit of antinomianism has too often prevailed. Pope John Paul II faces the embarrassing legacy of his predecessor as he tries to explain to the world why a majority of his American adherents tell the pollsters they practice artificial means of birth control when a papal encyclical explicitly forbids such methods. One must ask how people can confess their belief in an "infallible" leader of their church and at the same time obstinately refuse to submit to that leader.

Within the Protestant churches, individuals frequently become irate when called to moral accountability. They often declare that the church has no right to intrude into their private lives. This, in spite of the fact that in their membership vows they publicly committed themselves to submit to the moral oversight of the church.

Antinomianism should be more rare in the evangelical Christian community than anywhere else. Sadly, the facts do not fit the theory. So blasé is the typical "evangelical" toward the law of God that the prophecies of doom that Rome thundered at Luther are beginning to come true. Some "evangelicals" are indeed using justification by faith alone as a license to sin; these can only be deemed properly as pseudoevangelicals. Anyone who has the most rudimentary understanding of justification by faith knows that authentic faith always manifests itself in a zeal for obedience. No earnest Christian can ever have a cavalier attitude toward the law of God. Though obedience to such laws does not bring justification, the justified person will surely endeavor to obey them.

To be sure, there are times when the commandments of men are on a collision course with the laws of God. In those instances Christians not only *may* disobey men, but *must* disobey men. I am not talking here of isolated moral issues but of attitudes. Christians must be particularly careful in this era of antinomianism not to get caught up in the spirit of the age. We are not free to do what is right in our own eyes. We are called to do what is right in his eyes.

Freedom should not be confused with autonomy. As long as evil exists in the world, the moral restraint of law is necessary. It is an act of grace by which God institutes government, which exists to restrain the evildoer. It exists to protect the innocent and the righteous. The righteous are called to support it as much as they possibly can without compromising their obedience to God.

While we understand that the decretive will and

the preceptive will of God are part of his overall
will, other aspects of the mystery of his sovereignty
still remain. One such aspect is "the will of disposition." It is tied up with the ability of man to disobey
God's preceptive will.

God's Will of Disposition

This aspect of the will of God refers to what is
pleasing and agreeable to God. It expresses something of the attitude of God to his creatures. Some
things are "well pleasing in his sight," while other
things are said to grieve him. He may allow (but
not via moral permission) wicked things to tran-
spire, but he is by no means pleased by them.

To illustrate how these differing aspects of the
will of God come into play in biblical interpretation, let us examine the following verse which
says that the Lord is "not willing that any should
perish" (2 Peter 3:9, KJV). Which of the above-
mentioned meanings of *will* fits this text? How is
the meaning of the text changed by the application
of the nuances?

Try first the decretive will. The verse would then
mean, "God is not willing in a sovereign decretive
sense that any should perish." The implication
would then be that nobody perishes—a proof text
for *universalism* with its view that hell is utterly
vacant of people.

The second option is that God is not willing in a preceptive way that any should perish. This would mean that God does not *allow* people to perish in the sense that he grants his moral permission. This obviously does not fit the context of the passage.

The third option makes sense. God is not willing in the sense that he is not inwardly disposed to, or delighted by, people's perishing. Elsewhere Scripture teaches that God takes no delight in the death of the wicked. He may decree what he does not enjoy; that is, he may distribute justice to wicked offenders. He is pleased when justice is maintained and righteousness is honored, but takes no personal pleasure in the application of such punishment.

A human analogy may be seen in our law courts. A judge, in the interest of justice, may sentence a criminal to prison and at the same time inwardly grieve for the guilty man. His disposition may be *for* the man, but against the crime.

But you say, God is not merely a human judge, working under the constraints of the criminal justice system. God is sovereign—he can do what he pleases. If he is not pleased or willing that any should perish, why then does he not exercise his decretive will accordingly? How can there be a hiatus between God's decretive will and his will of disposition?

All things being equal, God does desire that no

one perishes. But all things are not equal. Sin is real.
Sin violates God's holiness and righteousness. God
also is not willing that sin go unpunished. He desires as well that his holiness be vindicated. It is
dangerous to speak of a conflict of interests or of a
clash of desires within God. Yet in a certain sense
we must. He wills the obedience of his creatures.
He wills the well-being of his creatures. There is a
symmetry of relationship ultimately between obedience and well-being. The obedient child will
never perish. Those who obey God's preceptive
will enjoy the benefits of his will of disposition.
When the preceptive will is violated, things are no
longer equal. Now God requires punishment while
not particularly enjoying the personal application
of it.

But again—does this not beg the ultimate question? Where does the decretive will fit in? Could
not God originally have decreed that no one would
ever be *able* to sin, thus insuring an eternal harmony among all elements of his will: decretive,
preceptive, and dispositional?

Often the answer to this question is superficial.
Appeals are made to the free will of man, as if by
magic man's free will could explain the dilemma.
We are told that the only way God could have
created a universe guaranteed to be free from sin
would be to make creatures without free will. It is
then argued that these creatures would be nothing

more than puppets and would lose their humanity if devoid of the power or ability to sin. If that is the case, then what does it suggest about the state of our existence in heaven? We are promised that when our redemption is complete, sin will be no more. We will still have an ability to choose, but our disposition will be so inclined toward righteousness that we will, in fact, never choose evil. If it is possible in heaven after redemption, why could it not have been possible *before* the Fall?

The Bible gives no clear answer to this thorny question. We are told that God created people who, for better or for worse, have the ability to sin. We also know from Scripture that there is no shadow of turning in the character of God and that all of his works are clothed in righteousness. That he chose to create man the way he did is mysterious; but we must assume, given the knowledge we have, that God's plan was good. What conflict should arise among his commandments to us, his desire that we should obey him, and our failure to comply does not destroy his sovereignty.

We have already distinguished among the three types of the will of God: his decretive will, his preceptive will, and his will of disposition. Another distinction must be established between what is called God's *secret*, or hidden, will and his *revealed* will. This secret will of God is subsumed under the decretive will because, for the most part, it remains

undisclosed to us. There is a limit to the revelation
God has made of himself. We know certain things
about God's decretive will that he has been pleased
to set forth for our information in Holy Scripture.
But we, as finite creatures, do not comprehend the
total dimension of divine knowledge or the divine
plan. As the Scriptures teach, the secret things belong to the Lord, but that which he has revealed
belongs to us and to our "seed forever."

Protestant theologians have made use of the distinction between the hidden God (*Deus-Obsconditus*)
and the revealed God (*Deus-Revelatus*). This distinction is necessary, yet it is fraught with peril since
some have found within it a conflict between two
kinds of gods. A god who reveals his character to be
one thing, but who is secrectly contrary to that revealed character, would be a supreme hypocrite. The
distinction is valuable and indeed necessary when
we realize that not all that can be known of God has,
in fact, been revealed to us. There is a sense in which
God remains hidden from us, insofar as he has not
been pleased to reveal all there is to know about
himself.

If we say that God has no secret will and proposes to do only what he commands and nothing
more, then we would perceive God as one whose
desires and plans are constantly thwarted by the
harassment of human beings. Such a god would be
impotent, and no god at all.

If we distinguish between the secret aspect of God and the revealed aspect of God, we must hold these as parts of the whole, not as contradictions. That is to say, what God has revealed about himself does not lie; it is trustworthy. Our knowledge is partial, but it is true as far as it goes. What belongs to the secret counsel of God does not contradict the character of God which has been revealed to us. The distinction of God's revealed will and hidden will raises a practical problem: the question of whether or not it is possible for a Christian to be acting in harmony with God's decretive (hidden) will and at the same time be working against his preceptive will.

In a certain sense, we must admit that such a possibility does exist. For example, it was in God's decretive will and by his determinate counsel that Jesus Christ was condemned to die on the cross. The divine purpose, of course, was to secure the redemption of God's people. But that purpose was hidden from the view of men who sat in judgment over Jesus. When Pontius Pilate delivered Jesus to be crucified, Pilate acted against the preceptive will of God but in harmony with the decretive will of God. Does this make nonsense of God's preceptive will? God forbid. What it does is bear witness to the transcendent power of God to work his purposes sovereignly in spite of, and by means of, the evil acts of men.

Consider the story of Joseph whose brothers, out of jealousy and greed, sold their innocent brother into slavery in Egypt. At their reunion years later, and upon the confession of sin made by the brothers to Joseph, Joseph replied, "You meant evil against me; but God meant it for good." Here is the inscrutable majesty of God's providence. God made use of human evil by bringing to pass his purposes for Joseph and for the Jewish nation. Joseph's brothers were guilty of willful and malicious sin. By directly violating the preceptive will of God, they sinned against their brother. Yet in their sin, God's secret counsel was brought to pass, and God brought redemption through it.

However, what if Joseph's brothers had been obedient? Joseph would not have been sold into slavery; he would not have been taken captive into Egypt; he would not have been sent to prison from which he was recalled to interpret a dream. What if Joseph had not become prime minister? What would have become the historical reason for the brothers' settling in Egypt? There would have been no Jewish settlement in Egypt, no Moses, no exodus from Egypt, no law, no prophets, no Christ, no salvation.

Can we, therefore, conclude that the sins of Joseph's brothers were, in fact, virtues in disguise? Not at all. Their sin was sin, a clear violation of the preceptive will of God, for which they were held responsible and judged to be guilty; but God brought good out of evil. This reflects neither a contradiction in God's character nor a contradiction between his precepts and his decrees. Rather it calls attention to the transcendent power of his sovereignty.

Is it possible for us in this day and age to obey the preceptive will of God and yet at the same time be in conflict with the secret will of God? Of course, such a possibility exists. It may be the will of God, for example, that he use a foreign nation to chastise the United States for sinning against God. It may be in the plan of God to have the people of the United States brought under judgment through the aggressive invasion of the Soviet Union. In terms of God's inscrutable will, he could sovereignly, for purposes of judgment, be "on the side of the Russians." Yet at the same time, it would remain the duty of the civil magistrate of the American nation to resist the sinful transgression of our borders by a conquering nation.

We have a parallel in the history of Israel where God used the Babylonians as a rod to chastise his people Israel. In that situation it would have been perfectly proper for the civil magistrate of Israel to have resisted the wicked invasion of the Babylonians. In so doing, the Israelites would have been, in effect, resisting the decretive will of God. The book of Habakkuk wrestles with the severe problem of

God using the evil inclinations of men to bring
judgment upon his own people. This is not to suggest that God favored the Babylonians. He made it
clear that judgment would also fall upon them, but
he made use of their evil inclinations in order to
bring about a corrective discipline to his own
people.

Knowing the Will of God for Our Lives

Pursuing knowledge of the will of God is not an
abstract science designed to titillate the intellect or
to convey the kind of knowledge that "puffs up"
but fails to edify. An understanding of the will of
God is a desperately important matter for every
Christian seeking to live a life that is pleasing to his
or her Creator. It is a very practical thing for us to
know what God wants for our lives. A Christian
asks, "What are my marching orders? What should
my role be in contributing to the establishment of
the kingdom of God? What does God want me to
do with my life?" It is inconceivable that a Christian could live for very long without coming face-
to-face with these gripping questions.

Having been a Christian for some twenty-five
years, with the study of theology my main vocational pursuit, I find that practical question pressing
upon my mind quite frequently. I doubt if a fortnight
passes without my being seriously engaged by the

question, At this point in my life am I doing what God wants me to do? The question haunts and beckons all of us. It demands resolution, and so we must ask ourselves, How do we know the will of God for our lives?

The practical question of how we know the will of God for our lives cannot be solved with any degree of accuracy unless we have some prior understanding of the will of God in general. Without the distinctions that we have made, our pursuit of the will of God can plunge us into hopeless confusion and consternation. When we seek the will of God, we must first ask ourselves which will we are seeking to discover.

If our quest is to penetrate the hidden aspects of his will, then we have embarked upon a fool's errand. We are trying the impossible and chasing the untouchable. Such a quest is not only an act of foolishness, but also an act of presumption. There is a very real sense in which the secret will of the secret counsel of God is none of our business and is off limits to our speculative investigations.

Untold evils have been perpetrated upon God's people by unscrupulous theologians who have sought to correct or to supplant the clear and plain teaching of sacred Scripture by doctrines and theories based on speculation alone. The business of searching out the mind of God where God has remained silent is dangerous business indeed. Luther put it this way, "We must keep in view his word and leave alone his inscrutable will; for it is by his word and not by his inscrutable will that we must be guided."

Christians are permitted, in a sense, to attempt to discern the will of God by means of illumination by the Holy Spirit and by confirmation through circumstances that we are doing the right thing. However, as we will discover, the search for providential guidance must always be subordinate to our study of the revealed will of God. In our search, we must also come to terms with the dynamic tensions created by the concept of man's will *versus* predestination. Before our inquiry can lead us into such practical avenues as occupation and marriage, we must face the thorny issues involved in the free will—predestination issue. We have seen what the will of God entails. What about the will of man? How do the two relate? How free is man, after all?

CHAPTER 11

THE MEANING OF MAN'S WILL

The term *free will* as applied to man is often glibly declared with little or no understanding of its meaning. There is actually no unified theory of man's free will, but a variety of competing, and often conflicting, views about it.

The question of man's free will is made more complicated by the fact that we must examine it in man, in terms of how the will functioned before and after the fall of Adam. Most important for us today is how the Fall affected man's moral choices.

It was St. Augustine who gave the church a close analysis of the state of freedom that Adam enjoyed before the Fall. Augustine's classic concept of freedom distinguished four possibilities. In Latin, they are:

1. *posse pecarre*—referring to the ability to sin.

2. *posse non-pecarre*—referring to the ability not to sin, or to remain free from sin.

3. *non-posse pecarre*—referring to the inability to sin.

4. *non-posse, non-pecarre*—referring to the inability not to sin.

Considering Adam before the Fall, Augustine argued that Adam had possessed both the ability to sin (*posse pecarre*) and the ability not to sin (*posse non-pecarre*). Adam lacked the exalted state of the inability to sin that God enjoys (*non-posse pecarre*). God's inability to sin is based not on an inner powerlessness of God to do what he wants, but rather on the fact that God has no inner desire to sin. Since the desire for sin is utterly absent from God, there is no reason for God to choose sin.

Before the Fall Adam did not have the moral perfection of God; neither did Adam have the inability to refrain from sin (*non-posse, non-pecarre*). During his time of "probation" in the garden, he had the ability to sin *and* the ability not to sin. He chose to exercise the ability to sin and thus plunged the race into ruin.

As a result, Adam's first sin was passed on to all his descendants. *Original sin* refers not to the first sin but to God's punishment of that first transgression. Because of the first sin human nature fell into a morally corrupt state, itself partially a judgment of God. When we speak of original sin, we refer to the fallen human condition which reflects the judgment of God upon the race.

Christians differ in their views concerning the extent and seriousness of the Fall. It is, however, almost universally conceded that in dealing with mankind, we are dealing with a fallen race. Augustine located the depths of man's fallenness in his loss of original powers of righteousness. No longer does man have the *posse non-pecarre*. In his fallen state the plight of man is found in his inability to keep from sinning (*non-posse, non-pecarre*). In the Fall, something profoundly vital to moral freedom was lost.

Augustine declared that in his prefallen state man enjoyed both a free will (*liberium arbitrium*) and moral liberty (*libertas*). Since the Fall, man has continued to have a free will, but has lost the moral liberty he once enjoyed.

Perhaps the most insightful study of the question of fallen man's free will was produced in the epic work of Jonathan Edwards, *On the Freedom of the Will*. Edwards and Augustine differ in terminology, but their meaning is essentially the same. Edwards distinguished between the *natural ability* of freedom and the *moral ability* of freedom. Natural ability deals with the powers of action and choice that we possess by nature. Man's natural abilities include the power to think, to walk, to speak, to eat, and so on. Man lacks the natural ability to fly, to live beneath the sea as a fish, or to hibernate for months without food. We may desire to fly, but lack the natural equipment necessary to live out our desire. Our freedom has a certain built-in restriction relegated to the limitations of our natural faculties.

With respect to the making of choices, fallen man still has the natural ability and the natural faculties necessary to make moral choices. Man can still think, feel, desire. All of the equipment necessary for the making of choices remains. What fallen man lacks is the moral disposition, the desire, or the inclination of righteousness.

Stated simply, man still has the ability to choose what he wants, but lacks the desire for true righteousness. He is *naturally free*, but *morally enslaved* to his own corrupt and wicked desires. For both Edwards and Augustine, man is still free to choose; but if left to himself, man will never choose righteousness, precisely because he does not desire it.

Edwards took the question a step further. Man still has not only the ability, but also the built-in *necessity*, to choose according to his desires. Not only *can* we choose what we want, but we *must* choose what we want. It is at this point that the protest is sounded: Is free choice an illusion? If we *must* choose what we choose, how can such a choice be called *free*? If we are free to choose what we want but want only what is evil, how can we still speak of free will? This is precisely why Augustine distinguished between free will and liberty, saying that fallen man still has free will but has lost his liberty. It is why Edwards said that we still have natural freedom but have lost moral freedom.

Why talk of freedom at all, if we can choose only sin? The crux of the matter lies in the relationship between choice and desire, or disposition. Edwards's thesis is that we always choose according to the strongest inclination, or disposition, of the moment. Again, not only can we choose according to our strongest desires, but we must choose according to our strongest desires of the moment. Such is the essence of freedom—that I am able to choose what I want when I want it.

If I *must* do something, then in a sense my actions are determined. If my actions are determined, then how can I be free? The classic answer to this difficult question is that the determination of my choices comes from within myself. The essence of freedom is *self-determination*. It is when my choices are forced upon me by external coercion that my freedom is lost. To be able to choose what I want by virtue of self-determination does not destroy free will but establishes it.

To choose according to the strongest desire, or inclination, of the moment means simply that there is a reason for the choices I make. At one point

Edwards defined the will as "the mind choosing." The actual choice is an effect, or result, which requires an antecedent cause. The cause is located in the disposition, or desire. If all effects have causes, then all choices likewise have causes. If the cause is apart from me, then I am a victim of coercion. If the cause is from within me, then my choices are self-determined or free.

Think about Edwards's thesis that we always choose according to the strongest inclination, or desire, of the moment. Think, if you will, of the most harmless choice that you might make in the course of a day. Perhaps you attend a meeting of a group and choose to sit on the left side in the third seat from the end of the fourth row at the front of the room. Why did you choose to sit there? In all probability, when you entered the room, you did not engage in a thorough analysis of your seating preferences. You probably did not make a chart to determine which was the best seat. Your decision was probably made quickly, with little or no conscious evaluation and with a sense of apparent spontaneity. Does that mean, however, that there was no reason for your choice? Perhaps you sat where you did because you are comfortable sitting on the left side of the room in such meetings. Perhaps you were attracted to that seat because of its proximity to a friend or its access to the exit. In situations like this, the mind weighs a host of contributing factors so quickly that we tend to think our responses are spontaneous. The truth is that something in you triggered a desire to sit in a certain seat or else your choice was an effect without a cause.

Perhaps your seat selection was governed by forces outside of your control. Perhaps the seat you chose was the only seat left in the room so that you had no choice in the matter at all. Is that completely true? The option to stand at the back of the room was still there. Or the option to leave the meeting altogether was still there. You chose to sit in the only seat available because your desire to sit was stronger than your desire to stand; your desire to stay was stronger than your desire to leave.

Consider a more bizarre illustration. Suppose on the way home from the meeting you encounter a robber who points a gun to your head and says, "Your money or your life." What do you do? If you accede to his demand and turn over your wallet, you will become a victim of coercion, and yet in some measure you will have exercised free choice. Coercion enters by virtue of the fact that the gunman is severely restricting your options to two. The element of freedom that is preserved stems from the fact that you still have two options and that you choose the one for which you have the strongest desire at the moment.

All things being equal, you have no desire to

donate your money to an unworthy thief. You have even less desire, however, to have your brains poured out on the sidewalk by the gunman's bullet. Given the small number of options, you still choose according to the strongest inclination at the moment. We always do what we really want to do.

The Bible teaches, some will say, that we do not always do what we want to do. The apostle Paul laments in Romans 7 that the good he would do he does not do, and the thing he does not want to do is the very thing he does. Paul's frustration over the wretchedness of his condition would seem totally to refute Edwards's thesis of the relationship of choice to desire. Paul, however, is not giving expression to an analysis of the causal relationship between desire and choice. He is expressing a profound frustration that centers on the complex of desires that assault the human will.

We are creatures with a multitude of desires, many of which are in violent conflict with each other. Again consider the "all things being equal" dimension of our moral choices. As a Christian I have a profound desire to please Christ with my life and to attain righteousness. That good desire for obedience to God is neither perfect nor pure as it struggles daily with other desires in my sinful personality. If I had no conflicting desires, I would, of course, never be disobedient. If the only desire I had, or if the strongest desire I had, were continuously the desire to obey

God, I would never willfully sin against him. But there are times when my desire to sin is greater than my desire to obey; when that happens, I sin. When my desire to obey is greater than my desire to sin, then at that moment, I refrain from sinning. My choices reveal more clearly and more certainly than anything else the level of my desire.

Desire, like appetite, is not constant. Our levels of desire fluctuate from day to day, from hour to hour, and from minute to minute. Desire moves in an ebb-and-flow pattern like the waves of the sea. The person who goes on a diet experiences intensifying pangs of hunger at various times of the day. It is easy to make a resolution to diet when one is satiated; it is easy to swear off alcohol in the middle of a hangover. It is easy to resolve to be righteous in the middle of a moving spiritual experience of prayer. But we are creatures of changing moods and fleeting desires who have not yet achieved a constancy of will based upon a consistency of godly desires. As long as conflict of desire exists and an appetite for sin remains in the heart, then man is not totally free in the moral sense of which Edwards spoke, nor does man experience the fullness of liberty described by Augustine.

Over against the Augustinian view of free will is the classical notion that describes the action or activity of choice in purely spontaneous terms. In this concept the will chooses and is free from not only external forces of coercion, but also any internal rule of disposition, or desire. The choice of the moment proceeds freely in the sense that no inclination or prior disposition controls, directs, or affects the choice that is made. It is safe to say that this view of the will is the dominant view of free will in Western culture and is the view Calvin had in mind when he stated, "Free will is far too grandiose a term to apply to man." At bottom it implies that man can make choices that are effects without any causes. Here it is suggested that the power of man to produce an effect without a cause exceeds even the creative power of God Almighty. Moreover, the cardinal rule of causality—*ex nihilo, nihil fit* (out of nothing, nothing comes)—is broken. Such a view of freedom is repugnant not only to Scripture, but to reason as well.

To understand freedom as purely spontaneous choice with no prior disposition controlling it is to rob freedom of any moral significance. That is, if I act with no prior motive or no previous inclination toward or away from righteousness, then how can it be said that my act is moral at all? Such activity would be without reason or motive behind it; it would be a purely random action, with no moral virtue attached to it.

But a deeper question remains: Is such a spontaneous action possible at all? If the will is inclined neither to the right nor to the left, how could it choose at all? If there is no disposition toward, or away from, the action, then the will suffers from complete paralysis. It is like the donkey who had set before him a bale of hay and a bucket of oats. The donkey's inclination with respect to the hay and the oats was exactly equal with not the slightest degree of preference toward one or the other. The story is told that the donkey in such circumstances starves to death with a banquet feast in front of him because he has no way to choose between the two.

The practical problem that remains with the classical view of freedom is one raised by behavioristic psychology. If man is indeed self-determined or free, does that not imply that if his desires were completely known, man's action in every given circumstance would be completely predictable? There is a sense in which we must agree that such a predictability would be implied. However, there is no way that we or a collection of mankind or any genius short of God and his omniscience could possibly know all the complex factors present in the human mind weighing a choice.

We recognize with psychologists that preferences and inclinations are shaped in many respects by past experience and environment, but we cannot predict with certainty what any human being will do. Hidden variables within the complex of human personality make for this unpredictability. It nevertheless remains a fact that there is always a reason for our actions, a cause for our choices. That cause stems partly from ourselves and partly from the forces operating around and over against us.

The safest course to steer is to define freedom as the church fathers, such as Augustine, did: "the ability to choose what we want." God's sovereignty does not extinguish that dimension of human personality, but certainly rules over it.

Out of rigid forms of determinism comes the cry of despair: "If the complex factors that make up personality completely determine my choices, then what value is self-improvement or the search for righteousness? If my will is enslaved by my dispositions and desires, what hope do I have of ever breaking out of the patterns of sin that are so destructive to my present mode of behavior?"

In a real sense the process of sanctification involves a radical reprogramming of the inner self. We are not the victims of blind mechanical forces that control our destiny. As intelligent beings, we can do something to change the disposition of our heart and the inclination of our mind.

It is important to remember that desire is not a fixed and constant power that beats within our souls. Our desires change and fluctuate from moment to moment. When the Bible calls us to feed the new man and starve the old man, we can apply this injunction by taking advantage of the ebb and flow of moods to strengthen the new man when our desire for Christ is inflamed and to kill the old man's desires by starving him in times of satiation. The simplest way to state the mechanism of sin is to understand that at the moment I sin, I desire the sin more than I desire to please God. Stated another way, my love for the sin is greater at the moment of its intense desire than is my love for obedience to God. Therefore, the simple conclusion is that to overcome the power of sin within us, we need either to decrease our desire for the sin or to increase our desire to obey God.

What can we do to effect such changes? We can submit ourselves to the discipline of a class or a teacher and devote ourselves to a rigorous study of the law of God. Such disciplined study can help renew our mind, equipping us with a new understanding of what pleases and displeases God. Having a renewed mind is the biblical definition of spiritual transformation.

The mind and the will are linked, as Edwards noted. By understanding more deeply how abhorrent our sin is to God, we can have our own attitudes toward sin changed or reprogrammed. We are to follow the biblical injunction to concentrate on whatever things are pure and good. It may be too much to expect that a man in the midst of an attack of profound lust will switch to pure thoughts. It would be difficult for him to push a button and change the inclination of his desire at that moment. But in a more sober mood, he may have the opportunity to reprogram his mind by filling it with high and holy thoughts of the things of God. The end result is that he may well strengthen the disposition of his heart toward God and weaken the disposition of his fallen nature toward sin.

We need not surrender to a superficial form of rigid determinism or behaviorism that would cause us to despair of any hope of change. Scripture encourages us to work out our salvation "with fear and trembling," knowing that not only are we applying the means of grace by our own effort, but we are also confident that God himself is working within us to bring about the necessary changes to conform us to the image of his Son.

But what about man's will with respect to the sovereignty of God? Perhaps the oldest dilemma of the Christian faith is the apparent contradiction between the sovereignty of God and the freedom of man. If we define human freedom as *autonomy* (meaning that man is free to do whatever he pleases, without constraint, without accountability to the will of God), then of course we must say that free will is contradictory to divine sovereignty. We cannot soft-pedal this dilemma by calling it a mystery; we must face up to the full import of the concept. If free will means autonomy, then God cannot be sovereign. If man is utterly and completely free to do as he pleases, there can be no sovereign God. And if God is utterly sovereign to do as he pleases, no creature can be autonomous.

It is possible to have a multitude of beings, all of whom are free to various degrees but none is sovereign. The degree of freedom is determined by the level of power, authority, and responsibility held by that being. But we do not live in this type of universe. There is a God who is sovereign—which is to say, he is absolutely free. My freedom is always within limits. My freedom is always constrained by the sovereignty of God. I have freedom to do things as I please, but if my freedom conflicts with the decretive will of God, there is no question as to the outcome—God's decree will prevail over my choice.

It is stated so often that it has become almost an uncritically accepted axiom within Christian circles that the sovereignty of God may never violate human freedom in the sense that God's sovereign will may never overrule human freedom. The thought verges on, if not trespasses, the border of blasphemy because it contains the idea that God's sovereignty is constrained by human freedom. If that were true, then man, not God, would be sovereign, and God would be restrained and constrained by the power of human freedom. As I say, the implication here is blasphemous because it raises the creature to the stature of the Creator. God's glory, majesty, and honor are denigrated since he is being reduced to the status of a secondary, impotent creature. Biblically speaking, man is free, but his freedom can never violate or overrule God's sovereignty.

Within the authority structure of my own family, for example, I and my son are free moral agents; he has a will and I have a will. His will, however, is more often constrained by my will than is my will constrained by his. I carry more authority and more power in the relationship and hence have a wider expanse of freedom than he has. So it is with our relationship to God; God's power and authority are infinite, and his freedom is never hindered by human volition.

There is no contradiction between God's sovereignty and man's free will. Those who see a contradiction, or even point to the problem as an unsolvable mystery, have misunderstood the mystery. The real mystery regarding free will is how it was exercised by Adam before the Fall.

If Augustine was correct that pre-Fall Adam possessed an ability to sin and an ability not to sin and was created with no prior disposition or inclination toward sin, then the question we face is, How was it possible for such a creature with no prior disposition toward evil actually to take the step into evil? As we grapple with this mystery, let me present several options that have served as explanations in the past.

We can hypothesize that Adam fell because he was duped by the craftiness of Satan and simply did not know what he was doing. The inspiration for this hypothesis is the biblical emphasis on the craftiness of Satan. Satan, in his guile, was able to seduce Adam and Eve by confusing their thought patterns. Thus, the weakness of our primordial parents was not moral in nature, but intellectual, inasmuch as they failed to perceive the chicanery of the serpent. What complicates the picture is the fact that the Scriptures in this instance do not describe Adam and Eve as having been completely duped by their adversary; rather they had full knowledge of what God allowed them and did not allow them to do. They could not plead ignorance of the command of God as an excuse for their transgression.

There are times when ignorance is excusable, namely when such ignorance cannot possibly be helped or overcome. Such ignorance is properly described by the Roman Catholic church as "invincible ignorance"—ignorance that we lack the power to conquer. But invincible ignorance excuses and gives one reprieve from any accusation of moral wrongdoing. The biblical record gainsays this option, for God pronounces judgment upon Adam and Eve; and unless that judgment were arbitrary or immoral on the part of God himself, we can only conclude that Adam and Eve were inexcusable. A just God does not punish excusable transgressions. Indeed, *excusable* transgressions are not transgressions.

A second option is that Adam and Eve were coerced by Satan to disobey God. Here we see the original instance of the statement "The devil made me do it." If, however, Satan, in fact, fully and forcibly coerced Adam and Eve to transgress the law of God, then once again we would find an excuse for their actions. We would have to conclude that they did not act with a reasonable measure of freedom, a measure which would at least have delivered them from moral culpability. Such a theory, however, violates the clear teaching of the biblical text, which hints at no coercive manipulation on the part of Satan.

Consistently, the Scriptures place the responsibility, the blame, and the full culpability upon Adam and Eve themselves. They committed evil. Their choice was an evil one.

By what means did Adam and Eve make an evil choice? If we apply the analysis of choice common to Augustine and Edwards to pre-Fall Adam, we face an insoluble dilemma. If Adam had been created with a purely neutral disposition (with no inclination toward either righteousness or evil), we would still face the same rational impasse that Edwards notes for those who would impose it for post-Fall man. A will with no predisposition would have no motivation to choose. Without motivation, there could actually be no choice. Even if such a choice were possible, it would have no moral import to it.

We must examine the other two alternatives—that Adam was created either with a predisposition toward evil or with a singular predisposition toward good. Both of these options end at the stone wall of intellectual difficulty. If we assume that Adam was created with a predisposition toward evil, we cast a horrible shadow over the character of God, for this would mean that God had created man with a predisposition toward evil and then had punished man for exercising that disposition that God himself had planted within his soul. This would, in a real sense, make God the author of, and the one ultimately responsible for, human wickedness. Every page of Holy Scripture recoils from such a thesis, as it would transfer the blame from man to God himself, who is altogether good. Many take this option, following in the footsteps of the implied criticism of the first man, Adam, who excused himself before the Creator by saying, "The woman *you* put here with me—she gave me some fruit from the tree, and I ate it." Men from Adam onward have, as a manifestation of their fallenness, tried to transfer the blame for that fallenness to the Creator.

A third option is that God created man with a disposition toward only righteousness. If this were the case, then we have an effect without a sufficient cause. How is it possible for a creature created with the disposition toward only righteousness to have chosen a wicked act?

I have a built-in antipathy to dialectical theology—theology that proclaims the beauty of contradictions and nonsense statements. Thus, I must swallow hard to agree with one neoorthodox theologian about the origin of Adam's sin: Karl Barth calls the sin of Adam the "impossible possibility." Barth, of course, is calling attention to the utterly inexplicable mystery of Adam's transgressions—what was rationally impossible and inconceivable happened and remains a bona fide and impenetrable mystery to us so far.

Other attempts have been made to seek a complex and sophisticated answer to the mystery of iniquity. One suggestion is that the sin of Adam was like all sin, namely a privation, a corruption, or a negation of something that was inherently and intrinsically good. In other words, Adam was created with a good moral disposition. His appetites and desires were continuously good, and as a result, one would expect his activities to have been equally good. However, it is suggested that in the complexity of moral choices, sometimes a good will (which has a desire that in itself is good) can be misused and abused toward an evil end. The supreme example of such a twisting occurred at the temptation of Jesus, the second and new Adam.

In Jesus' temptation experience in the wilderness, Satan came to him in the midst of a prolonged fast. It is probably safe to assume that at that point Jesus had a consuming passion for food. That natural human desire to eat in and of itself carried no immoral overtones. One expects a hungry man to have a disposition to eat. However, in the context of a fast, Jesus wanted to obey God through this act of self-deprivation. When Satan came to Jesus and suggested that he turn stones into bread, Satan was appealing to a perfectly normal appetite and desire within Jesus. However, Jesus' desire to obey the Father was deeper than his desire to partake of food. Thus, filled with an altogether righteous desire, he was able to overcome the temptation of Satan.

Now the theory goes like this: Perhaps it was something good that caused Adam to fall—something that in and of itself was good, but which could have been misused and abused by the seductive influences of Satan. Such an explanation certainly helps make the Fall more understandable, but it goes only so far before it fails. At its most vital point, the explanation does not account for how this good desire could have become distorted, overruling the prior obligation to obey God. At some point before the act of transgression took place, Adam must have had to desire disobedience to God more than obedience to God; therein the Fall had already taken place because the very desire to act against God in disobedience is itself sinful.

I leave the question of explaining the Fall of Adam by virtue of the exercise of his free will to the hands of more competent and insightful theologians. To blame it on man's finite limitations is really putting blame on the God who made man finite. Biblically, the issue has been, and always will be, a moral one. Man was commanded by the Creator not to sin, but man chose to sin, not because God or anyone else forced him to. Man chose out of his own heart.

Consequently, to probe the answer to the *how* of man's sin is to enter the realm of deepest mystery. Perhaps all we can do in the final analysis is to recognize the reality of our sin and our responsibility for it. Though we cannot explain it, certainly we know enough to confess it.

We must never attribute the cause of our sin to God, neither must we adopt any position that would excuse us from the moral responsibilities that Scripture clearly assigns to us.

Some have criticized the Christian faith for its inability to give a satisfying answer to the question of sin. The fact is that other religions must come to terms with this same question. Some respond simply by denying the reality of evil—a convenient but absurd way out. Christianity alone deals head-on with the reality of sin by providing an escape from its consequences.

The Christian solution to the problem of sin is a radical departure from what other religions provide, for it is centered in the person and work of Jesus Christ. Through his perfect sacrifice, which has the efficacy of blotting out believers' sins, we have become righteous in God's eyes. However, that righteousness does not give us the license to do as we please. We must still seek to do God's preceptive will, especially as we swim through the perilous waters of the moral, ethical, and social dilemmas of our age.

While we have discussed the more theological aspects of man's will and God's will, two other topics now beckon us: God's will for our job and for our marital status. These two practical concerns take center stage in the drama of our personal lives. What can we learn about God's will and man's will in relation to these vital aspects of living? The next chapter offers guidelines to facilitate our decision making in these all-important areas.

CHAPTER 12

GOD'S WILL AND YOUR JOB

When we are introduced to people, the following three questions are generally asked: What is your name? Where are you from? What do you do? The third question is the one that concerns us in this chapter.

What do you do? is obviously about one's occupation, career, or vocation. People want to know what task or service constitutes our livelihood or helps fulfill our personal aspirations.

We are all familiar with the aphorism "All work and no play makes Jack a dull boy." We understand that life is more than work. We devote periods of time to recreation, sleep, play, and other activities not directly part of our principal employment or labor. However, the element of our lives that is taken up by work is so encompassing and time-consuming that we tend to understand our personal identity in the light of our work.

Whatever else we are, we are creatures involved in labor. This was the design of creation—God himself is a working God. From the very moment of creation he conferred upon our original parents the responsibilities of work. Adam and Eve were called to dress, till, and keep the earth, to name the animals, and to have dominion by way of managerial responsibility over the earth. All of these activities involved the expenditure of time, energy, and resources—in short, work.

Sometimes we fall into the trap of thinking that work is a punishment that God gave us as a result of Adam's fall in the Garden of Eden. We must remember that work was given *before* the Fall. To be sure, our labor has added burdens attached to it. A mixture of thorns and thistles is found among the good plants we seek to cultivate. Our labor is accomplished by the sweat of our brow. These were the penalties of sinfulness, but work itself was part of the glorious privilege granted to men and women in creation. It is impossible to understand our own humanity without understanding the central importance of work.

Most of us spend the early years of our lives preparing and training for a lifelong activity of work. The sensitive Christian understands that in the labor of his occupation, he is responsible to make a contribution to the kingdom of God, to fulfill a divine mandate, to embark upon a holy calling as a servant of the living God. Such a Christian is keenly aware of the question, How can I best serve God with my labor?

Vocation and Calling

The idea of vocation is based on the theological premise of a divine call. The word *vocation* comes from the Latin word meaning "calling." In our secular society the religious meaning of the term has lost its significance, having become merely a synonym for *career*. We will be using the term *vocation* in its original sense: a divine call, a holy summons to fulfill a task or a responsibility that God has laid upon us. The question we as Christians wrestle with is, Am I in the center of God's will with respect to my vocation? In other words, Am I doing with my life what God wants me to do? Here the question of the will of God becomes eminently practical, for it touches on that dimension of my life that fills most of my waking hours and has the greatest impact upon the shaping of my personality.

If the Bible teaches anything, it teaches that God is a calling God. The world was created through the call of the omnipotent Creator: "'Let there be light'; and there was light." God also calls his people to repentance, to conversion, and to membership in his family. In addition he calls us to serve him in his kingdom, making the best possible use of our gifts and talents. But still the question faces us: How do I know what my particular vocational calling is?

One of the great tragedies of modern society is that, although the job market is vast and complex with an infinite number of possible careers, the educational systems that train us tend to guide and direct us to a very small number of occupational choices. As a high school graduate embarking upon college, I remember that a great deal of discussion centered on one's major and career aspirations. At that time it seemed as if everyone were setting out to become an engineer. The mechanized culture of the fifties was one that opened up literally thousands of lucrative positions in engineering. College campuses were flooded with young aspirants for degrees in the field of engineering.

I also remember the engineer glut on the market that occurred in the seventies. Stories circulated about Ph.D.'s in engineering who were collecting unemployment or washing dishes in the local diner because there simply were not enough engineering jobs available. The same could be said for education majors. Positions in education became fewer and fewer while the number of applicants became greater and greater. The problem was heightened by misguided publicity and counseling that steered people into occupational roles that society already had filled.

A hundred years ago the choices were much less difficult since the vast majority of American children spent their time preparing for a life in agricultural labor. Today roughly 3 percent of the population is now employed in farming—a radical decrease in one particular occupation that has opened the door for a vast number of other occupations.

Finding Your Vocation

The question of vocation becomes a crisis at two major points in life. The first is in late adolescence when a person is pressured into deciding what skills and knowledge he should acquire for future use. Some college freshmen feel pressured to declare a major in their first year, before knowing the available options and the limits of their ability.

The second period in life when vocation becomes critical is in mid-life when a person experiences a sense of frustration, failure, or a lack of fulfillment in his current position. He may ask, Have I wasted my life? Am I sentenced forever to a job that I'm finding meaningless, unfulfilling, and frustrating? Such questions highlight the fact that vocational counseling is a major part of pastoral counseling in America, second only to marital counseling.

We must also consider the fact that vocational frustration is a major contributing cause of marital disharmony and family upset. Thus, it is important to approach the matter of vocation with great care, both in the early stages of adolescent development and in the latter stages when the sense of frustration hits home.

The problem of discerning one's calling focuses heavily on four important questions:

1. What *can* I do?

2. What do I *like* to do?

3. What would I like to be *able* to do?

4. What *should* I do?

The last question can plague the sensitive conscience. To begin to answer it, we need to take a look at the other three questions because they are closely linked to the ultimate question, What should I do?

What can I do? Reasonably assessing our abilities, skills, and aptitudes is a crucial and basic part of the decision-making process in choosing a vocation. What are my abilities? What am I equipped to do? We may ask and then protest, immediately saying, "Wait a minute. What about Moses? What about Jeremiah? Didn't both of these men protest against God's call by saying that they were not equipped for the task?" Moses protested that he had limited speaking ability, and Jeremiah reminded his Creator of his youthfulness. Both experienced God's rebuke for seeking to evade a divine calling on the basis of the flimsy claim that they lacked the ability to do the job.

A couple of things need to be said about Moses and Jeremiah. Neither one had a full understanding of what was needed to carry out the summons God gave him. Moses protested that he lacked speaking skill, but God had already prepared Aaron to meet that part of the task. What God was looking for was obedient leadership from Moses. Public speaking could easily be delegated to another. God certainly took into consideration Moses' gifts, ability, and aptitude before he called him.

We must remember that God is the perfect Manager. He is efficient in his selection, calling people according to the gifts and talents that he has given them. Satan's strategy is to manipulate Christians into positions for which they have no ability or skill to perform well. Satan himself is very efficient in directing Christians to inefficiency and ineffectiveness.

What can I do? can be answered by proficiency examinations, analysis of our strengths and weaknesses, and a sober evaluation of our past performance. Abilities and performances can be, and are, measured in sophisticated ways in our society. We need to know what the parameters of our abilities are.

Often people apply for positions for which they have no skill. This is particularly and sadly true within the church and related Christian service. Some hunger and thirst to be in full-time Christian service, but lack the ability and the gifts required for the particular job. For example, they may have the academic training and credentials for the pastorate but lack the managerial skills or the people skills to help make them effective pastors.

Perhaps the most important principle in Scripture regarding abilities is found in the apostle Paul's injunction that we ought to make a sober analysis of ourselves, not thinking too highly of ourselves. Through sober analysis we can make a serious, honest, and clear evaluation of what we can and cannot do, and we should act accordingly.

The young person has a different question: What would I *like* to be able to do? Such a person may have developed very few skills or little educational background but realizes that he has enough time to acquire skills and talents through education or vocational training.

At this point the concept of aptitude is relevant. Aptitude involves a person's latent abilities as well as his acquired abilities. A person may have a certain aptitude for mechanical things and have no aptitude whatsoever for abstract things. This person may desire to be a philosopher, but would make a far better investment of his time by learning to be an airplane mechanic. But preferences are still important. Here

we tread into that critical and frightening area of
human experience called the realm of motivation.

Motivated Abilities

Research indicates that most people have more
than one ability and that their abilities can be divided into two basic types: *motivated* abilities and
non-motivated abilities. A non-motivated abililty is
a skill or a strength that a person has but is not
motivated to use. Some people are very good at
doing certain things, but find no particular fulfillment or enjoyment in doing them. Performing
them is sheer drudgery and pain. They may be
proficient in what they do, but for one reason or
another find the task odious.

I know of one young woman who in her early
teenage years attracted national attention because of
her proficiency at the game of golf. While still a
teenager, she won a national tournament. Yet when
the time came for girls her age to turn professional,
she chose a different vocation, not out of a higher
calling to seek a more spiritual enterprise than professional athletics, but because she had found the game
of golf to be very unpleasant. Her displeasure came
as the result of fierce pressure her father had placed
upon her in pushing her to become a proficient
golfer at a young age. When she became of age and
was out from under parental authority, she decided

to do something else. She had the ability to become a professional golfer, but lacked the motivation.

We might ask, "But how could she have become so proficient in the first place if she had not been motivated to perform well in golf?" We have to realize that she had been motivated to become proficient, but the motivation was largely based on fear of her father's wrath. In order to please him, she disciplined herself to acquire a skill that she would never have pursued on her own. Once free from the driving force of his authority, she turned her vocational pursuits in another direction. The moral to the story is obvious. The person who gives his full measure of time and energy to a nonmotivated ability is a walking pressure cooker of frustration.

It is true that, as Christians, we don't always have the luxury of doing the things we want to do. God does call us to sacrifice and to be willing to participate in the humiliation of Christ. To be sure, we live in the midst of warfare, and as Christians we have signed up for the duration. We should never neglect our awesome responsibility to the kingdom of God. Called to be servants, we are also called to obedience. Sometimes we are called to do things that we don't particularly enjoy doing. Nevertheless, the overriding consideration is to bring both our motivation into conformity with our call and our call into conformity with our motivation.

All things being equal, Jesus did not want to go to the Cross as he expressed in his agony in the Garden of Gethsemane. Yet at the same time, he had an overarching desire and motivation to do the will of his Father. That was his "meat and drink," the focus of his zeal. When it was confirmed to him that it was the Father's will that he lay down his life, Jesus was, in a very real and vital sense, motivated to do it.

Let us extend the concept of service and obedience to the analogy of human warfare. A crisis besets a nation, and people are summoned in the cause of national defense. Leaving the security and comfort of their homes and jobs, they make sacrifices by enlisting in the armed services. Are not Christians called to do the same? Certainly there is a sense in which we are. Yet within the context of the earthly military, there are a vast number of jobs, some for which we would be suited and others for which we would not. Some military tasks would be in line with our motivated skills and patterns of behavior while others would be completely at odds with our motivated skills and behavior. Even within the context of sacrificial service, consideration of motivation is a vital ingredient in determining our vocation.

Some rugged individualists in our society are self-employed and find it totally unnecessary to fit into an organizational working structure that involves supervisors, bosses, staff, and lines of authority. Most of us, however, carry out our working lives within the context of an organization. Here we face the problem of *fitting*. Does our job fit our gifts, talents, and aspirations? Do our motivated abilities fit our job? The degree to which our job requirements and our motivated abilities fit often determines the usefulness of our contribution and the extent of our personal satisfaction.

When personal motivations do not fit job descriptions, many people suffer. The first who suffers is the individual because he is laboring in a job that does not fit his motivated abilities. By being in a job for which he is unsuited, he tends to be less efficient and less productive. He also creates problems for others in the organization because his frustration spills over and has a negative effect on the group.

Some of us are "sanctified" enough to perform assigned tasks for which we lack motivation, doing them as proficiently as we do other tasks that are more enjoyable. However, the people who are so sanctified make up an infinitesimal minority within the work force. Research shows again and again that there is a strong tendency for people to do what they are motivated to do regardless of what their job description calls for. That is, they will spend the majority of their time and effort doing what they want to do rather than what the job, in fact, calls them to do. Such an investment of time and energy can be quite costly to a company or an organization.

The following simple diagrams show the relationships between motivated ability patterns and job description. They have been borrowed from People Management, a Connecticut-based organization. It helps people to discern their motivated ability patterns and helps organizations to coordinate people's gifts and motivations with the needs and aims of their organization. This kind of guidance works not only in secular industry but also within the structures of the church and sacred vocations.

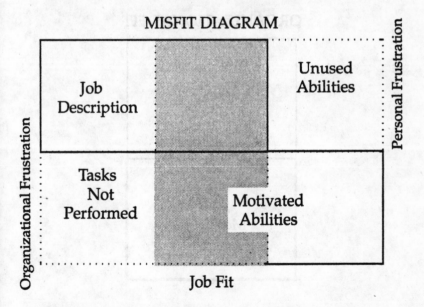

MISFIT DIAGRAM

In this diagram the top left block represents the job description of the employee, including the tasks required for optimal organizational functioning.

The lower right block represents the motivated abilities of the employee. The shaded area represents the area of job fit. It is not in balance. A large portion of the employee's motivated abilities are not being used. This produces frustration for the employee.

A large portion of the organizational job description is either left unperformed or performed at a low degree of proficiency. The result is organizational frustration. This pattern spells problems for both the individual employee and the organization. Changes must be made.

ORGANIZATIONAL FIT

Job Description

Motivated
Abilities

In this ideal matchup between job description and motivated abilities, the result is fulfillment for both the employee and the organization.

Through the influence of the world-denying spirit of Manichaeism, Christians got the idea that the only way they could possibly serve God would be to live their lives on a bed of nails. It was assumed that to embark upon a pathway of service involved self-denial. Real virtue could be found only in being as miserable as possible in one's job. However, if God indeed calls us to devote ourselves to the most unpleasant tasks possible, he would have to be the cosmic Chief of bad managers.

The Scriptures describe God's management style differently. God manages by building us into a body according to our abilities and our desires. He gives gifts to each one of his people. Every Christian is gifted of the Lord to fulfill a divine vocation. Along with the gift, God gives us a desire or a motivation to make use of that gift.

This brings us to the final and paramount question, What should I do? The most practical advice I can give is for you to do what your motivated ability pattern indicates you can do with a high degree of motivation. If what you would like to do can be of service to God, then by all means you should be doing it.

One vital constraint is at work: the preceptive will of God. If a woman's great ability and motivation were to be a prostitute and a man's motivated ability were to be the world's greatest bank robber, then obviously vocational goals would have to be adjusted. To fulfill such motivated abilities would bring individuals into direct conflict with the preceptive will of God.

If we carefully analyze the root causes for the motivated ability of the bank robber and the motivated ability of the prostitute, we would find root abilities and motivations of a sort that could profitably and productively be channeled into godly enterprises. We must not only bring our motivated abilities into conformity with the law of God, but also make sure that the vocation we choose has the blessing of God.

There is certainly nothing wrong, for example, with devoting one's life to the practice of medicine, for we see the good that medicine can do in terms of alleviating suffering. We also understand that the world needs bread to eat and that the vocation of baker for someone who is motivated and able to bake is a godly enterprise. Jesus himself spent a vast number of his years not in preaching and teaching but in being a carpenter, a craftsman in a legitimate trade. During those years Jesus was in "the center of God's will."

Any vocation that meets the need of God's world can be considered a divine calling. I underscore this because of the tendency in Christian circles to think that only those who go into "full-time Christian service" are being sensitive to divine vocation—as if preaching and teaching were the only legitimate tasks to which God calls us. A cursory reading of the Bible would reveal the flaw in such thinking. The temple was built in the Old Testament through not only the wise oversight of Solomon but also the craftsmanship of those who were divinely gifted in carving, sculpting, and so on.

David's vocation as shepherd, Abraham's vocation as a caravan trader, Paul's vocation as tentmaker—all were seen as part of God's plan to bring about the redemption of the world. When God made Adam and Eve, neither was called to be a full-time professional worker in the ecclesiastical structure; they were basically called to be farmers.

A vocation is something that we receive from God; he is the one who calls us. He may not call us in the way that he called Moses, by appearing in a burning bush and giving a specific set of marching orders. Instead, he usually calls us inwardly and by means of giving us the gifts and talents and aspirations that we have. His invisible sovereign will is certainly working in the background to prepare us for useful tasks in his vineyard.

In addition to the inner call of God, we recognize that there is such a thing as an external call to labor, a call that comes from people who request our services for their particular mission or purpose. We may be called by the church to be preachers or by a company to be foremen or shippers. Every time an organization places a want ad in a newspaper, a human call is going out for able workers to come and match their gifts and talents to a presented need.

Some Christians have argued that the need always constitutes the call. They say that there is a need for evangelists in the world and therefore everyone should be an evangelist. I agree that we must consider the needs of the kingdom of God as we make vocational decisions. However, the very fact that the world needs evangelists does not necessarily imply that everyone in the world is called to be an evangelist. Again the New Testament makes it clear that not all are called to be preachers or administrators. The church is composed of people with a diversity of gifts, talents, and vocations. We must not make a simplistic, passive assumption that the need constitutes the call.

Certainly the presence of a need requires that the people of God strive to meet that need. However, it does not necessarily mean that people who are not equipped to meet the need are thereby forced into the gap. For example, it is every Christian's responsibility to help carry out the mandate for evangelism. It is not every Christian's responsibility to be an evangelist. I am not an evangelist, though I contribute to evangelism by teaching evangelists theology and by contributing money for the church's task of evangelism. I do those things so that those who do have the gift and the motivation can be called out, trained, equipped and sent into the world as evangelists. I participate in the responsibility of the body of Christ to see that the task is met, but I myself am not the one who delivers the goods as the practicing evangelist. I could say the same regarding a host of other vocations.

How do others affect our vocational calling? We do need to listen to the community of believers and friends. Sometimes our gifts and abilities are more evident to those around us than they are to ourselves. The counsel of many and the evaluation of the group are important considerations in our search for our vocation. However, we must put up a red flag of warning. The group's judgment is not always correct. The fact that a particular individual or group thinks we should be doing a certain task is not a guarantee that it is the will of God.

I went through a period in my life of being unemployed for six months. During that time I had five different job offers in five different cities in the United States. Five different friends came to me and said out of sincerity and urgent zeal that they were sure God wanted me to take each of the particular jobs. This meant that if all five of them had a direct pipeline to the will of God, God wanted me to hold five full-time positions and live in five different cities in the United States at the same time. I explained to my friends that I knew I was iniquitous (full of sin) but had not yet discovered the gift of being ubiquitous (being everywhere at the same time). I simply could not possibly do all five jobs. Somebody was wrong in his estimation of the will of God for my life.

I find it very difficult to resist the pressures that come from people who are sure they know what God wants me to do with my life. We all experience that kind of pressure, and so we must be careful to pay attention to those whose judgment we trust. We must be able to discern between sound judgment and the vested personal interests of other people.

As it turned out, I accepted a sixth position for which no one came to me in the middle of the night with a telegram from God. I was convinced that the sixth position was the one that matched my abilities with the job that needed to be done.

One last consideration that is often neglected but is of crucial importance is *the foreseeable consequences of the job*. To take a job simply for money or for geographical location is a tragic mistake. All things being equal, I would like to have a salary of a million dollars a year, to be a teacher of theology, and to live where the climate is mild twelve months of the year. At the present time I am a teacher of theology living in Florida, but I make far less than a million dollars a year. Somewhere along the way I had to make a decision about my priorities. Did I want to make a million dollars, or did I want to heed my vocational calling? My residence was determined by the locale of my vocation.

Job decisions have both short-range and long-range consequences. Consider the case of Abraham and his nephew Lot, who lived and worked together in the Promised Land. Conflict between their hired hands made it necessary for them to divide the territory they were occupying. Abraham gave Lot the first choice, offering any half that he chose. Lot gazed toward the barren area of Transjordan and then looked toward the fertile valley near the city. He thought for a moment, *If I take the fertile valley, my cows can graze there and become fat. It's a short distance to the city market. My profit will be great.* In consideration of his business, Lot opted for the fertile areas around the city and left Abraham the barren land. Lot's choice was brilliant—from the perspective of raising cattle. He didn't ask questions like "Where will my family go to school? Where will my family go to church?" The city he chose was Sodom—a great place to raise cows. The short-term consequences were fine, but long-term living in Sodom turned out to be a disaster in many ways.

How will our job decisions be conducive to fulfilling our other responsibilities? The person who chooses a vocation purely on the basis of money or location or status is virtually guaranteeing his later frustration.

Much of the confusion we often experience in the job arena would be dispelled by asking ourselves one simple question: What would I most like to do if I didn't have to please anyone in my family or my circle of friends? Another good question is, What would I like to be doing ten years from now? These questions are good to keep in mind even after one has settled into a particular job.

Another thing to remember is the promise of God's Word that the Holy Spirit will guide us into all truth. As his children, that includes the area of our work. God's peace is also promised as we seek to do his will. While God's decretive will may not necessarily always be clear to us even in our occupational pursuits, his preceptive will is more easily discerned. Wherever we are, in whatever work we find ourselves, his preceptive will must be done.

Finally, what does God expect of us in relation to our work? As Christians we have been called to be spiritual salt in a decaying world, to be spiritual light in the midst of darkness. We are to be wise stewards of God's gifts and talents. That means striving to be the most honest, patient, hard-working, and committed workers we can be. It means settling for nothing less than excellence. God help us to live up to his high call for each of us.

CHAPTER 13

GOD'S WILL IN MARRIAGE

God's will. Man's will. Our work. The other topic of perennial concern is our marital status. Should we marry or remain single?

Perhaps in no other area of human activity do Christians expend more decision-making energy than in the area of marriage. No wonder, since the decisions relevant to the marital relationship have such far-reaching effects on our lives. How a person feels about his marital status determines, in large part, his sense of fulfillment, his productivity, and his self-image. The reality and the seriousness of the marital relationship are brought home when we realize that the one who knows us most intimately; the one before whom we are the most fragile and vulnerable; and the one who powerfully shapes and influences our lives—this one is none other

than our marriage partner. That is why entering
into the marital relationship is not something anyone should take lightly.

Now, before we tackle the general question, Is it
God's will for me to marry? several specific questions need to be considered.

Should I Get Married?

The answer to this question is often assumed by
our culture. From early childhood most of us ab-
sorb the idea that marriage is a natural and integral
part of normal life. From the fairy-tale characters
Snow White and Prince Charming, the romantic
plays of Shakespeare, and the mass media heroes
and heroines, we receive signals that society expects us to be numbered among the married.
Should we fail to fulfill this cultural expectation,
we are left with the nagging feeling that perhaps
something is wrong with us, that we are abnormal.

If a young man reaches the age of thirty without
getting married, he is suspected of having homosexual tendencies. If a woman is still single by
thirty, it is often tacitly assumed that she has some
defect that makes her unattractive as a marriage
partner, or worse, has lesbian preferences. Such
assumptions are by no means found in the Scriptures.

From a biblical perspective the pursuit of celibacy

is indicated in some instances as a legitimate option. Under other considerations it is viewed as a definite preference. Though we have our Lord's blessing on the sanctity of marriage, we also have his example of personal choice to remain celibate, obviously in submission to the will of God. Christ was celibate not because of homosexual leanings or from a lack of the masculine traits necessary to make him desirable as a life partner. Rather, his divine purpose obviated the destiny of marriage, making it crucial that he devote himself entirely to the preparation of his bride, the church, for his future wedding.

The most important biblical instruction that we have regarding celibacy is given by Paul in a lengthy passage from 1 Corinthians 7:25-40.

> *Now concerning the unmarried, I have no command of the Lord, but I give my opinion as one who by the Lord's mercy is trustworthy. I think that in view of the present distress it is well for a person to remain as he is. Are you bound to a wife? Do not seek to be free. Are you free from a wife? Do not seek marriage. But if you marry, you do not sin, and if a girl marries, she does not sin. Yet those who marry will have worldly troubles, and I would spare you that. I mean, brethren, the appointed time has grown very short; from now on, let those who have wives live as though they had none, and*

those who mourn as though they were not mourning, and those who rejoice as though they were not rejoicing, and those who buy as though they had no goods, and those who deal with the world as though they had no dealings with it. For the form of this world is passing away.

I want you to be free from anxieties. The unmarried man is anxious about the affairs of the Lord, how to please the Lord; but the married man is anxious about worldly affairs, how to please his wife, and his interests are divided. And the unmarried woman or girl is anxious about the affairs of the Lord, how to be holy in body and spirit; but the married woman is anxious about worldly affairs, how to please her husband. I say this for your own benefit, not to lay any restraint upon you, but to promote good order and to secure your undivided devotion to the Lord.

If any one thinks that he is not behaving properly toward his betrothed, if his passions are strong, and it has to be, let him do as he wishes: let them marry—it is no sin. But whoever is firmly established in his heart, being under no necessity but having his desire under control, and has determined this in his heart, to keep her as his betrothed, he will do well. So that he who marries his betrothed does well; and he who refrains from marriage will do better.

A wife is bound to her husband as long as he

lives. If the husband dies, she is free to be married to whom she wishes, only in the Lord. But in my judgment she is happier if she remains as she is. And I think that I have the Spirit of God.

The teaching of the apostle Paul in this matter of marriage has been subjected to serious distortions. Some observe in this text that Paul is setting forth a contrasting view of marriage that says celibacy is good and marriage is bad, particularly for Christians called to service in the interim period between the first advent of Christ and his return. However, even a cursory glance at the text indicates that Paul is not contrasting the good and the bad, but rival goods. He points out that it is good to opt for celibacy under certain circumstances. Moreover, it is also good and quite permissible to opt for marriage under other circumstances. Paul sets forth the pitfalls that a Christian faces when contemplating marriage. Of prime consideration is the pressure of the kingdom of God on the marriage relationship.

Nowhere has the question of celibacy been more controversial than in the Roman Catholic church. Historically Protestants have objected that the Roman Catholic church, by imposing upon its clergy a mandate beyond the requirements of Scripture itself, has slipped into a form of legalism. Though we agree that Scripture permits the marriage of clergy, it indicates, at the same time, that one who is married and serving God in a special vocation does face the nagging problems created by a divided set of loyalties—his family on one hand; the church on the other. Unfortunately the dispute between Protestants and Catholics over mandatory celibacy has become so heated at times that Protestants have often reacted to the other extreme, dismissing celibacy as a viable option. Again let us return to the focus of Paul's word which sets forth a distinction between rival goods. His distinction, in the final analysis, allows the individual to decide what best suits him or her.

Paul in no way denigrates the honorable "estate" of marriage, but rather affrrms what was given in creation: the benediction of God over the marriage relationship. One does not sin by getting married. Marriage is a legitimate, noble, and honorable option set forth for Christians.

Another aspect regarding the question, Should I get married? moves beyond the issue of celibacy to whether a couple should enter into a formal marriage contract or sidestep this option by simply living together. In the last thirty years the option of living together, rather than moving into a formal marriage contract, has proliferated in our culture. Christians must be careful not to establish their precepts of marriage (or any other ethical dimension of life) on the basis of contemporary community standards. The Christian's conscience is to be governed not merely by what is socially acceptable or even by what is legal according to the law of the land, but rather by what God sanctions.

Unfortunately, some Christians have rejected the legal and formal aspects of marriage, arguing that marriage is a matter of private and individual commitment between two people who have no further legal or formal requirements. These view marriage as a matter of individual private decision apart from external ceremony. The question most frequently asked of clergymen on this matter reflects the so-called freedom in Christ: Why do we have to sign a piece of paper to make it legal?

The signing of a piece of paper is not a matter of affixing one's signature in ink to a meaningless document. The signing of a marriage certificate is an integral part of what the Bible calls a *covenant*. Biblically, there is no such thing as a *private* marriage contract between two people. A covenant is done publicly before witnesses and with formal legal commitments that are taken seriously by the community. The protection of both partners is at stake; there is legal recourse should one of the partners act in a way that is destructive to the other.

Contracts are signed out of the necessity spawned by the presence of sin in our fallen nature. Because we have an enormous capacity to wound each other, sanctions have to be imposed by legal contracts. Contracts not only restrain sin, but also protect the innocent in the case of legal and moral violation. With every commitment I make to another human being, there is a sense in which a part of me becomes vulnerable, exposed to the response of the other person. No human enterprise renders a person more vulnerable to hurt than does the estate of marriage.

God ordained certain rules regulating marriage in order to protect people. His law was born of love and concern and compassion for his fallen creatures. The sanctions God imposed upon sexual activity outside of marriage do not mean that God is a spoilsport or a prude. Sex is an enjoyment he himself has created and given to the human race. God, in his infinite wisdom, understands that there is no time that human beings are more vulnerable than when they are engaged in the most intimate activity known to human beings. Thus he cloaks this special act of intimacy with certain safeguards. He is saying to both the man and the woman that it is safe to give one's self to the other only when there is a certain knowledge of a lifelong commitment behind it. There is a vast difference between a commitment sealed with a formal document and declared in the presence of witnesses before family, friends, and authorities of church and state, and a whispered hollow promise breathed in the backseat of an automobile.

Do I Want to Get Married?

Paul states in 1 Corinthians 7:8-9: "To the unmarried and widows I say that it is well for them to remain single as I do. But if they cannot exercise self-control, they should marry. For it is better to marry than to be aflame with passion." The distinction is between the good and the better. Here Paul introduces the idea of burning, not of the punitive fires of hell, but of the passions of the biological nature, which God has given us. Paul is speaking very candidly when he points out that some people are not made for celibacy. Marriage is a perfectly honorable and legitimate option even for those who are most strongly motivated by sexual fulfillment and relief from sexual temptation and passion.

The question, Do I want to get married? is an obvious, but very important one. The Bible does not prohibit marriage. Indeed it encourages it except in certain cases where one may be brought into conflict with vocation; but even in that dimension, provisions are left for marriage. So, to desire marriage is a very good thing. A person needs to be in touch with his own desires and conscience.

If I have a strong desire to marry, then the next step is actively to do something about fulfilling that desire. If a person wants a job, he must seriously pursue employment opportunities. When we decide to attend a college or a university, we have to follow the formal routine of making applications, of evaluating various campuses. Marriage is no different; no magic recipe has come from heaven that will determine for us the perfect will of God for a life partner. Here, unfortunately, is where Christians have succumbed to the fairy-tale syndrome of our society. It is a particular problem for young single women who feel that if God wants them to be married, he will drop a marriage partner out of heaven on a parachute or will bring some Prince Charming riding up to their doorstep on a great white horse.

One excruciating problem faced by single women is caused by the unwritten rule of our society that allows men the freedom actively to pursue a marriage partner while women are considered loose if they actively pursue a prospective husband.

No biblical rule says that a woman eager to be married should be passive. There is nothing that prohibits her from actively seeking a suitable mate. On numerous occasions, I've had the task of counseling single women who insist at the beginning of the interview that they have no desire to be married, but simply want to work out the dimensions of the celibacy they believe God has imposed upon them.

After a few questions and answers, the scenario usually repeats itself: the young woman begins to weep and blurts out, "But I really want to get married." When I suggest that there are wise steps that she can take to find a husband, her eyes light up in astonishment as if I had just given her permission to do the forbidden. I have broken a taboo.

Wisdom requires that the search be done with discretion and determination. Those seeking a life partner need to do certain obvious things such as going where other single people congregate. They need to be involved in activities that will bring them in close communication with other single Christians.

In the Old Testament Jacob made an arduous journey to his homeland to find a suitable marriage partner. Isaac did much the same thing. Neither of these patriarchs waited at home for God to deliver them a life partner. They went where the opportunity presented itself to find a marriage partner. The fact that they were men does not imply that such a procedure is limited to males only. Women in our society have exactly the same freedom to pursue a mate by diligent search.

What Do I Want in a Marriage Partner?

A myth has arisen within the Christian community that marriage is to be a union between two people committed to the principle of selfless love. Selfless love is viewed as being crucial for the success of a marriage. This myth is based upon the valid concept that selfishness is often at the root of disharmony and disintegration in marriage relationships. The biblical concept of love says no to acts of selfishness within marital and other human relationships. However, the remedy for selfishness is nowhere to be found in selflessness.

The concept of selflessness is originally one that proceeds from Oriental and Greek thinking where the ideal goal of humanity is the loss of self-identity by becoming one with the universe. The goal of man in this schema is to lose any individual characteristic, becoming one drop in the great ocean. Another aspect of Oriental absorption is the notion of the individual becoming merged with the great Oversoul and becoming spiritually diffused throughout the universe. From a biblical perspective the goal of the individual is not the annihilation or the disintegration of the self, but the *redemption* of the self. To seek selflessness in marriage is an exercise in futility. The self is very much active in building a good marriage, and marriage involves the commitment of the self with another self based on reciprocal sharing and sensitivity between two actively involved selves.

If I were committed to a selfless marriage, it would mean that in my search for a marriage partner I should survey the scene to find a person for whom I was willing to throw myself away. This is the opposite of what is involved in the quest for a marriage partner. When someone seeks a mate, he should be seeking someone who will enrich his life, who will add to his own self-fulfillment, and who at the same time will be enriched by that relationship.

What are the priority qualities to seek in a marriage partner? One little exercise that many couples have found helpful is based upon freewheeling imagination. While finding a marriage partner is not like shopping for an automobile, one can use the new car metaphor. When one purchases a new car, he has many models from which to choose. With those models there is an almost endless list of optional equipment that can be tacked onto the standard model.

By analogy, suppose one could request a made-to-order mate with all the options. The person engaged in such an exercise could list as many as a hundred qualities or characteristics that he would like to find in the perfect mate. Compatibility with work and with play, attitudes toward parenting, certain skills, and physical characteristics could be included. After completing the list, the person would have to acknowledge the futility of such a process. No human being will ever perfectly fit all the possible characteristics that one desires in a mate.

This exercise is particularly helpful for people who have delayed marrying into their late twenties or early thirties. Such a person sometimes settles into a pattern of focusing on tiny flaws that disqualify virtually every person he meets. After doing the made-to-order mate exercise, he can take the next step: reduce the list to the main priorities. The person involved in this exercise reduces the number of qualifications to twenty, then to ten, and finally to five. Such a reduction forces him to set in ordered priority the things he is most urgently seeking in a marriage partner.

It is extremely important that individuals clearly understand what they want out of the dating and eventually the marital relationship. They should also find out whether their desires in a marriage relationship are healthy or unhealthy. This leads us to the next question regarding counseling.

From Whom Should I Seek Counsel?

Many people resent the suggestion that they seek counsel in their selection of a marriage partner. After all, isn't such a selection an intensely personal and private matter? However personal and private the decision might be, it is one of grave importance to the future of the couple and their potential offspring, their families, and their friends.

Marriage is never ultimately a private matter because how the marriage works affects a multitude of people. Counsel can be sought from trusted friends, pastors, and particularly from parents.

In earlier periods of Western history, marriages

were arranged either by families or by matchmakers. Today the idea of arranged marriages seems primitive and crass. It is totally foreign to our American heritage. We have come to the place where we think that it is our inalienable right to choose one whom we love.

Some things need to be said in defense of the past custom of arranged marriages. One is that happy marriages can be achieved even when one has not chosen his own partner. It may sound outrageous, but I am convinced that if biblical precepts are applied consistently, virtually any two people in the world can build a happy marriage and honor the will of God in the relationship. That may not be what we prefer, but it can be accomplished if we are willing to *work* in the marital relationship. The second thing that needs to be said in defense of arranged marriages is that in some circumstances, marriages have been arranged on the objective evaluation of matching people together and of avoiding destructive parasitic matchups. For example, when left to themselves, people with significant personal weaknesses, like a man having a profound need to be mothered and a woman having a profound need to mother, can be attracted to each other in a mutually destructive way. Such negative mergings are repeated daily in our society.

It is not my intention to lobby for matched or arranged marriages. I am only hailing the wisdom of seeking parental counsel in the decision-making process. Parents often object to the choice of a marriage partner. Sometimes their objections are based upon the firm conviction that "no one is good enough for my daughter [or son]." Objections like these are based upon unrealistic expectations at best and upon petty jealousy at worst. However, not all parents are afflicted with such destructive prejudices regarding the potential marriage partners of their children. Sometimes the parents have keen insight into the personalities of their children, seeing blind spots that the offspring themselves are unable to perceive. In the earlier example of a person with an inordinate need to be mothered attracting someone with an inordinate need to mother, a discerning parent can spot the mismatch and caution against it. If a parent is opposed to a marriage relationship, it is extremely important to know why.

When Am I Ready to Get Married?

After seeking counsel, having a clear understanding of what we are hoping for, and having examined our expectations of marriage, the final decision is left to us. At this point some face paralysis as the day of decision draws near. How does one know when he or she is ready to get married? Wisdom dictates that we enter into serious premarital study, evaluation, and counseling with competent counselors so that we may be warned of the pitfalls that come in this new and vital human relationship. Sometimes we need the gentle nudge of a trusted counselor to tell us when it is time to take the step. With the breakdown of so many marriages in our culture, increasing numbers of young people fear entering into a marriage contract lest they become "statistics."

What things need to be faced before taking the actual step toward marriage? Economic considerations are, of course, important. The second greatest reason given for divorce is conflict over finances. Financial pressures imposed upon a relationship already besieged with emotional pressures of other kinds can be the straw that breaks the proverbial camel's back. That is why parents often advise young people to wait until they finish their schooling or until they are gainfully employed so that they can assume the responsibility of a family.

It is not by accident that the creation ordinance of marriage mentions that a man shall leave his father and mother and "cleave unto" his wife and the two shall become one flesh. The leaving and cleaving dimensions are rooted in the concept of being able to establish a new family unit. Here economic realities often govern the preparedness for marriage.

But entering into marriage involves far more than embarking upon new financial responsibilities. The marriage commitment is the most serious one that two human beings can make to each other.

I am ready to get married when I am prepared to commit myself to a particular person for the rest of my life, regardless of the human circumstances that befall us.

In order for us to understand the will of God for marriage, it is again imperative that we pay attention to God's *preceptive will.* The New Testament clearly shows that God not only ordained marriage and sanctified it—but he also regulates it. His commandments cover a multitude of situations regarding the nitty-gritty aspects of marriage. The greatest textbook on marriage is the sacred Scripture, which reveals God's wisdom and his rule governing the marriage relationship. If someone earnestly wants to do the will of God in marriage, his first task is to master what the Scripture says that God requires in such a relationship.

What does God expect of his children who are married or thinking about getting married? God expects, among other things, faithfulness to the marriage partner, provision of mutual needs, and mutual respect under the lordship of Christ. Certainly the couple should enhance each other's effectiveness as Christians. If not, something is wrong.

Now, while celibacy is certainly no less blessed and honorable a state to be in than marriage, we do have to recognize Adam and Eve as our models. God's plan involved the vital union of these two individuals who would make it possible for the earth to be filled with their "kind."

Basically I cannot dictate God's will for anyone in this area any more than I can or would in the area of occupation. I will say that good marriages require hard work and individuals willing to make their marriages work.

Ultimately what happens in our lives is cloaked in the mystery of God's will. The joy for us as his children is that the mystery holds no terror—only waiting, appropriate acting upon his principles and direction, and the promise that he is with us forever.

PART FOUR

HOW SHOULD I LIVE IN THIS WORLD?

Almost every major discussion of ethics these days begins with an analysis of the chaotic situation of our modern culture. Even secular writers and thinkers are calling for some sort of basic agreement on ethical behavior. Humanity's "margin of error," they say, is shrinking with each new day. Our survival is at stake.

These "prophets of doom" point out that man's destructive capability increased from 1945 to 1960 by the same ratio as it did from the primitive weapons of the Stone Age to the dropping of the atomic bomb on Hiroshima. The thawing of the Cold War has provided little comfort. Numerous nations have nuclear arms now or nearly have them. What, besides ethics, will keep them from using these weapons?

This stark reality is compounded by the profusion of social injustice in many areas, the rise of international terrorism, and the general decline of personal and social values. Who is to say what's right and wrong? One technical volume, Hill's *Contemporary Ethical Theories*, comes up with more than eighty different theories of ethics competing for acceptance in our modern world. It is not just a matter of "doing the right thing," but of figuring out what the right thing is. This proliferation of options generates confusion in our world and, for many, a sense of despair. Will we ever reach a cultural consensus that will stabilize the shifting sands of pluralism?

All this talk of "theories of ethics" may leave you cold. But the fact is, ethical decisions enter into every aspect of our lives. No field or career is immune from ethical judgments. In politics, in psychology, in medicine, ethical decisions are made regularly. The legislative action, the economic policy, the school board's curriculum, the psychiatrist's advice—all involve ethical considerations. Every vote cast in the ballot box marks an ethical decision.

On what basis do we make these decisions? That's where the "ethical theories" come in. The Christian may say, "I simply obey God's Word." But what about those issues where the Bible has no specific "thou shalt"? Can we find ethical principles in Scripture, and in the very nature of God, that will guide us through this difficult terrain? And then how can we communicate these principles to others? How does God's Word stand up against the eighty-some other standards?

Let us start by looking deeper into the field of ethics to consider how our society deals with such questions. Then we will see how God's Word fits in, and we will seek to apply biblical teaching to several modern dilemmas.

CHAPTER 14

ETHICS AND MORALS

In present word usage the term *ethics* is often used interchangeably with the word *morals* or *morality*. That the two have become virtual synonyms is a sign of the confusion that permeates the modern ethical scene. Historically, the two words had quite distinctive meanings. *Ethics* comes from the Greek *ethos*, which is derived from the root word meaning "stall," a place for horses. It conveyed the sense of a dwelling place, a place of stability and permanence. On the other hand, *morality* comes from the word *mores*, which describes the behavioral patterns of a given society.

Ethics is a normative science, searching for the principal foundations that prescribe obligations or "oughtness." It is concerned primarily with the imperative and with the philosophical premises upon which imperatives are based. Morality is a descriptive science, concerned with "isness" and the indicative. Morals describe what people do; ethics define what people ought to do. The difference between them is between the normal and the normative.

ETHICS	MORALS
1. *normative*	1. *descriptive*
2. *imperative*	2. *indicative*
3. *oughtness*	3. *isness*
4. *absolute*	4. *relative*

When morality is identified with ethics, the normal becomes the normative and the imperative is swallowed by the status quo. This creates a kind of "statistical morality." In this schema the good is determined by the normal and the normal is determined by the statistical average. The "norm" is discovered by an analysis of the normal, or by counting noses. Conformity to that norm then becomes the ethical obligation. It works like this:

Step #1. *We compile an analysis of statistical behavior patterns such as those integral to the Kinsey Report and the Chapman Report. If we discover that a majority of people are in fact participating in premarital sexual intercourse, then we declare such activity "normal."*

Step #2. We move quickly from the normal to a description of what is authentically "human." Humanness is defined by what human beings do. Hence, if the normal human being engages in premarital sexual intercourse, we conclude that such activity is normal and therefore "good."

Step #3. The third step is to declare patterns that deviate from the normal to be abnormal, inhuman, and inauthentic. In this schema chastity becomes a form of deviate sexual behavior and the stigma is placed on the virgin rather than the nonvirgin.

Statistical morality operates on the following syllogism:

Premise A—*the normal is determined by statistics;*
Premise B—*the normal is human and good;*
Conclusion—*the abnormal is inhuman and bad.*

In this humanistic approach to ethics the highest good (*summum bonum*) is defined by that activity which is most authentically human. This method achieves great popularity when applied to some issues but breaks down when applied to others. If we do a statistical analysis of the experience of cheating among students or lying among the general public, we discover that a majority of students have at some time cheated and that everyone has at some time lied. If the canons of statistical morality apply, the only verdict we can render is that cheating is an authentically human good and that lying is a *bona fide* virtue.

Obviously there must be a relationship between our ethical theories and our moral behavior. In a real sense our beliefs dictate our behavior. A theory underlies our every moral action. We may not be able to articulate that theory or even be immediately conscious of it, but nothing manifests our value systems more sharply than our actions.

The Christian ethic is based on an antithesis between what is and what ought to be. We view the world as fallen; an analysis of fallen human behavior describes what is normal to the abnormal situation of human corruption. God calls us out of the indicative by his imperative. Ours is a call to nonconformity—to a transforming ethic that shatters the status quo.

Even within relativistic claims, a serious inconsistency emerges. The decade of the sixties brought a moral revolution to our culture, spearheaded by the protests of the youth. Two slogans were repeated, broadcast side by side during this movement. The tension was captured by these twin slogans: "Tell it like it is" and "Do your own thing."

The cry for personal freedom was encapsulated in the "inalienable right" to do one's own thing. This was a demand for subjective freedom of self-expression. When the guns were turned on the older generation, however, a curious and glaring inconsistency was heard: "Tell it like it is." This slogan implies an objective basis for truth and virtue. The adult generation was not "allowed" to do their own thing if doing their own thing deviated from objective norms of truth. The flower children demanded the right to have their ethical cake and eat it too.

I was once maneuvered into an unenviable counseling situation by a distraught Christian mother, performing the role of a modern day Monica anguishing over the wayward behavior of her nonbelieving and rebellious son. The lad had retreated from his mother's constant religious and moral directives by moving out of the family home and into his own apartment. He promptly decorated his apartment with walls painted black and strobe lights flashing, then adorned the room with accoutrements designed for the liberal indulgence of hashish and other exotic drugs. His was a bacchanalian "pad" into which he promptly invited a willing coed to join him in luxurious cohabitation. All of this was to his mother's unmitigated horror. I agreed to talk with the young man only after explaining to the mother that such an encounter would probably engender further hostility. I would be viewed as the mother's "hired gun." The youth also agreed to the meeting obviously only to escape further verbal harassment from his mother.

When the young man appeared at my office, he was overtly hostile and obviously wanted to get the meeting over with as quickly as possible. I began the interview bluntly by asking directly, "Who are you mad at?"

Without hesitation he growled, "My mother."

"Why?" I inquired.

"Because all she does is hassle me. She keeps trying to shove religion down my throat."

I went on to inquire what alternative value system he had embraced in place of his mother's ethical system. He replied, "I believe everyone ought to be free to do his own thing."

I then asked, "Does that include your mother?" He was startled by the question and not immediately aware of what I was driving at. I explained to him that if he embraced a Christian ethic he could readily enlist me as an ally in his cause. His mother had been harsh, provoking her son to wrath and being insensitive to questions and feelings, issues which are indeed circumscribed by the biblical ethic. I explained that at several crucial points his mother had violated Christian ethics. However, I pointed out that on the boy's ethical terms he had no legitimate gripe. "Maybe your mother's 'thing' is to harass children by shoving religion down their throats. How can you possibly object to that?" It became clear that the boy wanted everybody (especially himself) to have the right to do his or her "own thing" except when or unless the other person's "thing" impinged on *his* "thing."

It is commonplace to hear the lament that some Christians, notably conservatives, are so rigidly bound by moralistic guidelines that everything becomes for them a matter of "black and white" with no room left for "gray" areas. Those who persist in fleeing from the gray, seeking refuge in the sharply defined areas of white and black, suffer from the epitaph "brittle" or "dogmatic." But the Christian must seek for righteousness and never be satisfied with living in the smog of perpetual grayness. He wants to know where the right way is located, where the path of righteousness lies.

There is a right and there is a wrong. The difference between them is the concern of ethics. We seek a way to find the *right*, which is neither subjective nor arbitrary. We seek norms and principles that transcend prejudice or mere societal conventions. We seek an objective basis for our ethical standards. Ultimately we seek a knowledge of the character of God, whose holiness is to be reflected and mirrored in our patterns of behavior. With God there is a definite and absolute black and white. The problem for us is to discover which things belong where. The model on the next page depicts our dilemma:

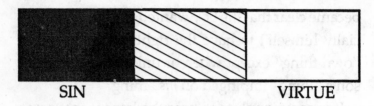

SIN   VIRTUE

The black section represents sin or unrighteousness. The white section represents virtue or righteousness. What does the gray represent? The gray area may call attention to two different problems of Christian ethics. It may be used to refer to those activities the Bible describes as being *adiapherous.* Adiapherous matters refer to those things which in themselves are ethically neutral. Such matters as eating food offered to idols are placed in this category. In themselves adiapherous matters are not sin, but there are occasions when they might become sin. Ping-Pong playing, for example, is not sinful. But if a person becomes obsessed with Ping-Pong to the extent that it dominates his life, it becomes a sinful thing for that person.

However, the second problem of the gray area is more important for us to grasp. Here the gray area represents *confusion:* it encompasses those matters where we are uncertain about what is right and wrong. The presence of gray calls attention to the fact that ethics is not a simple science, but a complex one. Finding the black and the white areas is a noble concern—jumping to them simplistically, however, is devastating to the Christian life. When we react to black/white approaches to ethics, we may be accurately assessing an annoying human tendency toward simplistic thinking. We must guard against the reactionary posture of leaping to the conclusion that there are no limits of black and white. Only within the context of atheism can we speak of no black and white. We desire competent and consistent theism, which demands a rigorous scrutiny of ethical principles in order to find our way out of the confusion of the gray.

The Ethical Continuum

Our graph may also be used to illustrate the ethical continuum. In classical terms, sin is described as righteousness run amok. Evil is seen as the negation, privation, or distortion of the good. Man was created to labor in a garden. In modern jargon the workplace is described as a jungle. What is the difference between a garden and a jungle? A jungle is merely a chaotic garden, a garden run wild.

Man was created with an aspiration for significance, a virtue. Man can pervert that drive into a lust for power, a vice. These represent the two poles on the continuum. At some point we cross over a line between virtue and vice. The closer we come to that line, the more difficult it is for us to perceive it clearly and the more our minds encounter the foggy gray area.

In teaching a course on ethics to clergymen working on Doctor of Ministry degrees, I posed the following ethical dilemma:

Suppose a husband and wife are interned in a concentration camp. They are housed in separate quarters with no communication between them. A guard approaches the wife and demands that she have sexual intercourse with him. The wife refuses. The guard then declares that unless the woman submits to his overtures, he will have her husband shot. The woman submits. When the camp is liberated and the husband learns of his wife's behavior, he sues her for divorce on the grounds of adultery. I then posed this question to twenty conservative clergymen: "Would you grant the man a divorce on the grounds of adultery?" All twenty answered yes, pointing to the obvious fact that the wife did have sexual relations with the guard. They saw extenuating circumstances in the situation, but the situation did not change the fact of the wife's immoral behavior.

I then asked, "If a woman is forcibly raped, may the husband sue for divorce on the grounds of adultery?" All twenty responded no. The clergymen all recognized a clear distinction between adultery and rape. The difference is found at the point of coercion versus voluntary participation. I pointed out that the prison guard used coercion (forcible compliance lest the husband be killed) and asked if the woman's "adultery" was not actually rape.

By merely raising the question, half of the clergymen changed their verdict. After prolonged discussion almost all of them did. The presence of the element of coercion threw the adultery issue into the gray area of confusion. Even those who did not completely change their verdict strongly modified it to account for the extenuating circumstances, which moved the woman's "crime" from the clear area of sin into the gray area of complexity. They all agreed that if it was sin, it was a lesser sin than adultery committed with "malice aforethought."

That a continuum exists between virtue and vice was the main thrust of Jesus' teaching in the Sermon on the Mount. He was teaching the principle of the complex of righteousness and the complex of sin. The Pharisees had embraced a simplistic understanding of the Ten Commandments. Their ethical judgments were superficial and therefore distorted. They failed to grasp the continuum motif.

Recently I read an article by a prominent psychiatrist who was critical of Jesus' ethical teaching. He expressed astonishment that the Western world had been so laudatory about Jesus as a "great teacher." He pointed to the Sermon on the Mount as exhibit A for the foolishness of Jesus' ethical teaching. He asked why we extol the wisdom of a teacher who taught that it is just as bad for a man to lust after a woman as it is to commit adultery with her. He questioned how a teacher could argue that it is just as bad to be angry at a man or to call him a fool as it is to murder him. He then belabored the difference between the destruction caused by lust as opposed to adultery and that caused by slander as opposed to murder.

The answer to the psychiatrist should be clear. Jesus did not teach that lust was as bad as adultery, or that slander was as bad as murder. (Unfortunately, many Christians have jumped to the same erroneous conclusion as the psychiatrist, obscuring the point of Jesus' ethical teaching.)

Jesus was correcting the simplistic view of the law held by the Pharisees. They had embraced an "everything but" philosophy of technical morality, assuming that if they avoided the most obvious dimension of the Commandments, they had fulfilled the law. Like the rich young ruler they had a simplistic and external understanding of the Decalogue. Because they had never actually murdered anyone, they thought they had kept the law perfectly. Jesus spelled out the wider implications or the complex of the law. "You shall not kill" means more than refraining from homicide. It prohibits the entire complex that goes into murder. It implies its opposite virtue: "You shall promote life." In our continuum, we see the following range:

VICE	VIRTUE
MURDER-HATRED-SLANDER	SAVING LIFE

DESTROYING LIFE	PROMOTING LIFE

A similar continuum moves from the virtue of chastity to the vice of adultery. In between are lesser virtues and lesser sins, but sins nevertheless.

Slander doesn't kill the body or leave the wife a widow and the children orphans. It does destroy a man's good name, which robs him of a quality aspect of life. Slander murders the man "in spirit." Jesus' teaching is to reveal both the spirit and the letter of the law. The Pharisees had become crass literalists, ignoring the spirit of the law and missing the wider concerns of the complex of the sin of murder.

Degrees of Sin?

To speak of an ethical continuum or a complex of righteousness and evil is to plunge us into the debate over degrees of sin and righteousness. The Bible teaches that if we sin against one point of the law we sin against the whole law. Does this not imply that sin is sin and that ultimately there are no degrees? Has not Protestantism repudiated the Roman Catholic distinction between mortal and venial sins?

These are the issues that come to the surface as soon as we begin to speak of degrees of sin. Certainly the Bible teaches that if we sin against one point of the law we sin against the whole law, but we must not infer from this that there are no degrees of sin. Sinning against the law is in reality sinning against the God of the law. When I violate one point of God's law, I bring myself in opposition to God himself. This is not to say that sinning against one point of the law is the equivalent of sinning against five points of the law. In both cases I violate the law and do violence to God, but the frequency of my violence is five times as great in the latter as in the former.

It is true that God commands perfect obedience to the whole law, so that by a single transgression I stand exposed to his judgment. The lightest sin exposes me to the wrath of God and in the smallest peccadillo I am guilty of cosmic treason. In the least transgression I set myself above the authority of God, doing insult to his majesty, his holiness, and his sovereign right to govern me. Sin is a revolutionary act in which the sinner seeks to depose God from his throne. Sin is a presumption of supreme arrogance in that the creature vaunts his own wisdom above that of the Creator, challenges divine omnipotence with human impotence, and seeks to usurp the rightful authority of the cosmic Lord.

It is true that historic Protestantism has rejected the Roman Catholic schema of mortal and venial sin. The rejection, however, is not based on a rejection of degrees of gradations of sin. Calvin, for example, argued that all sin is mortal in the sense that it rightly deserves death, but that no sin is mortal in the sense that it destroys justifying grace. Considerations other than the degrees of sin were in view in the Protestant rejection of the mortal and venial sin distinction. Historic Protestantism retained the distinction between ordinary sins and sins that are deemed gross and heinous.

The most obvious reason for the Protestant retention of degrees of sin is that the Bible abounds with such gradations. The Old Testament law had clear distinctions and provisions of penalty for different levels of criminal acts. Some sins were punishable by death, others by corporal penalties, and still others by the levying of fines. In the Jewish criminal justice system, distinctions were made between types of murder that would correspond to modern-day distinctions such as first- and second-degree murder, and voluntary and involuntary manslaughter.

The New Testament lists certain sins that demand the forfeiture of Christian fellowship for the impenitent continuance of them. At the same time,

the New Testament advocates a kind of love that
covers a multitude of sins. Warnings abound concerning a future judgment that will take into account both the number (quantity) and the severity
(quality) of our sins. Jesus speaks of those who will
receive many stripes and those who will receive
few; of the comparatively greater judgment that
will befall Chorazim and Bethsaida as opposed to
the judgment on Sodom and Gomorrah; and the
greater and lesser degree of rewards that will be
distributed to the saints. The apostle Paul warns the
Romans against heaping up wrath against the Day
of Wrath. These and a host of other passages indicate that God's judgment will be perfectly just,
measuring the number, the severity, and the extenuating circumstances that attend all of our sins.

CHAPTER 15

REVEALED ETHICS

At the heart of Christian ethics is the conviction that our firm basis for knowing the true, the good, and the right is divine revelation. Christianity is not a life system that operates on the basis of speculative reason or pragmatic expediency. We assert boldly that God has revealed to us who he is, who we are, and how we are expected to relate to him. He has revealed for us that which is pleasing to him and commanded by him. Revelation provides a supernatural aid in understanding the good. This point is so basic and so obvious that it has often been overlooked and obscured as we search for answers to particular questions.

The departure from divine revelation has brought our culture to chaos in the area of ethics. We have lost our basis of knowledge, our epistemological foundation, for discovering the good. This is not to suggest that God has given us a code book that is so detailed in its precepts that all ethical decisions become easy. That would be a vast oversimplification of the truth. God has not given us specific instructions for each and every possible ethical issue we face, but neither are we left to grope in the dark and to make our decisions on the basis of mere opinion. This is an important comfort to the Christian because when dealing with ethical questions we are never working in a vacuum. The ethical decisions that we make touch the lives of people and mold and shape human personality and character. It is precisely at this point that we need the assistance of the superiority of God's wisdom.

To be guided by God's revelation is both comforting and risky. It is comforting because we can rest in the assurance that our ethical decisions proceed from the mind of one whose wisdom is transcendent. God's law not only reflects his righteous character but also manifests his infinite wisdom. His knowledge of our humanity and his grasp of our needs for fullness of growth and development far exceed the collective wisdom of all of the world's greatest thinkers. Psychiatrists will never understand the human psyche to the degree the Creator understands that which he has made. God knows our frames; it is he who has made us so fearfully and wonderfully. All of the nuances and complexities that bombard our senses and coalesce to produce a human personality are known in their intimate details by the divine mind.

Taking comfort in divine revelation is risky business. It is risky precisely because the presence of hostility in the human heart to the rule of God makes for conflict between divine precepts and human desires. To take an ethical stand on the foundation of divine revelation is to bring one's self into serious and at times radical conflict with the opinions of men. Every day throughout this nation clergymen give counsel and advice that run contrary to the clear mandates of God. How can we explain such a hiatus between God's Word and ministerial counsel?

One critical factor in this dilemma is the fact that ministers are profoundly pressed to conform to acceptable contemporary standards. The person who comes to the minister for counsel is not always looking for guidance from a transcendent God, but rather for permission to do what he or she wants. The Christian counselor is vulnerable to sophisticated forms of manipulation coming from the very people who seek his advice. So often what is desired is a license to sin, and the minister is placed in that difficult pressure point of either acquiescing to the desires of the people or being considered unloving and fun-squelching. Add to this the cultural emphasis that there is something dehumanizing in discipline and moral restraints imposed upon us by God. Thus, to stand with God is often to stand against men and to face the fiery trials that go with such convictions.

Ethics involves the question of authority. The Christian lives under the sovereignty of God, who alone may claim sovereignty over us. Christian ethics is theocentric as opposed to secular or philosophical ethics, which tend to be anthropocentric. For the humanist, man is the norm, the ultimate standard of behavior. Christians, however, assert that God is the center of all things and that his character is the absolute standard by which questions of right and wrong are determined.

The sovereignty of God deals not only with abstract principles but with real lines of authority. God has the right to issue commands, to impose obligations, and to bind the consciences of men. Christians live in the context of theonomy. Debates about law and ethics tend to focus on two basic options—autonomy and heteronomy. Autonomy declares that man is a law unto himself. The autonomous man creates his own value system, establishes his own norms, and is answerable and accountable to man and to man alone. Heteronomy means "ruled by another." In any system of heteronomy, the individual is considered to be morally responsible to obey limits and proscriptions imposed upon him by someone else. This someone else might be another individual, a group such as the state, or even a transcendent God. When we speak of theonomy, or the rule of God, we are distinguishing a specific kind of heteronomy. Theonomy is rule by another who is identified as God. This distinction between autonomy and theonomy is the most fundamental conflict of mankind. When theonomy surrenders to autonomy, the biblical description of that surrender is sin. It is the creature's declaration of independence from his Creator.

There is an important difference between freedom and autonomy. Though autonomy is a kind of freedom, it carries the dimensions of freedom to the level of the absolute. Christianity asserts that man is given freedom by God, but that his freedom has limits. Our freedom never moves us to the point of autonomy. Some have viewed the Fall of man in Eden as a result of man's primordial grasp for autonomy—man's basal sin, the attempt to usurp the authority that belongs to God.

Friedrich Nietzsche, in trying to locate the most basic of human characteristics, located it in what he called man's lust or will to power. For Nietzsche the authentic man was the one who refused to submit to the herd morality of the masses—an existential hero who had the courage to create his own values. For man to create his own values absolutely, the first thing he must do is to declare the death of God. As long as God exists, he represents the ultimate threat to man's pretended autonomy. Jean-Paul Sartre also addressed this theme when he declared that unless freedom reaches the full measure of autonomy, it is not true freedom. Thus, Sartre stands with those who would dismiss God from the ethical arena.

Our concept of liberty has changed drastically from eighteenth-century America to twentieth-century America. The change has much to do with our understanding of autonomy. The quest for autonomy is considered by modern man to be a noble and virtuous declaration of human creativity. From the Christian vantage point, however, the quest for autonomy represents the essence of evil as it contains within its agenda the assassination of God.

The contemporary existentialist cries that "cowering in the shadow of the Almighty" is the worst thing man can do. Such human dependency upon divine assistance, he says, encourages weakness and inevitable decadence. To be sure, many people flee to Christianity because of moral weakness, but the fundamental issue is not what we regard to be preferable states of mind or psychological attitudes. The ultimate issue centers on the existence of God. It matters not whether I enjoy submitting to God. What matters first is the question, Is there a God? Without God the only possible end of ethical reflection is chaos. Dostoyevski captured this idea in *The Brothers Karamazov*, where he has one of his characters say, "If there is no God, all things are permissible."

The God of Christianity is sovereign, wise, righteous, and ultimately concerned with justice. Not only is God concerned with justice, but he assumes the role of Judge over us. It is axiomatic to Christianity that our actions will be judged. This theme is conspicuously absent in much Christian teaching today, yet it fills the New Testament and touches virtually every sermon of Jesus of Nazareth. We will be called into account for every idle word we speak. On the final day it is not our consciences that will accuse or excuse us, but God himself.

Christian ethics cannot be established in a vacuum. The Christian is not concerned with ethics for ethics' sake. We understand that rules for conduct are established in the context of God's will for human redemption. There is a real sense in which grace precedes law. The very giving of commandments by the Creator is in the context of a covenant God makes on the basis of grace. The purpose of divine commandments is redemption. The law of the Old Testament and of the New Testament is fundamentally person-oriented. To isolate this law from its basic concern for persons is to fall into the abyss of legalism. Christian ethics is built upon obedience of persons to a personal God. When God first gave the law, he did so by means of a personal introduction: "*I* am the LORD *your* God; *you* are *my* people. Therefore, *you* shall not . . ." We see that this is not law for law's sake, but for people's sake.

CHAPTER 16

LEGALISM AND ANTINOMIANISM

The continuum of ethics is divided sharply by a fine line, the razor's edge. This fine line of demarcation is similar to what Jesus described as the "narrow way." The New Testament makes frequent reference to Christians living according to "the way." Christians in the first century were called "people of the way." Jesus called his disciples to walk by the narrow way and enter by the straight gate that leads to life, while warning against the broad way that leads to destruction. There is a difference between a narrow way and narrow-mindedness. Narrow-mindedness reveals a judgmental attitude, a critical mind-set, which is far from the biblical ideal of charity. Walking the narrow way involves not a distorted mental attitude, but a clear focus of what righteousness demands.

One can deviate from the path of righteousness

by moving too far to the left or to the right. One can stumble from the narrow way by falling off the road in either direction. If we consider ethics again in terms of the model of the continuum, we know that the opposite poles, which represent distortions of authentic righteousness, may be labeled legalism and antinomianism. These twin distortions have plagued the church as long as it has been in existence. The New Testament documents reveal that struggles with both legalism and antinomianism were common in the New Testament church.

Legalism is a distortion that takes many forms. The first form of legalism involves the abstracting of the law of God from its original context. This variety of legalism reduces Christianity to a list of do's and don'ts, a codified system of rigid moralism that is divorced from the covenant context of love. To be sure, God gives rules. He pronounces do's and don'ts, but the purpose of these rules is to describe for us what is pleasing and displeasing to God. God is concerned with the attitude of the heart that one brings with him to the application of the rules. When the rules are kept for their own sake, then obedience is given to a cold abstraction known as the law rather than to a personal God who reveals the law.

A second dimension of legalism, closely related to the first, involves the divorce of the letter of the law from the spirit of the law. This is the distortion

Jesus constantly dealt with when confronting the Pharisees, and he rebukes it in the Sermon on the Mount. As we have indicated with respect to Jesus' expansion of the full import of the law in the Sermon on the Mount, it is not enough for the godly person to obey the mere externals of the law while ignoring the deeper implications of the spirit behind the law. The Pharisees became masters of external obedience coupled with internal disobedience.

The difference between spirit and letter touches the question of motive. When the Bible describes goodness, it does so in a complex way. Some are offended by the universal indictment brought against fallen mankind, which Paul articulates in his epistle to the Romans. The apostle declares that "none is righteous, no, not one; . . . no one does good, not even one" (Romans 3:11-12). Here the apostle echoes the radical statement with which Jesus replied to the question of the rich young ruler: "Why do you call me good? No one is good but God alone" (Mark 10:18). At face value, the Bible seems to teach that no one ever does a good thing in this world. This is a grim evaluation of the conduct of fallen human beings.

How are we to understand this radical judgment of human ethical conduct? The key is to be found in an analysis of the biblical definition of the good. For an action to be judged good by God, it must fulfill two primary requirements. The first is that the action outwardly corresponds to the demands of the law. In addition, the inward motivation is also considered by God. The motive for the act must proceed from a heart that is altogether disposed toward the glory of God. It is the second dimension, the spiritual dimension of motive, that disqualifies so many of our deeds from the evaluation of being good. A pagan, a person of profound corruption, may do acts externally conforming to the demands of the law. The internal motivation, however, is that of selfish interest or what the theologians call "enlightened self-interest," a motive that is not in harmony with the great commandment. Our external deeds may measure up to the external demands of the law, while at the same time our hearts are far removed from God.

Consider the example of a person driving his automobile within the context of legal speed limits. A person goes on a trip from one city to another, passing along the way a diversity of zones with differing speed limits. For cruising on the highway, the speed limit is established at sixty-five miles an hour; for moving through a suburban community's school zone, the speed limit drops to fifteen miles an hour. Suppose our driver has a preference for operating his vehicle at a speed of sixty-five miles an hour. He drives consistently at the speed he prefers. While driving on the highway, his activity is observed by policemen who note that he is driving in exact conformity to the requirements of the law, giving the appearance of the model safe driver and the upstanding and obedient citizen. He is obeying the law, however, not because he has a concern for the safety and well-being of others or out of a motive to be civilly obedient, but rather because he simply happens to enjoy driving his car at sixty-five miles an hour. This preference is noted when his car moves into the school zone and he keeps the accelerator pressed down, maintaining a speed of sixty-five miles an hour. Now, as he executes his preference, he becomes a clear and present danger, indeed a menace to children walking in the school zone. He is driving fifty miles an hour over the speed limit. His external obedience to the law vanishes when the law conflicts with his own desires.

The difference between our perception and God's is that our ability is limited to the observation of external modes of behavior. God can perceive the heart; God alone knows the deepest motives and intentions that undergird our practice and behavior. Legalism is concerned simply with external conformity and is blind to internal motivation.

Perhaps the most deadly and widespread form of legalism is that type which adds legislation to the law of God and treats the addition as if it were divine law. The Old Testament prophets expressed

God's fury at this form of behavior, lamenting the result of "binding men where God had left them free." It is a manifestation of man's fallenness to impose his own sense of propriety on other people, seeking mass conformity to his own preferences and adding insult to it by declaring these prejudices and preferences to be nothing less than the will of God. A frequent point of conflict between Jesus and the Pharisees centered on the Pharisees' traditions, which imposed hardships on the people who were bound by these man-made obligations. Jesus rebuked the Pharisees because they had elevated their traditions to the level of the law of God, seeking not only to usurp God's authority, but to oppress mankind.

The elevation of human preferences to the level of divine mandate is not limited to an isolated group of moralistic Pharisees in the first century. The problem has beset the church throughout its history. Not only do traditions develop that are added to the law of God, but in many cases they become the supreme tests of the faith, the litmus test by which people are judged to be either Christians or non-Christians. It is unthinkable in the New Testament that a person's Christian commitment would ever be determined by whether or not that person engaged in dancing, or in wearing of lipstick and the like. Unfortunately, so often when these preferences become tests of faith, they involve not only the elevation of nonbiblical mandates to the level of the will of God, but they represent the trivialization of righteousness. When these externals are elevated to the level of being measuring rods of righteousness, we begin to major in minors and obscure the real tests of righteousness.

Closely related to the elevation of human traditions to the norm of law is the problem of majoring in minors, which again was modeled by the Pharisees. The Pharisees distorted the emphasis of biblical righteousness to suit their own behavioral patterns of self-justification. Frequently Jesus confronts the Pharisees on this point. Jesus says to them, "You tithe mint and dill and cummin, and have neglected the weightier matters of the law, justice and mercy and faith." On numerous occasions Jesus acknowledges that some points of the law were scrupulously obeyed by the Pharisees. They paid their tithes, they read their Bible, they did a host of things the law required—and Jesus commended them for their actions, saying, "These you ought to have done." However, it was the emphasis that was out of kilter. They scrupulously tithed, but in doing so they used their obedience to this lesser matter as a cloak to cover up their refusal to obey the weightier matters of justice and mercy. That distortion occurs today.

Why do we have a perpetual struggle of majoring in minors? Certainly as Christians we want to be recognized for our growth in sanctification and for our righteousness. Which is easier to achieve, maturity in showing mercy and being righteous, or in the paying of tithes? To pay my tithes certainly involves a financial sacrifice of sorts, but there is a real sense in which it is cheaper for me to drop my money into the plate than it is for me to invest my life in the pursuit of justice and mercy. We tend to give God the cheapest gifts. Which is easier, to develop the gift of the fruits of the Spirit, conquering pride and covetousness, greed and impatience, or to avoid going to movie theaters or dancing? We also yearn for clearly observable measuring rods of growth. How do we measure our growth in patience or in compassion? It is much more difficult to measure the disposition of our hearts than it is to measure the number of movies we attend.

It is also our inclination as fallen creatures to emphasize as being most important those virtues in which we have achieved a relative degree of success. Naturally, I would like to think that my moral strong points are the important ones and my moral weaknesses are limited to minor matters. It is a short step from this natural inclination to a widespread distortion of where God places the emphasis.

One final type of legalism is what we call "loopholeism." Loopholeism involves getting around the law by legal and moral technicalities. Again we return to the Pharisees for the biblical model of loopholeism. The Pharisees had a clearly defined tradition about restrictions of travel on the Sabbath day. One was not permitted to travel more than a "Sabbath day's journey," which was defined by so many miles from one's home, on the Sabbath. If a Pharisee wanted to travel a distance exceeding these limits, he would take advantage of a technical provision in the law allowing one to establish separate residences during the week. He would have a traveling merchant take some articles of clothing or possessions, such as toothbrushes, and put them at strategic points along the road. Perhaps at the two-mile mark the Pharisee's toothbrush would be placed under a rock, thereby legally establishing "residence" at that rock. Now, with his legal residences defined in two-mile increments along the way, the Pharisee was free to travel from rock to rock—from "residence to residence"—and make his full trip without ever covering more than the prescribed distance from his home. Here the Sabbath-day journey principle was violated shamefully while technically being protected by the loophole.

In the decade of the sixties, Gail Green wrote a book describing the sexual behavior patterns of the American college woman. Dr. Green maintained that the prevalent ethical principle at that time was the "everything but" philosophy. Many forms of sexual activity were considered legitimate as long as the woman stopped short of actual intercourse. It seems almost naive today to think of a generation of college students who embraced an "everything but" philosophy, as those lines have fallen away since that earlier period. The mentality of the "everything but" philosophy is an example of technical loopholeism, where a person could be a virgin in the technical sense yet be involved in all sorts of premarital and extramarital sexual acts.

As legalism distorts the biblical ethic in one direction, so the opposite pole is the distortion of antinomianism. *Antinomianism* simply means "antilawism." As legalism comes in many shapes and sizes, so there are subtle forms of antinomianism that may also be delineated. We are living in a period of Christian history where antinomianism is rampant in the church.

The first type of antinomianism is libertinism, the idea that the Christian is no longer bound to obey the law of God in any way. This view of the law is often linked with the cardinal Protestant doctrine, justification by faith alone. In this view one understands justification by faith to mean that after a Christian is converted, he is no longer liable in any sense to fulfill the commandments of the law. He sees his justification as a license to sin, excusing himself by arguing that he lives by grace and not by law and is under no obligation to maintain the commandments of God.

It was the fear of such a distortion of the biblical concept of justification that was expressed by Roman Catholic theologians in the sixteenth century. They feared that Luther's insistence on justification by faith alone would open a floodgate of iniquity by those who would understand the doctrine in precisely these terms. The Lutheran movement was quick to point out that though justification is by faith alone, it is by a kind of faith that is not alone. Unless the believer's sanctification is evidenced by true conformity to the commandments of Christ, it is certain that no authentic justification ever really took place. Jesus stated it this way, "If you love me, you will keep my commandments." Christ is a commandment-giving Lord. If one has true justifying faith, he moves diligently to pursue the righteousness of obedience that Christ demands.

A second type of antinomianism may be called "gnostic spiritualism." The early gnostics, believing they had a monopoly on spiritual knowledge, plagued the Christian community. They claimed to be people "in the know," taking their name from the Greek word *gnosis*, which means "knowledge." They claimed a superior sort of mystical knowledge that gave them the right to sidestep or supplant the mandates given to the Christian community by the apostolic word. Though gnosticism as a formal doctrine has passed from the scene, many subtle varieties of this ancient heresy persist to this day. Evangelical Christians frequently fall into the trap of claiming that the Spirit of God leads them to do things that are clearly contrary to the written Word of God. I have had Christians come to me and report behavioral patterns that violated the commandments of Christ, but then say, "I prayed about this and feel at peace in the matter." Some have indeed committed outrage against the Spirit of truth and holiness by not only seeking to excuse their transgressions by appealing to some mystical sense of peace delivered to them by the Holy Ghost, but by actually laying the blame for the impulse of their sin at the feet of God the Holy Spirit. This comes perilously close to blasphemy against the Holy Spirit and certainly lies within the boundaries of grieving the Holy Spirit. The Spirit of God agrees with the Word of God. The Spirit of God is not an antinomian.

A third example of antinomianism that has made a profound impact on the Christian community in the twentieth century is the rise of situational ethics. Situational ethics is frequently known by another label, the "new morality." To identify this theory with one single individual would be a distortion. Dietrich Bonhoeffer's work on *Ethics*, Emil Brunner's *The Divine Imperative*, and Paul Lehmann's *Ethics in a Christian Context* all have contributed to situational ethics. Bishop John A. T. Robinson of *Honest to God* fame and Bishop James

Pike have also entered this discussion. But Joseph Fletcher, in *Situation Ethics*, has done more to popularize this theory than anyone else.

"There are times when a man has to push his principles aside and do the right thing." This St. Louis cabbie's remark is indicative of the style and mood of Fletcher's book. "You're so full of what's right, you can't see what's good." This is the Texas rancher's remark in *The Rainmaker*. He is one of the heroes of Fletcher's book.

The general basis for situation ethics is that there is one and only one absolute, normative ethical principle to which every human being is bound—the law of love, a law that is not always easy to discern. Fletcher realized that the word *love* is "a swampy one."

Fletcher argues that there are three basic approaches to ethical decision making: legalism, antinomianism, and situationism. He defines legalism as a preoccupation with the letter of the law. The principles of law are not merely guidelines or principles to illuminate a given situation; they are directives to be followed absolutely, preset solutions, and you can "look them up in a book." He charges that Judaism, Roman Catholicism, and Classical Protestantism have been legalistic in this sense. He points to such episodes of crass legalism in church history as the burning of homosexuals at the stake during the Middle Ages. Also in the Old Testament homosexuals were subject to the death penalty.

Antinomianism has no regard for law. Every decision is purely existential. Moral decisions are made in a random and spontaneous fashion. Fletcher sees that the legalist has too many maxims and the antinomian has none. He maintains that situationism is a middle ground for a more workable ethic. The situationist treats with respect the traditional principles of his heritage, but he is always prepared to set them aside if, in that situation, love seems better served by doing so.

Fletcher distinguishes between principles and rules: principles *guide*, rules *direct*. In working out applications of the law of love, he sets up the following working principles to serve as guidelines:

1. Pragmatism—*the good and the true are determined by that which works.*

2. Relativism—*the situationist avoids words like* never, always, perfect, *and* absolutely. *(The basic drift of secular man is to deny the existence of any absolutes. Fletcher asserts that there is one absolute as a reference point for a "normative relativism.")*

3. Positivism—*particularized,* ad hoc, *to-the-point principles. The situationist is not looking for universals; his affirmations are posited, not deduced. Faith propositions are affirmed voluntarily rather*

kind of absolutism. The limitation to *one* absolute facilitates decision making and eliminates a certain paralysis of the person who is considering many absolutes.

One of the most important insights that situation ethics offers us is that ethical decisions do not take place in a vacuum. They are made in a very real and often painful contexts. Those contexts must be considered. The high value placed on love and on the worth of persons is also a commendable trait of this position.

All these considered, however, there are still some serious inadequacies in this approach. What underlies the debate between orthodox Christianity and the situational ethicist is the question of the normativity of God's revelation in Scripture.

Fletcher oversimplifies the distinctions between and the definition of legalism, antinomianism, and situationalism. Legalism is a distortion of absolutism. Even Fletcher is an absolutist, though with just one absolute, and all of the legalistic dangers of absolutism are present in his system. One could easily legalistically obey the law of love. If this law is divorced from his context, legalism could easily emerge.

Why, when one holds more than one absolute, is the charge of legalism leveled? Haven't the situationists been simplistic and reductionistic in arbitrarily choosing love as the only absolute? God

God has not left us to make these decisions with unaided reason.

In Ephesians 5:1-3, we are given an imperative to be followers of God:

> *Therefore be imitators of God, as beloved children. And walk in love, as Christ loved us and gave himself up for us, a fragrant offering and sacrifice to God. But fornication and all impurity or covetousness must not even be named among you, as is fitting among saints.*

Here the biblical ethic is on a collision course with situationism. To be a follower of God is an absolute. At no point, in no situation, are we permitted to leave off the following of God. We are to walk in love, the kind of love embodied in the sacrificial ministry of Christ. Love stands here as an absolute—a norm. Its absolute call upon us, however, is not left entirely to the situation, informed by more "guides." The apostle immediately adds an absolute application to it involving fornication, uncleanness, and covetousness. He says, "Let it *not once* be named among you" (KJV). Paul falls into Fletcher's definition of legalism by making a universal prohibition. The apostle falls into the absolute realm of the "never."

Situationism stops with the injunction to walk in love. It must then allow for certain situations where

fornication is not only permitted but preferred. If love "demands it" in a given situation, then fornication must be practiced. How perilous is this "guideline," particularly in light of man's most ancient ploy of seduction, "If you love me, you will . . ."

It is difficult to conceive of concrete situations in which idolatry would be virtuous or coveting an expression of love. Paul concludes his admonition with a caveat: "Let no one deceive you with empty words, for it is because of these things that the wrath of God comes upon the sons of disobedience" (Ephesians 5:6).

Situationism makes the precepts of God relative, leaving us with the mandate to walk in love but to figure it out for ourselves by means of the guidelines of pragmatism, relativism, positivism, and personalism. At this point situationism is exposed as a virulent form of antinomianism masquerading as a legitimate option between legalism and antinomianism. We cannot realistically expect legalists to call themselves legalists or antinomians to plead their guilt before the world. Though Fletcher protests to the contrary, the substantive elements of antinomianism are rife in his thought.

The Christian ethicist asserts that not only does the Bible require us to do what love demands, but it reveals quite precisely at times what it is that love demands. We have directive content in the

Scriptures. We are not left with illuminators, but with divine commands.

Consider certain of the Ten Commandments from the standpoint of situationism:

"You shall have no other gods before me" unless it would seem in some situation to be the loving thing to do.

"You shall not make for yourself a graven image" unless, on the basis of foreseeable ends, means, motives and consequences, love would be best served by making a graven image. Consider Daniel's dilemma in the lions' den. He could have refrained from praying to God. Certainly the people needed his leadership. What good would he do God's people in the lions' den? Should he sell out the people and leave them without God's agent of revelation for a simple principle of prayer? The end that he wants is survival. His means are to obey the king. His motive is to serve the people of God. The foreseeable consequences would be that some people might be disappointed, but he would be able to make up for that by being a leader and guide to them. So Daniel should receive the blessing of God for doing the loving thing and abstain from prayer to his God.

One of the uniquenesses of the true people of God is not legalism, but fidelity, trust, and obedience to God. Obeying the law to love God is not legalism. When we consider Christ's obedience to

God and to the law, it seems impossible not to regard situationism as a serious heretical distortion of the biblical ethic.

There is a principle in the biblical ethic that is rarely seen in the writings of the situationists. They fail to emphasize, as does the Bible, that doing what love demands, what Christ commands, often means the bearing of unspeakable suffering. It means to participate in radical humiliation and to count one's life as nothing for the exaltation of Christ. It may mean spending a life rotting in a cell in a concentration camp rather than to violate the commandment of Christ.

Christ's statement about love is our norm: "If you love me, you will keep my commandments" (John 14:15). The proof of our love is obedience to Christ's commandments. Situation ethics establishes a false dichotomy between love and obedience. Situation ethics fails because it does not take love seriously enough.

We turn our attention now to specific questions of ethics that have become particularly controversial in our times—questions of materialism, capital punishment, war, and abortion.

CHAPTER 17

THE ETHICS OF MATERIALISM

Materialism has become a controversial issue in the church today, especially with the emergence of Christian youth movements. Several groups have made this a central issue of debate, speaking of materialism, not in the metaphysical sense, but rather in the economic sense: "That world view which places the accumulation of material things at the zenith of private and corporate concern." The pursuit of wealth is seen as the highest good in materialism.

At the other end of the spectrum is a view called "spiritualism," or better, "idealism," which sees that only spiritual values are worthy of human pursuit.

The biblical position repudiates both of these positions. Though material things are not the highest

good, neither are they intrinsically evil. There is no room for radical asceticism or monasticism in the church, as these positions are world denying and creation denying. It is important to recognize that in the Old Covenant and in the New, many of God's redemptive promises relate to creation—promises to redeem the physical world. The promise to Abraham and to his seed includes at its heart the promise of land and the promise of prosperity.

The principle of private property is pivotal to discussions of materialism. Many have argued that some kind of communal living or equal distribution of wealth is the only acceptable Christian norm, based on the presupposition that the concept of private property is illegitimate for the Christian. However, the concept of private property is inseparably related to the creation ordinance that sanctifies labor. Karl Marx did something of inestimable and lasting value for the history of the development of thought for Western man by making it impossible to conceive of the history of man without considering man's labor and the fruit of his labor as having influenced his development greatly. This is not to endorse Marxism but to recognize the crucial relationship between man and his labor. When man involves himself in labor, he involves himself with his responsibility of being made in the image of God.

The sanctity of labor is first of all instituted by the

labor of God himself in creation. Labor, in creation is a duty and a blessing, not a curse. The curse that is attached to labor after the Fall has to do with the quality of work and the difficulty of our labor by which we bring forth fruit. The thorns and the sweat, not the work itself, are the curse. Pre-Fall man existed in a condition where he labored, and that labor produced fruit, which he had the right to enjoy.

Even after the Fall, we have no indication that private property (the fruit of one's labor) is condemned or prohibited by God. Indeed, the first liturgical acts observed in the Old Testament are Cain and Abel presenting their offerings. Notice that the offerings were considered valid because they gave from what actually belonged to them. The offertory system of the Old Testament makes no sense when divorced from the system of private property. The right of human ownership is something God has assigned as part of our covenant partnership with him in creation. Though all ownership is answerable to divine ownership in the long run, this does not invalidate the concept of private property.

Examining the Decalogue, we see that private property is assumed in several situations. The prohibition against stealing presupposes private property, as does the prohibition against covetousness.

We can get a better understanding of the relationship between labor and property by examining the

Sabbath commandment. One of the things that is often overlooked is that not only does the commandment concern itself with the seventh day, but also with the first six. "Six days you shall labor" (Exodus 20:9). The day of rest makes no sense apart from the six days of labor preceding it. The sanctity of labor is the basis for private property. In both the Old and New Covenants, the call to labor is an emphatic one, bringing forth fruit as its just reward. The avoidance of labor is regarded as sin. Paul commands labor as an ethical norm. Idleness has no place in the New Testament ethic. In 2 Thessalonians 3:12, Paul says that persons should "earn their own living." In 1 Timothy 5:8, Paul adds that lack of provision for one's household makes one worse than an unbeliever.

There are two important conclusions to be drawn from these statements. First, there is the right of private property as the fruit of one's labor. Second, there is the responsibility of *honest* and *diligent* labor. Because we live to the glory of God, we have the responsibility to render an "honest day's labor." Our labor must not be for the simple end of the acquisition of wealth, but it should be for the glory of God.

This raises the problem of wealth, that is, the accumulation of material goods beyond the level of necessity. Are we permitted to earn and keep more than we need? We are indeed. The possession of

wealth is nowhere condemned in either Old Testament or New Testament. The means of acquiring wealth are clearly regulated: exploitation, fraud, dishonesty, oppression, and power politics are all condemned. Prosperity and wealth are seen as an aspect of God's providence. This is one of the reasons why covetousness is such a weighty matter. When I covet, I am protesting against God's distribution of wealth. Abraham was perhaps one of the richest men in antiquity. Noah and Job were both wealthy men. Not only does God never condemn this wealth, but he legitimizes the passing of the wealth from generation to generation by means of inheritance. The patriarchal blessings, which pass on the material blessings, are part of the messianic redemptive promise, including the promise of land.

In the New Testament we encounter wealthy men who are praiseworthy. Note the care of the body of Christ, after the Crucifixion, by Joseph of Arimathea, obviously a man of means.

What the New Testament says is that wealth imposes severe temptations. Jesus' statement about the camel going through the gate of Jerusalem, "the eye of a needle," indicates that a rich man who would enter heaven faces a huge task. Practically speaking, the maintenance and protection of wealth takes time and concentrated energy. The parable of the rich fool illustrates the perils of preoccupation with riches. It is easy for the rich man to

confuse his priorities. It is also easy for the poor man. It is not merely the rich who are susceptible to the siren call of materialism; its seductive power crosses all of the socioeconomic borders.

What about the Christian's responsibility to the poor? This, of course, touches the heart of the matter of materialism. Obviously, the provision for the needs of the poor is a Christian responsibility. In the Old Testament the needs of the poor were met somewhat by the laws, which included provisions for gleaners. The principle of bringing offerings to the needy is a practice enjoined by both covenants. The collection of provisions by the Gentile Christians for famine-struck Jerusalem was one of the most notable and dramatic episodes in the first century. Both the Corinthian and the Philippian churches are praised by Paul for their generosity. The interesting thing is that the need was prophesied and a relief fund established in advance. The principle of almsgiving is important to both covenants. When my brother is in need, I must attempt to meet that need.

Who Are the Poor?

"You always have the poor with you." This statement by Jesus has been taken by some as a license to neglect the poor as if Jesus were saying, "Oh, well, we always have poverty in our midst, so

than rationally, being more acts of the will than of the mind. We cannot prove our concept of love. The end product of our ethic is a decision, not a conclusion.

4. Personalism—*ethics deal with human relationships. The legalist is a "what-asker": what does the law say? The situationist is a "whoasker": who is to be helped? The emphasis is on people rather than on ideas or principles in the abstract.*

We still have the question, What do we ask ourselves to discover what love demands in a given situation? How do we protect ourselves from a distorted view of love? Fletcher offers four questions to consider.

1. The end: *for what result are we aiming?*

2. Means: *how may we secure this end?*

3. Motive: *why is that our aim?*

4. Consequences: *what forseeably might happen?*

All of these need to be considered before an ethical decision can be made.

There are some positive aspects about this system of situation ethics, as some of the principles involved are commendable. First, situation ethics is not absolute relativism. It is a normative ethic, a

LEGALISM AND ANTINOMIANISM

has laid more than one absolute requirement upon man. There is nothing in reason *or* revelation that would cause one to isolate love as the only absolute. When questioned, these men appeal to Scripture and the teachings of Jesus and Paul. But they are quite selective about their appeal to Scripture, falling into the quandary of the ethically arbitrary.

Related to this, the most serious deficiency of Fletcher's system is the problem of how we determine what love demands. We agree with the principle that one should do what love demands. But Fletcher has problems in determining these demands. Certainly the Bible teaches us to do what love commands, and the content of love is defined by God's revelation. Doing what love demands is the same as saying, "Do what God commands." If we obeyed the Scriptures like a sterile book of rules, we would be legalists. But if we see the Bible as being the revelation of the one who is Love, then we must take seriously what Love has commanded.

When we are left to make an ethical decision, knowing that we are fallen; knowing that we are given over to vices; knowing that we can never perfectly read our own motives; knowing that we are limited to foreseeable consequences; knowing that we can never comprehensively analyze the ends and the means; knowing all these things, we have a very precarious situation on our hands *if* we have rejected the Bible as normative revelation.

don't worry about it." Jesus recognized the perpetual plight of the poor, not to ignore it, but to call the Christian community to constant diligence in dealing with the problem.

In identifying the "poor" described in the Bible we can distinguish at least four different major categories of "poor" people. What follows is a brief description of these groups.

1. *The Poor As a Result of Slothfulness.* The Bible speaks of those who are poor because they are lazy, refusing to work. This indolent group receives sharp criticism from God and comes under his holy judgment. Karl Barth listed sloth as one of the primary and foundational sins of man, along with pride and dishonesty. It is to the slothful that God says, "Go to the ant, O sluggard; consider her ways" (Proverbs 6:6), shaming the lazy by telling them to go to insects for instruction. It is this group Paul undoubtedly has in mind when he says, "If any one will not work, let him not eat."

Since the Bible does criticize the lazy poor, some have jumped to the conclusion that indolence and poverty are synonymous. Some assume that poverty is always and everywhere a sign of sloth. Thus the poor can be righteously shunned as they are left to suffer their "just penalty for sloth." Such attitudes reflect a woeful ignorance of or callous disregard for distinctions the Bible forces us to make. There are other reasons for poverty.

2. *The Poor As a Result of Calamity.* The Scriptures recognize that many are left in poverty because of the ravages of disease or disasters. The man born blind or the person left crippled by an accident, the farmer whose crops have been destroyed by flood or drought, all have just cause for their impoverished estate. These people are victims of circumstances not of their own making. For these "poor" the Bible adopts an attitude of compassion and genuine charity. It is the responsibility of the people of God to see to it that the suffering of these people is ameliorated. They are to be a priority concern of the church. These are the hungry who are to be fed, the naked who are to be clothed.

3. *The Poor As a Result of Exploitation.* This group of poor are also oppressed. These are the masses who are frustrated daily by their inability to "fight city hall," the ones who live out the mournful slogan "the rich get richer and the poor get poorer." This group suffers indignities when they live in societies where the social and political institutions, and especially the judicial systems, favor the rich and the powerful and leave the poor without advocacy. Such was the condition of Israel in the eighth century B.C. when God thundered against his people. The word of God came via prophetic criticism that demanded justice and righteousness in a time when the poor were being sold "for a pair of shoes." This was Israel's status when in bondage to

Egypt. This kind of poverty moves God himself as he hears the cries and groans of his oppressed people and says, "Let my people go!" Such injustice and inequity should always "move" God's church. This is the church's basis for necessary and legitimate social action.

4. *The Poor As a Result of Personal Sacrifice.* These poor people are designated by the New Testament as being poor "for righteousness' sake." This group, whose chief representative is Jesus himself, is made up of people who are voluntarily poor. Their poverty is a result of a conscious decision to choose life-styles or vocations with little or no financial remuneration. This class of poor is promised special blessings from God. They are poor because the priorities of their lives may not mesh with the value standards of the culture in which they live. It is Jonathan Edwards, writing in almost microscopic print in order to conserve paper because of his meager stipend (ultimately costing the church and universities hundreds of thousands of dollars to retrieve and reconstruct the priceless treasures of his words); it is Martin Luther, forgoing a promising and lucrative career to wear the habit of the monk; it is the modern businessman who passes up the windfall deal because he has scruples about hidden unethical elements.

What can we learn from these four designations? In the first instance we should be warned not to lump all the poor together in one package. We must resist the tendency to generalize about poverty. An equally insistent warning must be voiced about the same kind of unjust grouping together of the rich. It would be slanderous to maintain that all rich people are corrupt, as if all riches were achieved through evil means or through exploiting the poor. Not all rich people are avaricious or ruthless. To indict the rich indiscriminately would be to condemn the likes of Abraham, Job, David, and Joseph of Arimathea.

Second, we must avoid a theological glamorizing of poverty. Throughout church history there have been repeated efforts to make poverty the precondition for entrance to the kingdom. It has been seen as a form of works righteousness whereby the poor have an automatic ticket into heaven. This substitutes justification by poverty for justification by faith.

Third, we must recognize that God cares deeply about human poverty and the consequent suffering. Our duty is to be no less concerned than God himself. As long as the poor are with us, we are called to minister to them, not only via charity, but by seeking and working for the reformation of social and political structures that enslave, oppress, and exploit.

The basic principle regarding wealth is the principle of stewardship, that a man is responsible for what he does with what he receives. He is not called to liquidate his assets; he is called to give as the Lord prospers him. The characteristic of Christian living is not communism, but charity.

The New Testament word for stewardship is the Greek *oikonomia*, from which we derive the English term *economy*. It comes from a combination of two Greek roots, *oikos*, which means "house," and *nomos*, which means "law." Literally, *economy* means "house rule." In antiquity the steward was not the owner of the house but its manager. He was responsible for the care and management of the house. Biblical economics recognizes God's ultimate ownership of the earth and man's duty to manage the earth responsibly.

The science of economics is not a neutral science divorced from ethical considerations. Economics involves questions of stewardship, the use of wealth, and private and public decisions of value, all of which impinge upon ethics. Each time we make a value judgment or render a decision to make use of material goods, we have made an ethical decision. That God is concerned with the material well-being of the world is axiomatic. Man has been called to be a steward of the earth.

The science of economics has become so complex in our day that it has obscured some of the primary principles found in the Scriptures. Though the Bible is not a textbook on economics, it does set forth basic principles that touch upon economic endeavor. As already mentioned, the Bible clearly sets forth the right of private property. But in addition to this right we also see a concern for equity, for industry, and for compassion. It is not by accident that virtually every major economic system in Western culture has appealed at one point or another to the Bible for its sanctions. Historic capitalism tends to emphasize the principles of private property, equity, and industry, while sometimes neglecting the responsibility for compassion. On the other hand, socialistic forms of economics have emphasized compassion, at times obscuring the rights of private property and undermining the importance of industry and equity. The socialist's ultimate goal is not equity but equality. That is, the socialist seeks a transfer society with the ideal of an egalitarian or equalized distribution of wealth. The goal is noble and virtuous; we would expect that in an idealized society, every member would have equal participation in the wealth of the society. But we live in a fallen world, where the only way we can have equality of economic welfare is to shut our eyes to the biblical principle of equity. To achieve equality we would have to penalize the producer and the industrious by taking their goods from them and distributing them to those who have been less than responsible stewards. Such a principle does violence to the biblical notion of justice.

If we look at the most elementary principles of economics in their foundational form we see a causal nexus, a formula that must not be violated if we are to grapple with the economic issues of our day. The formula may be seen in the following diagram:

MAN'S MATERIAL WELL-BEING
↓
PRODUCTION
↓
TOOLS
↓
INVESTMENT CAPITAL
↓
PROFITS

We see that there is a causal relationship among these factors. The single most important ingredient for man's material well-being is production. If we are going to feed the hungry, clothe the naked, and give shelter to the homeless, we must be able to produce the goods necessary to meet these needs. Man's physical life is dependent upon production for human survival. Unless we produce food, we will starve; unless we manufacture clothes, we will be naked. Unless homes are built, we will be shelterless. God does care about the human body as well as the human soul, and so production becomes a vital ethical concern for Christians.

If we follow our causal reasoning and ask what is

the single most important necessary ingredient for production, we would answer tools. Marx was astute in his understanding of the central significance of tools to man's increased capacity for production. The reason a peasant in an underdeveloped country cannot produce as much food as a farmer in the industrialized West is not that the body of the Western farmer is stronger, but that the Western farmer has at his disposal labor-saving devices that increase production. The machine more than any other single factor has been responsible for the explosion of man's ability to produce.

The next question we raise is, What is the most important single ingredient for the acquisition of tools? Obviously that ingredient is capital. The primary difference between the peasant in the underdeveloped nation and the Western farmer is at the level of tools. It is not that tools are not available in the world to be used by underprivileged persons, but rather that those without money cannot purchase the tools they need for increased production. Tools cost money to build, to buy, and to maintain.

Where does one get the money to purchase tools? The needed capital is what we would call surplus capital. Surplus capital is a result of profits. Thus, profit is the single most important ingredient necessary for capital to be available to buy tools, to increase production, and to increase the material welfare of a nation. But the term *profit* has become virtually an obscenity in the vocabulary of modern man, particularly among Christians. What we often fail to take into account is that the profit motive is not restricted to large industrial corporations or the superrich magnates and tycoons of industry. The profit motive is at the heart of all economic exchange. The goal or purpose of economic exchange is always and everywhere profit. This statement may appear on the surface to be outrageous, but let us take a moment to examine its implications.

When a business transaction takes place, when a customer buys a pair of shoes, for example, who realizes a profit? Often the answer is that the shoe salesman or the owner of the shoe store makes the profit. But the shoemaker cannot make a profit unless first the customer considers it profitable for him to buy the shoes. The business transaction takes place when the customer values the shoes more than he values the money he must pay for them. Then trade takes place. The customer trades his money for the shoemaker's shoes. The shoemaker can in turn exchange that money for other goods that he values more than the money. Thus, in any business transaction the goal is mutual profit. Both sides must profit or the exchange will not take place, unless the exchange is made necessary by some form of external coercion. This principle is based on the fact that material values are subjective to the extent that not every person values everything to the same degree.

The man who has a surplus of shoes but a lack of food will be eager to make a trade with the man who has a surplus of food but needs shoes. In the transaction one man values shoes more than meat, while the other values meat more than shoes, so a trade situation exists in which both persons profit according to the values they are seeking.

Profit is good in the sense that it is necessary for the whole community of mankind to survive in a relationship of mutual interdependence. No man is altogether self-sufficient. Each person is dependent to some degree on the gifts and talents of production of other people. The marketplace is where these gifts and talents are exchanged—a place of mutual profit, if the coercive dimension is absent. It is from the surplus of profit that tools can be purchased, production increased, and the general wealth of a nation strengthened. Christians must remember this lest they become participants in schemes by which surplus capital is siphoned off and redistributed in a way that quenches the ability of a nation or a community to be productive.

The protection of private property is so vital to the biblical ethic that repeatedly we have prohibitions and sanctions against stealing. But stealing can happen in a multitude of ways, some of which are very subtle. The outright grabbing and carrying off of another person's property is an obvious form of stealing, but stealing can also be accomplished through fraud, by failing to live up to contracts, by using false weights and measures, or even by intentional debasing of currency within a society. All of these means receive the severe indictment of God. One of the most subtle forms of theft is one that is perpetrated through the political system. When people use the power of the ballot box to vote for themselves subsidies from the general coffers, it is a sophisticated form of stealing. For example, if three people live together in a town and one is more wealthy than the other two, the two persons of lesser wealth can conspire together to pass a law forcing the wealthier person to distribute his goods to them. Here the power of political force is used to strip the wealthy man of his wealth and distribute it to the other two, who have voted for themselves this particular distribution of wealth. Christians need to be sensitive about how they use the power of the ballot.

CHAPTER 18

THE ETHICS OF
CAPITAL PUNISHMENT

The issue of capital punishment has been so volatile that it has set Christian against Christian,
church against church, conservative against conservative, and liberal against liberal. The problem
is complex, touching the deeper question of the
value, dignity, and sanctity of human life. Any
study of capital punishment must begin with an
understanding of the primary function of government as originally ordained by God. Romans 13:1-
7 is the classic text concerning God's ordination of
government. This text is the most comprehensive
and emphatic statement that the Scriptures give us
regarding the notion that the power of government
is rooted in the ordination of God. It is important
to note that the apostle is not speaking here of a

theocratic state but of secular government. The text of Romans reads as follows:

> Let every person be subject to the governing authorities. For there is no authority except from God, and those that exist have been instituted by God. Therefore he who resists the authorities resists what God has appointed, and those who resist will incur judgment. For rulers are not a terror to good conduct, but to bad. Would you have no fear of him who is in authority? Then do what is good, and you will receive his approval, for he is God's servant for your good. But if you do wrong, be afraid, for he does not bear the sword in vain; he is the servant of God to execute his wrath on the wrongdoer. Therefore one must be subject, not only to avoid God's wrath but also for the sake of conscience. For the same reason you also pay taxes, for the authorities are ministers of God, attending to this very thing. Pay all of them their dues, taxes to whom taxes are due, revenue to whom revenue is due, respect to whom respect is due, honor to whom honor is due.

The "governing authorities" are understood to be ordained by God. We are not privileged to obey only those authorities that we consider to be legitimate. It is a *de facto* matter, not a *de juro* matter. God certainly does not endorse everything civil magistrates do, but he does give them certain rights and requires our obedience to them. No government rules autonomously. All civil authorities must, and ultimately will, answer to God. We have the responsibility of obeying even corrupt governments except under certain conditions. Civil obedience is required repeatedly by the Word of God. The principle that governs our right and responsibility to disobey civil authority is this: we must obey those in authority over us unless they command us to do what God forbids or forbid us to do what God commands.

Biblically there are two basic rights that God has given to government: one, the right to levy taxes; two, the coercion of their subjects for the power of administering the state (the power of the sword).

Government was made necessary and legitimate because of the fall of man. The state was ordained to be God's deputy minister for the primary purpose of the restraint of evil. The first appearance of government in the Bible is found in the opening chapters of Genesis, when Adam and Eve were expelled from the garden and consigned to live east of Eden. The entrance to the garden was barred by the presence of an angel with a flaming sword. Here we see the appointment of a ministering agent, namely, the angel who is equipped by God with an instrument of restraint and is granted the power of coercion which is symbolized by the flaming sword.

The central duty of government is to enforce the laws that are designed to restrain evil. It was St. Augustine who said, "Sin is the mother of servitude and is the first cause of man's subjection to man." Augustine argued that government is a necessary evil, in fact, an evil made necessary by the prior presence of evil in the human heart. It is because men are prone to violating each other that government is established to check the strong and ruthless who exploit and oppress the weak and the innocent. Government is necessary because men do not live to the glory of God, loving him with all of their hearts and their neighbors as themselves. The only ultimate alternative to government is anarchy, in which each man lives for himself. Thus, government was instituted as an act of God's grace to protect the weak and the righteous from the wicked. The authority of the state is not an intrinsic authority but that which is derived from the authority of God.

The issue of capital punishment emerges when we examine the right of the state to bear the sword. In the first instance the sword is seen as an instrument of coercion. I once had a conversation with a United States senator who said to me, "No government ever has the right to coerce its subjects to do anything." I was shocked by the senator's statement and replied, "Senator, you have just stated that no government has the right to govern." The power of coercion is the essence of government. Perhaps the simplest definition we can find for *government* is the word "force." In a very real sense government is force. If you take away the government's right to coerce, you take away the government's right to govern, leaving the government with the impotent authority of rule by suggestion. The power of the sword is the arm of the government we call law enforcement, without which the law represents merely a list of suggestions. Nor did God give the sword to the civil magistrate as a means of intimidation for rattling only. In biblical categories the expression "power of the sword" is seen clearly as an idiomatic expression to indicate the power to kill.

At this point the issue of capital punishment comes to the fore. In the Old Testament we first read of the institution of capital punishment in the narrative of creation. In the garden there was one restraint, one prohibition given to man. The clear-cut punishment for disobedience of this command was instant death. "The day that you eat of it you shall die." It is important to note that when man sinned, God did not invoke the full measure of the punishment for disobedience. Indeed, capital punishment came upon the race, but it was postponed in terms of its implementation. Originally all sin was regarded as a capital offense. Capital punishment was the divine judgment for any and all sin. However, God reserved the right to replace justice with mercy according to his own prerogatives. Because God has not executed that punishment consistently and immediately—except on rare occasions such as the case of Uzza, Nadab and Abihu, Ananias and Sapphira—the world tends to take God's mercy for granted and has come to the place where in some circles capital punishment is considered to be cruel and unusual punishment for any crime.

In the old covenant God reduced the number of capital offenses and limited the penalty to approximately thirty-five specific crimes. The New Testament exhibits an even more gracious dispensation, with a further reduction of capital offenses.

Before the institution of the law at Sinai we have an even more important statement, found in the covenant God made with Noah. Here we see a covenant that renews the ordinances of creation, a renewal of God's rule for man as man. There is a certain sense in which the laws of this creation covenant are of far broader import than even that legislation found in Israel or in the New Testament. Here God proposes legislation for man as man, not for man as Jew or man as Christian. Man *qua* man is the one who receives the stipulations of the covenant of creation. It is therefore significant that capital punishment for murder is built into creation and presumably is binding as long as creation is intact. The renewal legislation is found in Genesis

9:6: "Whoever sheds the blood of man, by man shall his blood be shed; for God made man in his own image." This text is a command, not a future prediction. The sanction is clear. If a person murders another person, God requires that the murderer be put to death by human hands.

It is ironic that both sides of the dispute on capital punishment tend to base their arguments on the principle of the sanctity of life. The humanist argues that human life is so valuable that we are never justified in taking another person's life. From a biblical perspective the humanist view actually reflects a lower view of the sanctity of life than that found in Genesis 9:6. From the vantage point of the twentieth century we tend to view the Old Testament society as severe and savage, forgetting that it already manifested an enormous reduction in capital offenses. These reductions in capital offenses did not come about because God changed his mind and saw that his former policies were too cruel and severe, but partially because the responsibility for the execution of justice in the New Testament moved out of the hands of the theocratic state and into the hands of the secular state.

The question of how many crimes are considered "capital" in the New Testament is one that is open to lengthy debate. The only crime that we can be certain is a capital offense is first-degree murder. In the Decalogue of the Old Testament there is a clear prohibition against murder. But the broader legislation of Mount Sinai included within it several distinctions with respect to degrees of murder. The establishment of the cities of refuge, for example, dealt with the problem of involuntary manslaughter. The penalty for transgressing the prohibition in the Ten Commandments, "You shall not kill," was capital punishment.

It is ironic that many have appealed to the Ten Commandments as a basis for repudiating capital punishment, taking the prohibition "You shall not kill" as a universal mandate. This comes from a superficial reading of the Sinaitic legislation and a failure to observe that within the context of the Sinai covenant the penalty for violating that commandment was death. The holiness code of Israel clearly called for the death penalty in the case of the murder of another human being. The murderer must forfeit his own life. The reason given for the special sanctity of human life is the fact that man is created in the image of God. God is concerned with preserving the work of his creation, and at the top of his priorities is the preservation of the life of man. There is a sense in which the commission of murder is regarded by God as an indirect assault on him. Just as an attack on an ambassador of a king is seen as an affront to the king, so the murderer is guilty of committing an assault against the very life of God, inasmuch as he has desecrated one made in God's image. It is important to understand that power over life is not rescinded in the New Covenant but is mentioned again in Romans as a prerogative of the state. Thus, the Scriptures uniformly assert the propriety of capital punishment in the case of murder.

When we apply the principle of capital punishment to a given society or to a given culture, we must be careful lest we plunge into the matter without considering some of the other ramifications of the biblical sanctions. Though capital punishment was imposed in the Old Testament, it was circumscribed by other principles that were very important to the entire justice process. In the Old Testament, justice was truly blind under the law. The rich were to be given no special privileges before the bar of justice. That ideal exists in our own society, but at a practical level there are too many circumstances in which Lady Justice peeks or removes her blindfold altogether to take note of the rich and the powerful who are her suitors. Under the Old Covenant no one could be convicted of a capital offense on the basis of circumstantial evidence. Two or three eyewitnesses were required, and their testimony had to agree. If the witnesses who testified in a capital trial were found guilty of perjury, the penalty for bearing such false witness was itself death. There is no question that we need reforms to protect inequities of the application of capital punishment in our modern culture, but when we object to capital punishment in principle, we are objecting to a sanction God himself ordained.

CHAPTER 19

THE ETHICS OF WAR

The issue of a Christian's involvement in war is an extension of the more primary question of capital punishment. In a certain sense war is capital punishment on a grand scale. It involves the civil magistrates' widespread use of the power of the sword. Basically there have been three foundational positions taken regarding war in past Christian history:

1. *Activism*
2. *Pacifism*
3. *Selectivism*

Activism is a simplistic approach to war that views all wars as being permissible. It reflects the position that the subjects of the state are to give absolute obedience to the civil magistrate regardless of the situation. It reflects the simple cliché "My country, right or wrong." This is basically an uncritical approach that has little to do with the biblical ethic.

Pacifism, on the other hand, says that all wars are wrong and all people's involvement in war is wrong. The pacifist view would restrict Christians from participating in any kind of war.

The third variety is called selectivism, which maintains that involvement in some wars may be justifiable. It is within the context of selectivism that the basis for the just war theory has emerged in Christian history.

A sophisticated argument by pacifists who are Christians is based on the ethical mandates Christ gave his people, whereby he prohibited the Christian from the use of retaliatory violence and uttered a clear prohibition against building his kingdom with the sword. The pacifist transfers these prohibitions from the sphere of the church to the sphere of government. Here not only is the private citizen or the ecclesiastical authority forbidden the use of the sword but the state is prohibited as well. Some divide the question by admitting that the state has the power of the sword, but Christians are not to participate in the state's function. The question that is raised immediately is, On what grounds would a Christian refuse to obey a civil magistrate who calls the Christian to do something that is within the scope of righteousness? If God commands the state to bear the sword and the state conscripts the Christian to help him with that task, on what moral grounds could the Christian possibly refuse to comply?

The Swiss theologian Emil Brunner has remarked, "To deny on ethical grounds the elementary right of the state to defend itself by war simply means to deny the existence of the state itself. Pacifism of the absolutist variety is practical anarchy." Helmut Thielicke has added his judgment that pacifism is a moral cop-out. He draws a parallel between pacifism and a situation where the Christian is a witness to murder and stands by and allows it to happen without interference. Thielicke argues that it is not only our responsibility to minister to a man who has been mutilated by robbers, such as the man going down to Jericho, but we are to love our neighbor by preventing the crime as well.

Selectivism proceeds from the fundamental premise that all wars are wrong but that not everyone's involvement in a war is wrong. The particular circumstances and situations must be evaluated on each occasion to discern which side, if either, has a righteous cause to defend. The victim of a clear-cut act of aggression would have the right of self-defense, according to the selective view.

CHAPTER 20

THE ETHICS OF ABORTION

Abortion is a monumental issue that ignites heated debates. Divisions in the state and in the church are multiplying, with major denominational church bodies coming down on both sides of the issue. The fires of controversy show no signs of abating, but rather of intensifying.

In dealing with this issue, three major questions must be answered:

1. What is abortion?

2. Is abortion right or is it wrong? Or is it possibly without moral bearing?

3. Does the church have the right to advocate civil legislation on this question? Some church bodies have advocated a "middle way" under the rubric of "pro-choice," arguing that this should be a matter of conscience, not of civil legislation, and that it is wrong for the state to prohibit abortion.

The Biblical Basis for Discussion

No teaching in the Old Testament or New Testament explicitly condemns or condones abortion. Exegetically, the debate has been waged on implicit grounds. The Old Testament passage that has received the greatest attention concerning this matter is Exodus 21:22-24.

When men strive together, and hurt a woman with child, so that there is a miscarriage, and yet no harm follows, the one who hurt her shall be fined, according as the woman's husband shall lay upon him; and he shall pay as the judges determine. If any harm follows, then you shall give life for life, eye for eye, tooth for tooth, hand for hand, foot for foot.

There is a built-in ambiguity with this text, giving rise to differing interpretations of its precise meaning and application. The theological house is divided between "maximum" and "minimum" positions. The problem centers in the words *no harm follows*. To what "harm" does the verse refer? This problem is linked to another, namely the question of what is meant by the "miscarriage" of the pregnant woman. Is the text referring to an incident where the woman, being jostled by fighting men, is induced to a premature childbirth in which the anguish and inconvenience of premature delivery is recompensed by the law even though the premature child lives and thrives? Or is the text speaking of a case where the induced premature birth yields a stillborn fetus and further considerations come into play only if the mother suffers additional complications, even death?

The Old Testament scholar Keil adopts the maximum view, arguing that the "no harm follows" clause refers to both mother and child. The summary is that if the premature baby survives, recompense is limited to damages paid for the inconvenience and mental anguish provoked as claimed by the husband and awarded by the judge. But if the child is harmed or dies, the full measure of the *lex talonis* (eye for eye) is to apply. In this reading the unborn fetus is so highly valued by Scripture that the life-for-life principle is applied, and the unintentional causing of abortion "in the midst of another felonious act" warrants the death penalty. If this interpretation is correct, we would have decisive evidence that Scripture considers the unborn fetus as "life" in the fullest legal sense.

The minimal view of the text argues that the "no harm follows" clause refers exclusively to the mother. In this schema the net result would be that the aborted or premature birth of the fetus would not invoke the *lex talonis* or legally be considered murder or loss of life. Only if further complications affect the mother does the "eye for eye, life for life" equation apply. The inference then would be that Scripture does not regard the fetus as "life." The fetus is protected by the law, however, and its *value* may be established via a law suit. Some push it further by arguing that though legal indemnities *may* be imposed, they are initiated by the claims of the husband. The unspoken presumption is that the "value" of the fetus is determined to some degree by the subjective values attached by the parents. In this "case" the Scriptures deal with an abortion or miscarriage imposed from without, apart from the design of the parents, who presumably desire the pregnancy to reach its full term. The passage is then made of no consequence to the question of an intentional abortion performed according to the will and design of the parents. The minimal view thus protects the parents and not the fetus.

The difference between these interpretations covers the gamut of the contemporary debate. Though I am persuaded of the maximal interpretation, I must admit the problematic and ambiguous character of the text.

In the New Testament the word *abortion* is used only in a figurative sense. One passage often cited to support an antiabortion stance is Luke 1:39-42, when Mary visited Elizabeth and the child "leaped in her womb." Other passages that speak of persons being conceived in sin and known by God in the womb are also referred to. The question exegetically is whether or not these allusions are to be taken as religious hyperbole or poetry. However, the message of these passages clearly indicates that God is involved with man's history prior to his birth.

The question of when life begins has been pivotal to the discussion. Agreement is difficult because no consensus has emerged. Different points on the conception-birth continuum have been proferred, with the added problem of variant medical definitions of "life" itself.

There are some who maintain that the moment of birth is when a fetus becomes a person. There are good reasons for this argument. This is a rather clear line of demarcation, indicating a new status, a new moment of independent existence with *individuation* beginning with the snipping of the umbilical cord.

Another view points to the moment of "quickening"; another to the time when the circulatory system is fully developed. Others say that the principle of life in the Old Testament is the "breath" of life in man. Therefore, life would be present when the lungs develop and the fetus could breathe on its own.

The moment of conception has been seen by many groups to be the beginning of life, since all the potentiality of personhood is then present. David and others speak of their conception as part of their personal history.

What we conceive the fetus to be will determine what value we assign it. There are those who say that the embryo (the term usually used to refer to the product of conception during its first twelve weeks) is nothing more than a blob of protoplasm. Others argue that it is merely a highly specialized form of parasite. It has been compared to a cancer, a tissue growth foreign to the mother, which the body seeks to reject. If the mother fails to reject it, it would be fatal to her. Certainly these are emotive terms that greatly cloud the issue and represent an irresponsible approach to the question.

To refer to an embryo as a blob of protoplasm is to be guilty of a severe form of reductionism. The "parasite" term is equally inaccurate, as parasites have an independent life cycle that includes repro-duction. As for the analogy to cancer, a cancer left to natural development destroys life. An embryo left to natural development produces life—a differ-ence that cannot be ignored.

The crucial concern here is that we can say with certainty that at any stage of development the fetus is a potential life, a potential human being, with a high level of probability of becoming a human be-ing if left to the normal course of its life. With this in mind, let us look at the essence of the debate:

What is the relationship of abortion to the biblical prohibition against murder? Does the Bible have anything to say about the *destruction of a potential life?*

We remember that in the Old Testament there are five distinctions made in the broader application of the Decalogue's prohibition of killing, including distinctions for manslaughter and involuntary murder. In the New Testament, however, we have an authoritative application and interpretation of this prohibition.

The prohibition "You shall not kill" is not a universal prohibition against taking human life in *any* context, but it is wider in its scope than simple first-degree murder. Jesus includes in his understanding of this mandate a prohibition against hatred. Hatred is understood as murder of the heart. In effect Jesus says that the law implicitly prohibits *potential murder* (and *potential adultery*). Left to its own, hatred results in murder; lust, in adultery. He says that the law prohibits the *potential destruction of life.* This is not the same as prohibiting the *actual destruction of potential life.* But these two are very close to being the same, similar enough to raise serious questions about abortion. In terms of the sanctity of life, potentiality is clearly an issue with Jesus.

If we are seriously considering the spirit of the law, we must pay attention to the implications (implicit understanding) of a particular command-ment. The converse of a prohibition must be af-firmed: what the law implicitly affirms is a part of the complex of what the prohibition explicitly ne-gates. Wanton destruction of life is prohibited. This implies an implicit command to promote the sanc-tity and safeguarding of life. The sanctity of life is the supreme basis for the prohibition of murder. The question is, Does the sanctity of life include concern for potential life? There is no way we can prove decisively that it does. But in light of the overwhelming concern in the Scriptures for the safeguarding and preservation of life, the burden of proof must be on those who wish to destroy poten-tial life.

Perhaps the strongest case for the support of liberal abortion laws is the right of the mother. Some groups have countered this with the issue of the right of the unborn. But the root of the matter goes deeper. The issue biblically is between the concept of the woman's right and the woman's responsibility. Does the woman have the right to disrupt natural law? Is she responsible for the nat-ural consequences of her voluntary acts? Relative to this debate is the fact that we do not have abso-lute rights over our own bodies within the sphere of creation. Self-mutilation is forbidden within the Old Testament. If mutilation before conception is wrong, what about mutilation after conception?

Another argument used to support legalized abortion is the utilitarian argument, which opts for the lesser of two evils. The argument is that under the present restrictions, the only abortions that are available (apart from therapeutic abortions) are those obtained illegally, which are often hazardous. To protect people from their own foolish acts, wisdom would dictate legalizing abortion. This argument is irrelevant to the question of whether or not abortion is right. Committing a felony is also a dangerous business, but the danger is no justification for the legalization of bank robbery.

The issue of therapeutic abortions must be dealt with separately. Generally they are used in two situations: where there is clear and present danger to the life and physical health of the mother, and where there is concern for the psychological well-being of the mother, especially in the case where the woman has been victimized by a rapist. In the first instance, there are two basic points. Some argue that in the case of the danger to the life of the mother, it is better to destroy the fetus to save the mother. The actual life is more valuable than the potential life. Others say the fetus should be saved, basing this on the matter of certainty versus probability. Suppose that the death of the mother is 99 percent probable if the child is left to be born. If there is an abortion, that means 100 percent certainty of death for the fetus. If there is one chance in

100 for both to survive, this group holds that the chance should be taken.

The final question is that of church and state. Many Christians have taken the position that it is not the church's business what the state legislates, since the church is not to legislate morality. However, the state *does* have the responsibility of legislating morality. Traffic laws deal with the moral issue of how one drives one's car. Justice is a moral issue; laws are an attempt to promote justice. The essence of legislation is morality. The church has the responsibility to speak to the legislature. The state's primary function is the preservation of society and the preservation of life. When the state is involved in legislation that does not respect and promote the sanctity of life, the church must speak out. While we recognize the separation of power between church and state, we cannot recognize the autonomy of the state before God. The state is also a servant of God. If there is any legislation on which the church has the responsibility to speak, it is on this one, since the heart of the issue is the sanctity of life.

The debate within the church tends to focus on the *tertium quid*, the third option, known as the "Right to Choice" position, one that has steadily grown in popularity.

Evidence is emerging that the strategy of pro-abortionists, led by Planned Parenthood, has been the oldest strategy of all: "divide and conquer." Mainline Protestant bodies have been solicited to aid the cause of pro-abortion on the grounds that human rights are being violated by the oppressive tyranny of a Roman Catholic monolith. Eager to stand against tyranny and for human rights, countless Protestant clergy and denominations have endorsed the middle ground between the combatants of pro-life and pro-abortion. The *via media*, or moderate middle, has been defined as the pro-choice position.

Two vital questions must be faced by those wrestling with the premier moral issue of our day. The first question is, What is the practical difference between pro-abortion and pro-choice? In terms of legislation a vote for pro-choice is a vote for pro-abortion, which the pro-abortionists understand clearly. No one knows the exact figures, but it is obvious from the polls that a large group of voters, if not a plurality of them, favor the middle ground. Certainly it is this middle position that has swung the balance of legislative power and the weight of public opinion to the side of the pro-abortionists. We hear it said repeatedly, "I would not choose to have an abortion, but I think every woman has a right to make that choice for herself."

In this statement the focus is upon the concept of a human "right." The mother is said to have the right over her own body to bear a child or to dispose of the fetus. (The central issue is not about victims of rape or mothers endangered by childbirth; the issue before us is abortion-on-demand for convenience.) This presses the second question: What constitutes a moral right and from whence come moral rights?

As Christians we recognize, I hope, that there is a profound difference between a moral right and a legal right. Ideally, legal rights reflect moral rights, but such is not always the case. How does one establish the moral right to choose abortion? From the law of nature? From the law of God? Hardly. Natural law abhors abortion and divine law implicitly condemns it.

The real basis of the right to choose abortion is based on want. The unspoken assumption of the right-to-choice position is the assumption that I am free to choose whatever I want—an assumption repugnant to both God and nature. I never have the moral right to do evil. I may have the civil and legal right to sin but never the moral right. The only moral rights I have are to righteousness.

Is not the issue more complex? Does it not hang together with the broader issue of the extent of government intrusion into our private lives? Surely it does. I know few stronger advocates of limited government than myself. I abhor the proliferating tendrils of government pressing into our lives. But the primary purpose of government, biblically, is to exercise restraint on mankind in order to promote, preserve, and protect the sanctity of life. This is the very *raison d'être* of human government.

If abortion-on-demand is evil, no one has the moral right to choose it. If it is an offense against life, the government must not permit it. The day is being captured by the moderate middle who have not faced the ethical implications of this position. This is the moral cop-out of our day—the shame of our churches and her leaders. It is time to get off the fence. Pro-choice is pro-abortion. Be clear about that and abandon the muddled middle.

CHAPTER 21

ETHICS AND THE CONSCIENCE

The function of the conscience in ethical decision making tends to complicate matters for us. The commandments of God are eternal, but in order to obey them we must first appropriate them internally. The "organ" of such internalization has been classically called the conscience. Some describe this nebulous inner voice as the voice of God within. The conscience is a mysterious part of man's inner being. Within the conscience, in a secret hidden recess, lies the personality, so hidden that at times it functions without our being immediately aware of it. When Freud brought hypnosis into the palace of respectable scientific inquiry, men began to explore the subconscious and examine those intimate caverns of the personality. Encountering the conscience can be an awesome experience. The uncovering of the inner voice can be, as one psychiatrist notes, like "looking into hell itself."

Yet we tend to think of conscience as a heavenly thing, a point of contact with God, rather than a hellish organ. We think of the cartoon character faced with an ethical decision while an angel is perched on one shoulder and a devil on the other, playing tug-of-war with the poor man's head. The conscience can be a voice from heaven or hell; it can lie as well as press us to truth. It is a voice with two sides to its mouth, having the capacity either to *accuse* or to *excuse*.

Walt Disney made popular the jingle "Let your conscience be your guide." This is at best Jiminy Cricket theology. For the Christian the conscience is not the highest court of appeals for right conduct. The conscience is important, but not normative. It is capable of distortion and misguidance. It is mentioned some thirty-one times in the New Testament with abundant indication of its capacity for change. The conscience can be seared and eroded, being desensitized by repeated sin. Jeremiah described Israel as having the "brazen look of a prostitute" (Jeremiah 3:3, NIV). From repeated transgressions Israel had, like the prostitute, lost her capacity to blush. With the stiffened neck and the hardened heart came also the calloused conscience. The sociopath can murder without remorse, being immune to the normal pangs of conscience.

Though the conscience is not the highest tribunal of ethics, it is perilous to act against it. We remember Luther at the Diet of Worms, trembling in agony at the enormous moral pressure he was facing. When asked to recant, he included these words in his reply: "My conscience is held captive by the Word of God. To act against conscience is neither right nor safe."

Luther's graphic use of the word *captive* illustrates the visceral power the compulsion of conscience can exercise on a person. Once a person is gripped by the voice of conscience, a power is harnessed by which acts of heroic courage may issue forth. A conscience captured by the Word of God is both noble and powerful.

Was Luther correct in saying, "To act against conscience is neither right nor safe"? Here we must tread carefully lest we slice our toes on the ethical razor's edge. If the conscience can be misinformed or distorted, why should we not act against it? Should we follow our consciences into sin? Here we have a dilemma of the double-jeopardy sort. If we follow our consciences into sin, we are still guilty of sin inasmuch as we are required to have our consciences rightly informed by the Word of God. However, if we act against our consciences, we are also guilty of sin. The sin may not be located in what we do but rather in the fact that we committed an act we believed to be evil. Here the biblical principle that whatever is not of faith is sin comes into play. For example, if a person is taught and comes to believe that wearing lipstick is a sin and then wears lipstick, that person is sinning. The sin resides not in the lipstick but in the *intent* to act against what one believes to be the command of God.

The dilemma of double jeopardy demands that we diligently strive to bring our consciences into harmony with the mind of Christ lest a carnal conscience lead us into disobedience. We require a redeemed conscience, a conscience of the spirit rather than the flesh.

The manipulation of conscience can be a destructive force within the Christian community. Legalists are often masters of guilt manipulation, while antinomians master the art of quiet denial. The conscience is a delicate instrument that must be respected. One who seeks to influence the consciences of others carries a heavy responsibility to maintain the integrity of the other person's own personality as crafted by God. When we impose false guilt on others we paralyze our neighbors, binding them in chains where God has left them free. When we urge false innocence we contribute to their delinquency, exposing them to the judgment of God.

So where are we, at the end of this whirlwind tour of "practical theology"? We have gained some understanding of God's ways and God's commands. But, as we said at the beginning, true theology does not stay in the head; it is absorbed into the heart and is expressed in one's life. If this book remains merely theoretical knowledge and makes no difference in your life, then you have gone no farther than the skeptical academic.

The Christian life is lived by principles, principles drawn from the character of God as revealed in sacred Scripture. It is good for us to study these principles. But we fight a battle on two fronts. First, we must discern what is good, that is, we must know the right thing to do. Second, we must muster the moral courage to do the good.

Each step of our theological growth requires active commitment. We may learn all there is to know about who Jesus is, but unless we commit our lives to him, such knowledge does us little good. Even demons believe in the facts about Jesus. We need to bow in humble devotion before him.

The same thing is true of prayer. Once we have access to the Father through Jesus, do we "with confidence draw near to the throne of grace"? We may know everything about how to pray and how God answers, but it is all useless unless we get down on our knees and pray.

Similarly, we may understand God's will for

every facet of our lives. We may know what he wants for our jobs, our marriages, and so on. But are we growing in our obedience to God's revealed will? Are we truly following his desires?

Studying ethical questions in light of biblical principles helps clear away the gray areas of confusion. With greater assurance of what God requires we are less vulnerable to the seduction of moral compromise. Clarity of understanding strengthens the will as it enlightens the mind. To be sure, the clear understanding of the right does not guarantee the actual performance of it. For that we are dependent upon the grace of God. Yet the understanding assists and undergirds the will by strengthening the voice of a godly conscience. Our goal is to *do* the will of God, and "this," says the Scripture, "is the will of God, your sanctification" (1 Thessalonians 4:3).

My prayer is that the end of this book will be the beginning for you, the beginning of victory on both fronts. I pray both that the Father may "give you a spirit of wisdom and of revelation in the knowledge of him, having the eyes of your hearts enlightened, that you may know . . . the immeasurable greatness of his power in us who believe" (Ephesians 1:17-19).